THE DAILY STUDY BIBLE

(OLD TESTAMENT)

General Editor: John C.L. Gibson

DANIEL

DANIEL

D. S. RUSSELL

THE SAINT ANDREW PRESS
EDINBURGH

THE WESTMINSTER PRESS
PHILADELPHIA

Published by
The Saint Andrew Press
Edinburgh, Scotland
and
The Westminster Press ®
Philadelphia, Pennsylvania

Typeset in Great Britain
by Print Origination, Formby, England

Printed and Bound in the U.S.A.
by R. R. Donnelley & Sons Company, Crawfordsville, Indiana

ISBN (Great Britain) 0 7152 0464 5

552   2   3   4   5   6   7   8

Library of Congress Cataloging in Publication Data

Russell, D.S. (David Syme), 1916–
Daniel.

(The Daily study Bible series)
Bibliography: p.
1. Bible. O.T. Daniel —Commentaries. I. Title. II. Series: Daily study Bible series (Westminster Press)
BS1555.3.R87   224'.5077   81-1777
                                         AACR2

ISBN (U.S.A.) 0-664-21800-8
ISBN (U.S.A.) 0-664-24567-6 (pbk.)

GENERAL PREFACE

This series of commentaries on the Old Testament, of which Dr. Russell's volume on *Daniel* is one of the first, has been planned as a companion series to the much-acclaimed New Testament series of the late Professor William Barclay. As with that series, each volume is arranged in successive headed portions suitable for daily study. The biblical text followed is that of the Revised Standard Version or Common Bible. Eleven contributors share the work, each being responsible for from one to three volumes. The series is issued in the hope that it will do for the Old Testament what Professor Barclay's series succeeded so splendidly in doing for the New Testament—make it come alive for the Christian believer in the twentieth century.

Its two-fold aim is the same as his. Firstly, it is intended to introduce the reader to some of the more important results and fascinating insights of modern Old Testament scholarship. Most of the contributors are already established experts in the field with many publications to their credit. Some are younger scholars who have yet to make their names but who in my judgment as General Editor are now ready to be tested. I can assure those who use these commentaries that they are in the hands of competent teachers who know what is of real consequence in their subject and are able to present it in a form that will appeal to the general public.

The primary purpose of the series, however, is *not* an academic one. Professor Barclay summed it up for his New Testament series in the words of Richard of Chichester's prayer—to enable men and women "to know Jesus Christ more clearly, to love Him more dearly, and to follow Him more nearly." In the case of the Old Testament we have to be a little more circumspect than that. The Old Testament was completed long before the time of Our Lord, and it was (as it still is) the sole Bible of the Jews, God's first people, before it became part of the Christian Bible. We must take this fact seriously.

Yet in its strangely compelling way, sometimes dimly and sometimes directly, sometimes charmingly and sometimes embarrassingly, it holds up before us the things of Christ. It should not be forgotten that Jesus Himself was raised on this Book, that He based His whole ministry on what it says, and that He approached His death with its words on His lips. Christian men and women have in this ancient collection of Jewish writings a uniquely illuminating avenue not only into the will and purposes of God the Father, but into the mind and heart of Him who is named God's Son, who was Himself born a Jew but went on through the Cross and Resurrection to become the Saviour of the world. Read reverently and imaginatively, the Old Testament can become a living and relevant force in their everyday lives.

It is the prayer of myself and my colleagues that this series may be used by its readers and blessed by God to that end.

New College   JOHN C. L. GIBSON
Edinburgh   General Editor

AUTHOR'S PREFACE

When approached to contribute to the Daily Study Bible series made famous by the industry, scholarship and spiritual insight of the late Professor William Barclay, I felt honoured and at the same time apprehensive: honoured to have a share in the work he tackled so successfully in his writing on the books of the New Testament, and apprehensive because to do a similar work on the Old Testament—and particularly on the book of Daniel—is a daunting task. No attempt has been made here to copy Dr Barclay's approach or style; that would be quite futile. I only hope that this volume will, in some small measure at least, give the same kind of help that his writings give, and serve the same purpose.

Daniel is not the easiest Old Testament book to read or to understand or indeed to expound. Over the centuries it has been the happy hunting ground of serious scholars and cranks alike, and even today there are a number of unsolved problems. As is made clear in the Introduction, it is not the intention of this volume to enter into a critical examination of these problems or indeed of the text itself, but rather to try to see what the writer is saying to his contemporaries, and then to listen to what God may be saying through him to succeeding generations, not least our own. Daniel is an eminently readable book and, if I may drop a word in the preacher's ear, an eminently "preachable" book. It speaks clearly and powerfully to our day and to the condition of our modern world with a word from the God of history who rules over the nations of the earth.

In preparing this commentary I have taken a particular stance in dating Daniel in the time of Antiochus Epiphanes around the year 165 B.C., though recognising the presence in it of earlier material. This, I believe, is the generally accepted position. I hope, however, that even those readers who would give it a much earlier date will nevertheless find help in what has been written, and that all will find in it a word from God.

Writing this book in the midst of multifarious duties and "travels oft" has called for discipline and perseverance; and yet it has been an enjoyable task, as serious Bible study surely ought to be. I hope the pleasure and satisfaction I have had in writing these pages will come through. Above all I hope that what I have written will help the book of Daniel to "come alive" with its message of reassurance and encouragement for God's people today.

As will be obvious, I am deeply indebted to many scholars and interpreters. I would make special mention of the commentaries by E. W. Heaton and Norman Porteous, and of that lively and illuminating small volume by Adam C. Welch, *Visions of the End*. Most of the manuscript has been nobly deciphered and typed by Mrs. Barbara Chevill who has been assisted in this rather arduous task by Miss Gladys Shoebridge. I owe them both a deep debt of gratitude. For the patience of my wife when I have had to "live laborious days" I am truly thankful.

Baptist Church House
London, W.C.1

D. S. RUSSELL

CONTENTS

INTRODUCTION

Daniel is a fascinating book which speaks profoundly to our day as it did to the day it was first written. It raises for the reader a number of difficult historical, linguistic, and interpretative problems which can only be touched upon in a study of this kind. For a more thorough examination reference may be made to larger commentaries (see *Further Reading*).

DATE AND STRUCTURE

The book purports to have been written in the sixth century B.C. during the Babylonian exile by one, Daniel, himself one of the Jewish exiles. Most scholars, however, are agreed that as it now stands it is the product of the second century B.C. and was written probably around the year 165 towards the end of the troublesome reign of the Seleucid king, Antiochus IV Epiphanes (175–164 B.C.).

Evidence for this is found, for example, in the fact that the vocabulary and style of the Aramaic and Hebrew in which it is written cannot be as early as the sixth century B.C. but are akin to the usage of the second century B.C. Historical allusions, moreover, are increasingly accurate the nearer the writer comes to events of that particular era. There is a concentration of interest on the later years of Antiochus Epiphanes who died in 164 B.C., about which the writer shows fairly intimate knowledge. He knows, for example, of Antiochus' desecration of the Jerusalem Temple in 167 B.C., but his death in 164 B.C. is simply forecast and not described as having taken place. The convincing signs are that, in its present form at any rate, the book is to be dated around the year 165 B.C. This conclusion finds corroboration in the fact that prior to the second century B.C. there is no mention of the book in any literary sources, but from that time onwards it is known as a book of some importance, finding its way into the canon of sacred Scripture.

There is more, however, to its date of origin than this. To ask, How old is the book of Daniel? is like asking, How old is a brick wall? Is it to be dated by the year the individual bricks were baked in the kiln, or by the age of certain sections of the wall transported from somewhere else and built into it, or by the year in which the wall as it now is was put together? The composition of Daniel may have been in the second century B.C., but there are fairly clear indications that certain elements in it—particularly the stories contained in chapters 1–6—come from a much earlier period and may well have been handed down in oral form among the Jews of the Dispersion from the Persian and Greek periods. Unlike the visions recorded in later chapters, they do not seem to reflect a situation of open persecution such as is evident in the time of Antiochus but indicate simply the difficulties encountered by Jews compelled to live in a foreign land and in the midst of an alien culture. It has been argued that the author of Daniel—a faithful Jew belonging to the party of the *Hasidim* or Pious Ones who opposed the Hellenising tendencies which had become all-too-evident among the people in the time of Antiochus—wrote down these traditional tales, now contained in chapters 1–6, together with the visionary experiences recorded in chapter 7, which may also have been received in oral form, and added to these the visions contained in chapters 8–12 which reflect the period of persecution under Antiochus and are, in a sense, a commentary on chapter 7.

LANGUAGE

One intriguing problem associated with this is to be found in the language, or rather languages, of the book. Apart from 1:1–2:4a, the whole of chapters 1–7 is written in Aramaic, the rest of the book being in Hebrew. Many attempts have been made to solve this riddle. Perhaps the most attractive solution is that the author recorded anonymously in the vernacular Aramaic the stories now contained in chapters 1–6 to which he added chapter 7 (which has a great deal in common with chapter 2). Thereafter he wrote in the sacred language of Hebrew (in which he was not quite as well versed) the visions now contained in chapters 8–12. These visions, dealing in the main with "the end" and the coming of God's kingdom, he attributed to the hero of the earlier stories, thus indicating a common authorship for the whole book. A new introduction was then written in Hebrew consisting of 1:1–2:4a, at which point it is said that the Chaldeans replied to the king "in Aramaic" and the narrative continues in that language up to the end of chapter 7.

PSEUDONYMITY

If this explanation is correct it helps to explain the pseudonymous authorship of the book of Daniel—a Jew of the second century B.C. writing in the name of a Hebrew exile four hundred years before. His purpose was not to deceive his readers but simply to establish the single authorship of both parts of the book. Whatever the explanation may be, this phenomenon of pseudonymity was followed, often woodenly, by subsequent "apocalyptic" writers who, like the author of Daniel, recorded their own dreams and visions of "the end", and ascribed them to ancient worthies whose names were honoured in the long tradition of Israel. Thus during the period between the Old and New Testaments a fairly large number of such books appear in the names of such figures as Enoch, Moses, Baruch, Ezra etc. who, it is said, "sealed up" their visions till the time of "the end" was at hand.

The "ancient worthy" in whose name the book of Daniel appears is said to have lived in Babylon at the time of the exile. We know nothing from any other source concerning such a man, but we do know that an ancient hero of this name did belong to Hebrew tradition (cf. Jubilees 4:20). In Ezekiel, for example, the name appears in the form *Dan'el* who, together with Noah and Job, is praised for his righteousness (cf. 14:14,20) and is honoured for his wisdom and his knowledge of secret lore (cf. 28:3). The existence of such an ancient hero finds confirmation in the Ras Shamra tablets dating from the fourteenth century B.C. where *Dan'el* is mentioned as a righteous man who cares for widows and orphans. The relation of this ancient figure to the Daniel of the later apocalyptic tradition is not too clear, but it may be that the writer of our book had in mind the allusions to him in Ezekiel (a book with which he was very familiar) and chose the name Daniel as the hero of his stories.

LITERARY CLASSIFICATION

The book of Daniel is usually classified as belonging to that type of Jewish literature which goes by the name of "apocalyptic", from the Greek word *apokalupsis* meaning "an unveiling". Initially it referred to the unveiling or uncovering of divine revelation in the form of a vision and subsequently came to signify the books in which such visions were recorded. Generally speaking, books of this kind are esoteric in character, literary in form, symbolic in language, and pseudonymous in authorship. (For a fuller treatment of these "characteristics" see the writer's *The Method and Message of Jewish Apocalyptic,* chapter 4.) The book of Daniel in some measure shares these characteristics with subsequent apocalyptic writings, although the differences between them are also striking. Thus, both make use of the prophetic teaching of the Old Testament, but the book of Daniel is much more restrained in its use of the imagery found there and refrains from the flamboyant descriptions often found in later writers concerning the coming kingdom and the signs of its appearing.

E. W. Heaton has argued strongly for the inclusion of Daniel among the Wisdom books (e.g. Proverbs) which, by means of anecdote and aphorism, seek to make known the truth of God at work in the world. Norman Porteous comes to the balanced conclusion that "perhaps the wisest course is to take the book of Daniel as a distinctive piece of literature with a clearly defined witness of its own, and to take note of the various ways in which it borrows from and is coloured by the earlier prophetic literature, the Wisdom literature and the Psalms, and has its successors in the apocalypses, though these often exhibit an extravagance and a fantastic imagination which is less prominent in the book of Daniel."

MESSAGE

It is important to recognise that the book of Daniel was not written for some far-off age when God's kingdom would come, as the device of pseudonymity would have us believe, but for the age of crisis in which the author was then living. It is essentially a religious tract for the times, written for the encouragement of people who were being faced increasingly with the pressures of a Hellenistic culture which was in so many ways inimical to their Hebrew tradition and "the laws of the fathers"; written too for people who were having to face severe religious restrictions and even persecution and death by reason of their loyalty to God. Its message declared unequivocally that the sovereign Lord God was in control not only of history but also of the end of history, that mighty monarchs and great empires were allowed to hold sway only by his permissive will, that his people Israel would in the end be completely vindicated and that that end was about to break in upon them. The whole book demonstrates a deep piety and a trust and devotion which must surely reflect a like confidence in God on the part of many in Israel at that time. Indeed it is as true representatives of Israel that we are to see Daniel and his friends—suffering for their faith but assured of vindication at the hands of God. It is a vindication which breaks even the boundaries laid down by death and grasps the glorious hope of resurrection in God's eternal kingdom (cf. 12:1-4).

The fact that the author's dreams did not reach fulfilment in the way he had hoped for should not detract from the value of the message this book conveys. It is a dream of a kingdom which another, greater than Daniel, saw being fulfilled in himself, for the full realisation of which his Church continues to hope and pray. In him the kingdom has come; in him the kingdom will one day be revealed. *Maranatha.* 'Come, Lord Jesus' (Rev. 22:20).

DANIEL

DANIEL

THE PEOPLE OF GOD IN A FOREIGN LAND

Daniel 1:1–2

> In the third year of the reign of Jehoiakim king of Judah, Nebuchad-nezzar king of Babylon came to Jerusalem and besieged it. And the Lord gave Jehoiakim king of Judah into his hand, with some of the vessels of the house of God; and he brought them to the land of Shinar, to the house of his god, and placed the vessels in the treasury of his god.

(i)

The book of Daniel begins with a series of short stories concerning certain young men who had been taken captive following the fall of Jerusalem and the pillage of the Temple at the beginning of the sixth century B.C. and had been deported to Babylon (see *Note* 1). There they found themselves, as Jews, in the midst of an entirely alien culture, surrounded by a foreign people whose system of government and form of religion were altogether different from their own.

How were they to react to these new surroundings with all their political, social, cultural, and religious pressures? In particular, what were they to do now that they were deprived of the sacred Temple which for so long had been the focal point of their religion and indeed of their whole life? The "land of Shinar" (an archaic reference to Babylon) would remind them of the rebel Nimrod whose kingdom it had been (cf. Gen. 10:10) and recall the divine displeasure at the rebellious building of the Tower of Babel (cf. Gen. 11:1ff.). It was to this very place, as Zechariah records, that Wickedness had been exiled and had made its home (cf. Zech. 5:8). It was the centre for the worship of the god Bel (cf. Dan. 4:8; Isa. 46:1) or Marduk, whose worship was *anathema* to those who served the God of Israel. The sacred vessels of the Jerusalem Temple now lay in the treasury of the house of this same Bel, an added reminder of their subjection to an alien power.

What were they to do in such circumstances as these? They could follow the example of the exiles referred to in Psalm 137:1–2, who hung up their lyres on the willows and wept when they remembered Zion. Or they could take the advice of the prophet Jeremiah (ch. 29) in his famous letter to the exiles. There he bade them settle in Babylon, build houses, raise families and "seek the welfare of the city" where they were now to dwell. They were to continue to offer their worship to the God of their fathers as they had done in Jerusalem, for God was with them still. They were to remain loyal even under the pressures of this alien culture. These stories make clear the choice these young men were prepared to make; their decision would be a living example to all Israel. They would accept their situation, but would make the most of every opportunity to honour and serve the Lord their God.

(ii)

There is good reason to believe that around the year 165 B.C. a Jewish writer in Palestine, at a time of great stress to his people and his religion, sat down and wrote what we know as the book of Daniel, incorporating earlier material in the form of stories (see Introduction) which reflected a Babylonian setting and indicated the exploits of actual deportees and their life in the city of Babylon. As we shall see, the book of Daniel was written as "a tract for the times" to encourage the Jews living in Palestine and in the Dispersion during the reign of the Syrian tyrant, Antiochus Epiphanes (175–164 B.C.).

The readers would no doubt recognise in the Babylonian king Nebuchadnezzar an image, as it were, of Antiochus himself. The references to Nebuchadnezzar and the writer's criticism of him, however, are much more restrained than we might have expected if he had simply invented his own stories to illustrate his point. The fact that they are so restrained and do not tally in every respect with the conditions of the writer's day strengthens the suggestion that they were adopted from earlier times and, in some ways, adapted to suit the purpose of his writing.

These stories then (and indeed the rest of the book to follow) are to be understood against the background of the second century B.C. in the reign of Antiochus Epiphanes, their purpose being to comfort and encourage the Jewish people in a rapidly changing environment and in the midst of an alien culture which, in so many respects, was quite inimical to the teaching and practice of their fathers.

Ever since the time of Alexander the Great the Jews had become exposed in a new way to the so-called "Greek" culture which goes by the name of "Hellenism". Its syncretistic blend of various religions and philosophies built up a culture and a way of life quite different from that of the Jewish tradition and was to prove an increasing threat to the Jewish religion as it had been handed down. Throughout Palestine, as well as the Dispersion, Greek cities were founded, administered in the Greek style, imitating Greek government, creating a form of education and recreation based on the Greek gymnasium and youth centre, encouraging participation in the hippodrome and stadium where pagan "opening ceremonies" were performed, and sponsoring the music-hall and the theatre where everything was not "unto edification". Many Jews—especially among the young—were attracted by what they saw and heard, adopting the manner and even the distinctive dress of their pagan neighbours. They preferred to be called by Greek names and to conceal the fact that they had been circumcised. In course of time this whole Hellenistic culture was to find "official" support in the priestly class to be known as the Sadducees and was to lead to violent clashes between Syrian and Jew and indeed between Jew and fellow-Jew.

These stories in Daniel were told, or retold, to encourage the Jewish people in the writer's day to stand firm in the midst of *their* alien culture, as Daniel and his friends had done in theirs and to assure them that the time of their deliverance from such pressures was at hand.

(iii)

The New Testament writers would have had a fellow-feeling for the author of Daniel, for the emerging Church found itself at once in a similar state of tension, with pressures of many kinds crowding in upon it from the society round about. They belonged to the great Roman empire, and yet they were "a commonwealth of heaven" (Phil. 3:20); they belonged to this nation and that, and yet they knew themselves to be "a holy nation, God's own people" (1 Pet. 2:9). They were the people of God in a foreign land; in the midst of an alien culture they were sojourners, not settlers. Their home was in another country. They belonged to a city whose builder and maker is God (cf. Heb. 11:10) to which they owed supreme allegiance.

They were to be loyal citizens, "subject to the governing authorities" (Rom. 13:1), involved in the affairs of their society and open to its culture. They were to be well and truly *in* the world; and yet they were to be distinct from it. The Apostle Paul felt it right to issue a warning to his fellow-Christians in Rome: "Don't let the world squeeze you into its mould" (Rom. 12:1) (J. B. Phillips' translation). They were to be distinctive not just in their worship, but even in their style of life (cf.1 Pet. 1:15).

Jesus was under no illusions about the pressures that would come upon his followers: they would be arrested, beaten and betrayed (cf. Mark 13:9). But they would continue to recognise their responsibilities as the people of God in a foreign land: they were to be the salt of the earth (preserving what was good in society around them and saving it from going bad); they were to be the light of the world (revealing to society the truth about its own condition and God's redemptive purpose for its life); and they were to be as sheep in the midst of wolves (prepared if needs be to accept suffering and death, offering to God the daily sacrifices of their lives).

(iv)

Augustine reminds us that the Christian lives in two cities at one and the same time: the temporal and the eternal, the old Jerusalem and the new, life on earth and life in heaven. He is a citizen of both and both claim his allegiance.

The picture is not an unfamiliar one today. Very few are able, even if they choose to do so, to live in complete isolation from the world and its demands—like the holy order of nuns who, it is said, sleep at night in their coffins in which they will one day be buried, so as to remind themselves daily that they belong not to this world but to the next. For most Christians, however, there is no choice, nor would they wish it otherwise. They live as the people of God in a foreign culture.

The problem they face is perhaps most pronounced in officially atheistic countries or in societies where world religions, other than Christianity, are given state recognition. Pressures are often unobtrusive; but their accumulated strength is considerable: the accepted *mores* of the community, its political or religious presuppositions, its moral values, its religious or anti-religious stance, its social ethics and so on. When these are backed up by restrictive sanctions and legal pronouncements, the resulting situation can become oppressive in the extreme, straining loyalties and testing faith. In such circumstances, when does conformity become compromise and compromise collaboration and collaboration betrayal?

But pressures are not confined to such societies as these. They are to be found also to a marked degree in the secular societies of countries with a long Christian tradition behind them. Business and social ethics, the lowering of moral standards, the growth of a materialistic outlook, the weakening of Christian influence in private and public life—all these create a cultural climate that is hardly conducive to the practice of the faith or the propagation of the Gospel.

Today, as in the time of Antiochus, the stories of Daniel fortify the faith of God's people and strengthen their resolve.

KNOCKED DOWN, BUT NOT KNOCKED OUT

Daniel 1:1–2 (*cont'd*)

(i)

These verses refer to Nebuchadnezzar king of Babylon

(605–562 B.C.) who "came to Jerusalem and besieged it". At the beginning of the sixth century B.C. the power of the Babylonian Empire had reached its peak. The two great rival kingdoms of Assyria and Egypt had been defeated and Nebuchadnezzar turned his attention to Palestine, which was of considerable military and strategic importance and controlled the caravan routes between Egypt and the East. In 601 B.C. Jehoiakim of Judah was forced to pay tribute to Nebuchadnezzar for a period of three years. Thereafter he rebelled and in 592 B.C. Nebuchadnezzar marched west. Meanwhile Jehoiakim had died and was succeeded by his son Jehoiachin who had reigned for only three months when Nebuchadnezzar captured Jerusalem, stripped its Temple and carried off many of its people into captivity (597 B.C.)

Jehoiachin was succeeded by Zedekiah (597–586 B.C.) who, against the counsel of the prophet Jeremiah, rebelled against Babylon in 588 B.C. The Babylonians began the siege of Jerusalem which lasted for eighteen months. In 587 B.C. the city fell. Zedekiah's sons were slain in his presence before he was blinded and taken to Babylon. Jerusalem was destroyed by fire and many more of the people of Judah were taken captive. These two deportations of 597 B.C. (cf. 2 Kings 24:14–16) and 587 B.C. (cf. 2 Kings 25:8–11) were followed by a much smaller one in 581 B.C. (cf. Jer. 52:28ff.).

The exiles of 597 B.C. apparently represented the most cultured, intelligent and religious elements (cf. 2 Kings 24:14–16; Jer. 29:1) whom Jeremiah describes as "good figs" in contrast to the "bad figs" who remained behind (cf. Jer. 24:5). It is misleading to think of them as slaves. They were rather recognised foreigners who enjoyed a fair measure of freedom, were able to build their own houses in self-contained communities and were in communication with their kinsmen in Palestine.

These conditions prevailed for some years, but the evidence suggests that not all the exiles enjoyed comparable conditions. It is possible that the rebels of 587 B.C. were given sterner treatment and may have been used as forced labour in building operations of the Babylonian kings. Ezekiel 34:27, for example, prophesies that the day is coming when God will break the bars of their yoke and deliver them out of the hands of those that enslaved them. Isa. 14:3f. promises them rest from their pain, turmoil and hard service—conditions reflected also in later writings (cf. Isa. 42:22; 47:6; 51:23).

It is probable that their condition became worse in the closing years of the exile following the death of Nebuchadnezzar in 562 B.C. His long and prosperous reign was followed by the rapid decline of the Babylonian Empire. His son Evil-Merodach (562–560 B.C.) was murdered by Neriglissar (560–556 B.C.) whose reign was marked by rebellions and conspiracies. Labashi-Marduk, the king's son, was murdered after a reign of nine months by a conspiracy of the nobles who made Nabonidus king (556–539 B.C.).

Nabonidus was a native of Harran with Assyrian lineage, whose mother had been high priestess of the Moon-god Sin. He appears to have been a very religious man with a deep antiquarian interest. Soon after his accession he left Babylon for the west where he apparently remained for ten years. A good part of that time was spent in Tema in Arabia. It is not improbable that under his rule the conditions of the exiles in Babylonia took a turn for the worse as he was intolerant of religions other than his own and his many building operations would require much money and forced labour. In due course he returned to Babylon from Tema. His defeat by Cyrus the Persian in 539 B.C. brought the Babylonian Empire to an end. Nabonidus is of interest to the reader of the book of Daniel because, as we shall see later, there are indications here and there that traditions concerning this monarch may have been transferred by the writer to Nebuchadnezzar himself (see comments on 4:28–37; 5:1–4).

(ii)

This, then, is the background to the stories in the book of Daniel which spoke to the author and his readers about their own troubled situation in the second century B.C., not only as

Jews in an alien culture, but also as the people of God under foreign oppression. For the faith of their fathers was under attack, not just from the insidious influence of Hellenism, but also from the aggressive onslaught of Antiochus Epiphanes, the Syrian tyrant.

The account of Antiochus' dealings with the Jews is a very troubled one and would spring readily to mind as these stories were read. In the figure of Nebuchadnezzar/Nabonidus, for example, they would recognise Antiochus, and the spoiling of the Temple by the Babylonians would be a vivid reminder of a similar sacrilege perpetrated in their own day. In 169 B.C., because the people refused to recognise his protégé, Menelaus, as High Priest, Antiochus ordered a massacre among them, desecrated the Temple in Jerusalem and plundered its sacred vessels of silver and gold, together with the furnishings and other treasures. In that same year he assumed the title *Theos Epiphanes* ("God Manifest") and some few years later issued coins bearing the face of Zeus with a striking resemblance to his own! In 168 B.C. he attacked Jerusalem again, this time on the Sabbath Day when he knew the Jews would show no resistance, and let loose his troops who slaughtered many people. The city was plundered and set on fire; women and children were carried off as slaves; taxes were imposed and much land confiscated. The Temple came under the control of an alien power and the city itself became a place for the worship of foreign gods. But the worst was still to come. Antiochus' venom was re-directed from the political sphere to the religious. He decided to wipe out the Jewish religion altogether. The Jews were forbidden, under duress, any longer to live according to their ancestral laws. A ban was placed on the very things that marked them off from their neighbours—the rite of circumcision, the reading of the Law and the observance of sacrifices and festivals. Punishment for violation of the king's decree was death. Altars to idols were set up; Jews were ordered to eat swine's flesh and to offer sacrifices of ritually unclean animals. To crown all this infamy, in December 167 B.C. Antiochus set up in the Jerusalem Temple an altar to Zeus (together, apparently, with a cult-symbol or cult-image) on the altar of burnt offerings (see comments on 8:13–14; 9:25–27 (*cont'd*)) and commanded that swine's flesh be offered on it. Drunken orgies took place; acts of sensuality were perpetrated; Jews were forced to take part in heathen ceremonies and to share in processions in honour of the god Bacchus. All who refused to conform were threatened with death.

The High Priest Menelaus and many of his priests readily collaborated. Others submitted with the greatest reluctance. Others again "chose to die rather than to be defiled by food or to profane the holy covenant" (1 Maccabees 1:63). Many and grievous are the stories told—in 1 and 2 Maccabees especially—concerning the suffering of the Jewish people and the faithfulness of many even to the point of death. Very soon, however, the forces of Jewish resistance began to muster, led by an elderly priest named Mattathias and subsequently by his descendants, the Hasmoneans and the Maccabees. The Maccabean Revolt resulted and a new chapter in Jewish history came to be written.

Some pinned their hope on the power of armies; others looked to the intervention of God himself to deliver his people. The writer of Daniel was one of those latter. By the use of heroic stories of the past and by the recounting of visions and dreams unveiling the mysteries of God's providence and wisdom, he sought to encourage his fellow-Jews to stand fast in their faith and to have confidence in the speedy breaking in of God on their behalf. God was able to deliver them from their plight, but if not he would give them wisdom and strength to overcome.

(iii)

Modern history bears eloquent testimony to the relevance of all this to life in the twentieth century and not least to the plight of Jews and Christians under different kinds of tyrannical rule. In 1939, just before the outbreak of the Second World War, a Swiss writer, Walter Lüthi wrote a book entitled *The Church to Come* consisting of a number of expository sermons on Daniel. In the translator's note D. H. C. Read makes this observation: "In the following pages you will hear a voice from the cauldron of Central Europe, faithfully expounding the book of Daniel *in its stark modernity*". And in his foreword, the author himself comments: "The exposition of the book of Daniel involved the steadily growing conviction that it contains *a particular message for our time,* often in a very striking way...We are not dealing here with a burnt-out crater. Daniel is an active vulcano. Therefore if anyone thinks that it is a matter of playing with cold lava, for edification or otherwise, he should realise that he is playing with fire."

The relevance of the book of Daniel for the ghettos, labour camps and gas chambers of Europe under Nazi rule was all too apparent to members of, say, the Confessional Church in Germany, which, at great risk to itself, refused to remain silent in face of tyranny and oppression, but chose to suffer rather than conform. That relevance is perhaps no less real in situations today where the claims of the state can so readily clash with the claims of Christ. On the roof of the state building in Bucharest, facing the Patriarch's house, there stands a huge bronze statue of an eagle holding in its beak a tiny fragile cross. The symbolism was no doubt intended originally to represent the state as defender of the faith and an instrument of the Gospel. For many people today, however, such symbolism carries with it a quite different interpretation. The fragile cross has been crushed and broken and the people of God have shared in the sufferings of Christ.

In circumstances such as these the message of the book of Daniel rings out loud and clear, encouraging the faithful to stand firm and assuring them that God and the kingdom of God are at hand.

RECRUITS WANTED

Daniel 1:3–5

Then the king commanded Ashpenaz, his chief eunuch, to bring some of the people of Israel, both of the royal family and of the nobility, youths without blemish, handsome and skilful in all wisdom, endowed with knowledge, understanding learning, and competent to serve in the king's palace, and to teach them the letters and language of the Chaldeans. The king assigned them a daily portion of the rich food which the king ate, and of the wine which he drank. They were to be educated for three years, and at the end of that time they were to stand before the king.

(i)

The Babylonian king was not content to capture the bodies of those who had been deported from Judea, he had to capture their minds as well. And so he set about a process of conditioning and indoctrination. They were foreigners; nevertheless, given the right material, Nebuchadnezzar could do something really worthwhile with them. He was prepared to offer excellent prospects of promotion to the right people who were ready to submit themselves to his prescribed course of training.

Not everyone would do for what he had in mind. Only the very best would suit his purpose and these were to be found among the ranks of the Jewish nobility and the members of the royal family. But even good breeding was not enough. To fit in with his plans they must be young, able-bodied, good-looking, mentally alert, competent and well-mannered. With these gifts and qualities they would make the most of the opportunity presented to them.

This was to consist of a three years' course in "the letters and language of the Chaldeans". This word "Chaldean" was used in the days of Nebuchadnezzar to describe the dynasty founded in Babylon by his father Nabopolassar. In the writings of later times, however, it assumes a secondary meaning and refers rather to a class of influential Babylonian priests who were noted for their learning in astrology, divination, and magical arts—perhaps because by that time this priestly class was the only recognisable remnant left of the once-powerful dynasty. In all but two instances it is this secondary meaning that is implied in the book of Daniel. This tallies with the description given elsewhere in the book where the "Chaldeans" are introduced as wise men, soothsayers, sorcerers, magicians, and enchanters.

The "language" in which the young men were to be trained refers to the Sumerian tongue which was the sacred language used in the intricate and mysterious rituals performed by the priests and which required years of study to bring to perfection. The "letters" indicate its expression in a complicated cuneiform script imprinted on soft clay by means of a wedge.

Recruits were sought, then, to train for this high and influential office which would give them power with gods and men. Their privileges extended even to the provision of royal rations. The very food and drink served to the king would be theirs also. The story recalls that of Joseph and the food and drink allotted to his brothers (cf. Gen. 43:34) and of Jehoiachin, the captive king of Judah who, according to an extra-biblical source, was given the same kind of treatment. Babylon needed recruits. Money was no obstacle. Only the best would do—in personnel, in provision and in training.

The story is told, as we shall see, to demonstrate that the Babylonian wisdom cannot even begin to compare with the wisdom given by God to his own people.

(ii)

The importance of education was recognised by the Jews from quite an early stage and would be recognised by the writer and the readers of the book of Daniel in the second century B.C. Only at a later date is there evidence for the introduction into Jewish life of what we might call *formal* education. The beginnings of this are probably to be found in the latter half of the first century B.C. under the influence of one, Simeon ben Shetach, who, according to reliable tradition, founded the school system in Jerusalem whose influence spread rapidly, to the great advantage of the common people. Based on the study of the Law, it provided a comprehensive system of elementary education. This was further developed in the latter half of the first century A.D. under the influence of one, Joshua ben Gamala, under whose inspiration primary schools spread from Jerusalem into the Dispersion.

But long before such attempts at formal education scribal

schools had been established, having close association with the synagogue, in which young and old alike were taught the precepts of wisdom which springs from a study of the Law or Torah of God and finds expression in reverence and rectitude. This is clearly exemplified, just prior to the writing of the book of Daniel, in the writings of Ben Sira (Ecclesiasticus), around the year 180 B.C., which reflect the traditional Judaism of the scribal wisdom schools of that time. In the opening words of his book he asserts that "all wisdom comes from God" (Ecclesiasticus 1:1) and goes on to equate the Law with wisdom as God's supreme gift to men (cf. 24:23). The study of the Law is central and all-pervasive, covering the whole of life and all human interest and concern. This was the continuing emphasis in the schools and in the synagogues which had such a profound influence on the Jews in both Palestine and the Dispersion during the intertestamental period and beyond. It is well to remember in this connection that the synagogue was more than a place of prayer; it was essentially a "House of Study" *(Beth Hammidrash)* where the Law was read and studied, albeit in an atmosphere of praise and prayer.

This devotion to the Law and the study of the Law was expressed clearly at the time of the Maccabean Revolt when, for a period at any rate, the resistance movement had the support of the *Hasidim* (or "Pious Ones") to whose number the author of Daniel probably belonged. Indeed they were prepared, if needs be, to die in its defence. This was true wisdom and the only form of wisdom that really mattered. The education Nebuchadnezzar offered, with all its enticements and its initiation into secret lore, could not hold a candle to that wisdom to be found in the study of God's holy Law.

(iii)

The interest of Nebuchadnezzar in educating those who were "without blemish" in his "Three Years' Plan" has had many parallels in many generations. In his spiritual successors he has been active in every age in schools and Universities, in military academies and political institutions, in technical colleges and other places of higher learning—selecting the choicest young people for his purpose, neutralising and re-educating them according to a given philosophy, bending their minds to fit the accepted ideology, even breaking them in mental institutions if they refuse to comply. He decrees what they must think and determines what they must believe.

In most countries today this powerful yet delicate tool, which can so readily shape the minds of the young for good or ill, is in the hands of the institutions of state—powerful because it can have such a profound influence on the lives of so many, and delicate because it can so easily go wrong. In some countries compulsory lectures for children in military science and political ideology have caused concern to the Christian Church and also to non-Christians who value personal integrity and intellectual freedom. But the danger of indoctrination is there too in countries which pride themselves upon the freedom of their institutions and their people. Prejudice and propaganda can so readily slip into the teaching of such subjects as history, psychology, economics, biology, chemistry, and physics, not to mention religion.

Education has all along held a central place in the programme of the Christian Church. In the name of Christ it seeks to dispel ignorance as well as fear, to spread the light of knowledge, to encourage the grasp of truth. It has to be confessed, however, that it has not always succeeded and has all too often practised indoctrination, not intent on truth for truth's sake, indulging in prejudice and over-concerned about maintaining tradition or preserving doctrine. It, too, has to beware lest it go the way of Nebuchadnezzar, by distinguishing carefully between education and indoctrination, persuasion and coercion, truth and propaganda.

Education, then, can be made to serve the partisan purpose of Nebuchadnezzar or it can contribute to men's understanding of that wisdom which is God's supreme gift, and which is to be found in obedience to him and to his Law. The book of Daniel gives the assurance that the wisdom of God is stronger than men's, that truth is more powerful than falsehood, and that all the efforts of Nebuchadnezzar will be brought to naught.

A CHANGE OF NAME

Daniel 1:6–7

> Among these were Daniel, Hananiah, Misha-el, and Azariah of the tribe of Judah. And the chief of the eunuchs gave them names: Daniel he called Belteshazzar, Hananiah he called Shadrach, Misha-el he called Meshach, and Azariah he called Abednego.

(i)
> Sticks and stones may break my bones;
> Names will never hurt me.

Maybe. And maybe not. Be that as it may, the young men, now named in the story for the first time, could hardly have been happy with the decision of the chief eunuch to rename them. Their Hebrew names testified to Yahweh (or Jehovah), the God of their fathers, and to their faith in him. Two of them contain the word "El" meaning "God" and two the word "(y)ah", a form of the divine name "Yahweh". As they take up their new responsibilities they are given new, Babylonian, names which contain or have reference to Babylonian deities. Thus "Daniel", meaning "God has judged", becomes "Belteshazzar", meaning "May he (sc. Bel?) protect his life"; "Hananiah", meaning "Yahweh has been gracious", becomes "Shadrach", an obscure word apparently associated with the name of the god Marduk; "Mishael", meaning 'Who is what God is?', becomes "Meshach", a corrupt form whose meaning is also obscure; and "Azariah", meaning "Yahweh has helped", becomes "Abednego", which is probably a corruption for "Abed-nebo", meaning "Servant of Nebo", the Babylonian God mentioned, for example, in Isa. 46:1. (For the occurrence of the names elsewhere in the Old Testament and in extra-biblical sources, see *Note* 2).

It has been argued that the occurrence in the book of Daniel of Hebrew and of pagan names for these four young men is to

be explained not so much on religious as on literary grounds
and that what we have here is an attempt to weld together two
different traditions. Whether this be so or not, the Hebrew
forms predominate both in the present text and also in that of
"The Song of the Three Young Men", which appears in the
Apocrypha as an addition following 3:23.

Whatever the reasons for this change of names may have
been, the original readers of the book, in the second century B.C.,
may have detected in this story a covert allusion to the custom
that had grown up in their day of giving Jewish children Greek
as well as Hebrew names and of adults assuming Greek names
to express sympathy with the Greek culture within which they
lived. Two prominent examples of this were contemporaries of
the author of Daniel—the High Priests Joshua and Menahem
who were known by their Greek names Jason and Menelaus.

(ii)

The practice of name-changing is to be found, of course, quite
frequently in the case of conquered people in ancient historical
records. The name of the patriarch Joseph is a case in point (cf.
Gen. 41:45). The same is true also of countless minority groups
through the ages—from the forced labourers of Pharaoh to the
"guest-workers" of Europe, from the Hebrew slaves in Babylon
to the African slaves of the Western world, from "displaced
persons" in ancient civilisation to twentieth century immigrants
from the East—compelled by pressures of politics or religion or
poverty or war to lose their former identity and to assume the
life-style, the appearance, and even the names of those among
whom they have come to dwell.

(iii)

To the Hebrew mind the name is much more than simply a
"tag", an appellation. It contains within itself the "soul", the
character of a man, indicating what he is in the depths of his
being. As such it may be changed to correspond to a radical
change of circumstances on the part of the person concerned.
Thus Jacob, "the supplanter", after his life-changing encounter

with the angel of God, became Israel, "God prevails" (cf. Gen. 32:28); Simon became Peter, "the rock" (cf. Matt. 16:18) and Saul became Paul (cf. Acts 13:9). In each case a dramatic experience which gave life a totally new direction was marked by a change of name.

The Christian believer is given a new name (cf. Rev. 2:17); he is to bear God's name with him wherever he may go (cf. Rev. 22:4); he is to bear witness to that name (cf. Acts 8:12), not least by his manner of life among the heathen (cf. 1 Pet. 1:15); before that name every knee shall bow (cf. Phil. 2:10). Even in the midst of the alien culture of this world which does so much to destroy his faith and force him to conform, the Christian has the responsibility—and the high privilege—to bear and to share the name of Christ.

FOOD AND FAITH

Daniel 1:8–16

But Daniel resolved that he would not defile himself with the king's rich food, or with the wine which he drank; therefore he asked the chief of the eunuchs to allow him not to defile himself. And God gave Daniel favour and compassion in the sight of the chief of the eunuchs; and the chief of the eunuchs said to Daniel, "I fear lest my lord the king, who appointed your food and your drink, should see that you were in poorer condition than the youths who are of your own age. So you would endanger my head with the king." Then Daniel said to the steward whom the chief of the eunuchs had appointed over Daniel, Hananiah, Misha-el, and Azariah, "Test your servants for ten days; let us be given vegetables to eat and water to drink. Then let our appearance and the appearance of the youths who eat the king's rich food be observed by you, and according to what you see deal with your servants". So he hearkened to them in this matter, and tested them for ten days. At the end of ten days it was seen that they were better in appearance and fatter in flesh than all the youths who ate the king's rich food. So the steward took away their rich food and the wine they were to drink, and gave them vegetables.

(i)

Daniel and his friends are now faced with their first real test,
whether or not to take certain foods and drinks set before them
as part of their "grooming" to be pages and officials in the king's
service. The situation presented two difficulties. There were
certain foods forbidden to the faithful Jew in the Law of Moses
(cf. Lev. 11:4-12; Deut. 12:23f.) and there was no guarantee
that the "delicacies" now to be provided would avoid these.
Besides this, the food to be made available had no doubt been
offered to idols or was in some other way associated with idol
worship. On both counts it must be regarded as ritually unclean
and so to be avoided if, as Jews, they were to remain true to
their God.

So strong were their religious scruples that they asked to be
excused the food and drink laid on for them and instead to be
given vegetables and water. The chief of the eunuchs, despite his
friendly attitude to the young men, was loath to do as Daniel
requested. But a lesser official, here called a "steward", was
prepared to take the risk and agreed to the suggestion that they
be given a trial period of ten days to see how things might work
out. At the end of that time the faith of the young men and the
willingness of the steward to co-operate were vindicated, for
they looked healthier and more robust than the others who had
been fed on fine fare.

(ii)

The reference here to vegetables and water in place of rich food
and wine has, of course, nothing to do with either vegetarianism
or abstinence from alcohol! It relates rather to the ritual
punctiliousness of the young men concerned. Their request
vividly illustrates the importance to the faithful Jew of dietary
laws and of other regulations relating to food and drink laid
down in Scripture or accepted by tradition.

As early as the time of the prophet Hosea the food of Gentile
nations was regarded as ritually "unclean" (cf. Hos. 9:3) and
thus posed a considerable problem for Hebrews living away
from their native land. Scruples about partaking of such food

were no doubt accentuated during the early years of the exile, ceremonial laws and ceremonial ritual being given a prominent place in the required religious observances of the faithful Jew. But it is during the intertestamental period that dietary laws and regulations become really prominent. The Jews believed themselves to be distinct from their neighbours as recipients of the Law, and so of the revelation, of God. Their strict adherence to the laws of food and drink as laid down in the Torah was one way of demonstrating that difference openly and even defiantly. This is illustrated in the book of Tobit, written about 200 B.C., where Tobit himself records that whereas his brethren and his kinsmen, when carried captive to Nineveh "did eat of the bread of the Gentiles", he himself refrained from eating (cf. Tobit 1:10f.). Similarly in the book of Judith, the heroine declined the food and drink offered by Holofernes (cf. Judith 12:2), for even the smallest detail of dietary observance was of supreme importance (cf. 8:4–6; 12:1–9).

But even more graphic are the references that come from the time of the Maccabees (around the time of the writing of the book of Daniel) and the years that follow. As we have already seen, Antiochus Epiphanes, with the utmost callousness, forced the Jews on penalty of death to eat swine's flesh and to participate in ceremonies and practices which flouted the laws of God as understood and practised by loyal Jews. To many of them the principle involved was so important that they were willing, if need be, to die rather than betray their religious scruples. And many of them did just that. In 2 Maccabees 6:18, for example, the story is told of the aged Eleazar, a chief scribe, who "was constrained to open his mouth and to eat swine's flesh. But he, choosing rather to die gloriously, than to live stained with such an abomination, spit it forth, and came of his own accord to the torment." An even more celebrated account is given in chapter 7 which records the story of a mother and her seven sons who, one after another, were done to death on the orders of Antiochus because they refused to eat "unclean" food. A less emotional, but perhaps more historically accurate, account is given in 1 Maccabees 1:62, which tells of "many in

Israel" who refused to defile themselves with "unclean" foods and chose to die rather than "profane the holy covenant". In such circumstances as these the stand taken by the four young men in our story would not be lost on the first readers of the book of Daniel. God's holy laws must be maintained and he would, in due time, reward the loyalty of his faithful people.

(iii)

This whole question of ceremonial observance in general and dietary laws in particular posed a big problem for the early Christian Church which had to be resolved at an early stage if schism had to be avoided. The example and the teaching of Jesus must have been decisive factors in the great debate whether or not to adhere, as Christians, to Jewish legal requirements and customs. In the Gospels he is clearly set forth as one who gladly ate and drank with tax-collectors and sinners (cf. Matt. 9:11; Mark 2:16; Luke 5:30; 7:34), and he had some pointed things to say about ritual uncleanness. In Mark 7, for example, we are told that certain Pharisees criticised Jesus' disciples for eating food with "defiled" hands, i.e. with hands that had not been washed. The complaint is made not on the grounds of physical cleanliness, but rather on their failure to conform to the *tradition* relating to ritual purity which was as binding upon them as the Law itself. Jesus pronounces with regard to such food laws that "there is nothing outside a man which by going into him can defile him" (7:15). "Thus", says Mark, "he declared all foods clean" (7:19; cf. Luke 11:41). It is not what goes into a man's stomach that defiles him; it is what comes out of his heart: "evil thoughts, fornication, theft, murder, adultery, coveting, wickedness, deceit, licentiousness, envy, slander, pride, foolishness" (7:20ff.). Such teaching was revolutionary in its perceptiveness and in its simplicity. Small wonder his enemies regarded him as a menace to the accepted practice of their religion. What matters are not ritually correct acts but morally acceptable attitudes—a right response to the purity and holiness of God himself who requires that men be perfect as he himself is perfect (cf. Matt. 5:48). His followers must learn to distinguish between the outward and the inward, between the substance and the spirit, between legal observance and moral and spiritual worth.

But the lesson was hard to learn, as is clear from such a passage as Acts 10:9-16 where, it may be said, the Church is given its divine mandate to abandon food laws—and other "purity" laws—as binding upon them. In a vision Peter sees a great sheet lowered from heaven containing creatures of every kind. He is told to kill and eat, but protests that he has never eaten anything profane or unclean and implies he isn't going to begin to do so now! The divine voice issues a timely warning: "What God has cleansed you must not call common" (Acts 10:15).

The lesson was clear, but many were slow to learn. For a time the observance of the Jewish food laws by the Christian community continued to be a burning issue in the Church and was a subject of great controversy between Jewish Christians on the one hand and "Hellenising" Christians on the other (cf. Gal. 2:11-13; Col. 2:16). The celebrated Council of Jerusalem, after much heart-searching, arrived at a compromise solution. It was sufficient that Christians should "abstain from what had been sacrificed to idols, and from blood and from what is strangled, and from unchastity" (Acts 15:29; cf. 15:20).

The judgment of the Apostle Paul on such matters is an interesting and vitally important one: "Nothing is unclean in itself; but it is unclean for anyone who thinks it unclean. If your brother is being injured by what you eat, you are no longer walking in love...It is right not to eat meat or drink wine or do anything that makes your brother stumble" (Rom. 14:14,21). In other words, such legal requirements are nothing in themselves, but Christian love requires that the utmost sympathy be shown to those with tender consciences in such matters.

This is brought out in the story recorded in 1 Cor. 10. There we read of certain Christians in Corinth who prided themselves on their freedom from dietary laws and, in particular, regulations concerning food offered to idols. They felt themselves to be "liberated" people who knew what they were doing and

where they were going. Indeed, they give the impression
that they are a cut above their fellow-Christians who still
have a conscience about eating and drinking "unclean" food
and wine and then taking the bread and wine at the Lord's
table.

Paul agrees with them that they need have no qualms of
conscience about accepting an invitation to a meal at an
unbeliever's house and taking what is spread before them, for
after all "the earth is the Lord's and everything in it" (10:26).
But what if a fellow-Christian with a tender conscience on such
matters raises serious doubts about the propriety of such
action? Paul's answer is quite uncompromising: for the sake of
the other man's conscience, don't partake (cf. 10:29). All such
action may be lawful, but it is not necessarily expedient (cf.
10:23). The Christian, not least the "liberated" Christian, must
try to meet his "weaker" brother halfway (cf. 10:33), so as to
avoid giving offence to the Church of God (cf. 10:31). In the two
chapters which follow he spells out the reason for such counsel
and for such action. First, the Church is a fellowship in which, if
one member suffers, all the members must suffer with it (cf.
12:26); and second, the motivating power of Christian living
within that fellowship is not superior knowledge but sympathis-
ing love (cf. 14:1). It is significantly within this setting of mutual
caring and love that Paul narrates the tradition of the Lord's
Supper and warns against desecrating the body and blood of
Christ through a wrong attitude to one another. At this place
and in this act food and drink become sacramental and
indicate as nothing else can do the sacredness of God's provision.

The particular issues raised in these New Testament passages
are not those indicated in the story of Daniel and his friends,
whose sole purpose it is to demonstrate the loyalty of these
young men to their God. It is of interest, however, to see what
happens when a Jewish matter of this kind is transferred to a
Christian context. The message of Jesus is that the letter give
way to the spirit, that legal requirement be superseded by moral
response and mutual love.

THE REWARD OF LOYALTY

Daniel 1:17–21

As for these four youths, God gave them learning and skill in all letters and wisdom; and Daniel had understanding in all visions and dreams. At the end of the time, when the king had commanded that they should be brought in, the chief of the eunuchs brought them in before Nebuchadnezzar. And the king spoke with them, and among them all none was found like Daniel, Hananiah, Misha-el and Azariah; therefore they stood before the king. And in every matter of wisdom and understanding concerning which the king inquired of them, he found them ten times better than all the magicians and enchanters that were in all his kingdom. And Daniel continued until the first year of King Cyrus.

(i)

As we have seen, the story just told would remind Jews in the second century B.C. of the need to be scrupulously careful in the matter of diet if they were to remain ritually "clean" and so find favour with God. But the chief purpose of the story is somewhat different. It is to demonstrate that Jews, by remaining faithful to their hereditary laws, need not prejudice their standing in society or jeopardise their chances of promotion. This had been made quite evident in the stories of Joseph in Egypt and again in the case of Nehemiah who rose to a place of high eminence in the Persian court. This story of Daniel and his companions would come as an added incentive to all Jews throughout the Dispersion to remain loyal in the full assurance that God would look after his own.

But the benefits actually recorded here are not those of material success and high office, though they would surely have this result. They are rather the gifts of physical fitness and attractiveness and of mental ability. Not only were they healthier in appearance, but "in every matter of wisdom and understanding" they were ten times better than all the professional learned men of the king's court. Even in the very short time at their disposal they had mastered the learning and letters of the Chaldeans just as Joseph and Moses had done with Egyptian lore at the court of the Pharaohs. These were not simply acquired skills; they were divine gifts made possible through that wisdom which God imparts to his faithful people.

The reference here to learning, letters, skill, and wisdom no doubt, in the first instance, has to do with that secret tradition which, as we have seen, was the proud possession of the Babylonian priesthood. Even in this highly skilled field Daniel and his friends were so obviously better than them all! By the goodness of God they could beat the Babylonian experts at their own game. The secrets of Babylon were no secrets to Yahweh who made them known to whomsoever he willed.

But in one thing Daniel excelled even over his three companions: he was given "understanding in all visions and dreams". This reference recalls the part played by such experiences in the long history of Israel and particularly in the stories of Joseph. The reference here to visions and dreams prepares the reader for what is to follow in chapter 2 and beyond. We note, however, that in the stories contained in chapters 1–6 Daniel's gift is not so much that of personal visionary experience as it is that of *interpretation* of the visions and dreams of other people. In other words Daniel is presented not so much as the "the prophet" as "the wise man". Behind this we may perhaps detect an indication of the belief, current at the time of the writing of this book, that prophetic inspiration had dried up and prophecy itself had ceased. Daniel's wisdom did not express itself in the prophetic "Thus saith the Lord", but in his understanding and interpretation of mysteries revealed by God to men such as Nebuchadnezzar the king. (For comment on verse 21 see *Note* 3).

(ii)

It is a commonplace of Scripture that God rewards the faithfulness of his people and that loyalty to him will not go unrecompensed (cf. Matt. 19:29, etc.). But the same Scripture is well aware of the dangers lurking behind this confident belief. The prophet Jeremiah, faced with the hard realities of life, is forced to ask, "Why does the way of the wicked prosper?" (cf. Jer. 12:1), and the book of Job demonstrates quite clearly that, whatever may happen in the long run, the righteous man is not immune to suffering and sorrow. Jesus promised to his faithful disciples that they would receive "an hundredfold now in this time" houses and land and kinsmen they had willingly relinquished for his sake (cf. Mark 10:30). But it is significant that to this catalogue of blessings he adds the words "with persecutions". The Christian has to be on his guard against imagining that faithfulness to God will bring worldly success and must resist the blandishments of those who would offer Christianity as a talisman of good fortune. There are those who, by a postal ministry, have tried in recent years to spread this "Gospel of success" and to persuade the gullible to "believe and prosper". This is not the way of Jesus who bade his disciples "take up your cross" and who told at least one wealthy man to give away all that he had. Nor indeed was in the way of Daniel's companions, as subsequent testimony is to show. They were to accept uncomplainingly what God had to offer, be it of weal or of woe (cf. 3:18).

THE ASSURANCE OF FAITH

Daniel 1:17–21 *(cont'd)*

Daniel and his three companions had supreme confidence in God that he would vindicate their faith and, in his own way and in his own time, reward their faithfulness. As things turned out that confidence was fully justified and is affirmed in story after story throughout this book.

(i) There is good reason to believe that such an attitude reflects the mind of the author of Daniel himself and indeed of subsequent apocalyptic writers who, like Daniel, lived in troublous times. It has often been said that these writers were pessimists, discounting this life and looking for the next, laying little store by the events of history and staking their all on the supernatural intervention of God at the time of "the end". But this is surely at best only a half truth and so quite misleading. They believed firmly, as subsequent chapters in Daniel make quite plain, that "God is working his purpose out as year succeeds to year". As in so many other respects the story of Joseph has a parallel here also. Recalling his treatment at the hands of his brothers he says, "You meant evil against me; but God meant it for good" (Gen. 50:20). Their lives and the life of their people were in his hands; his sovereign rule would not be frustrated; in "the end" men would see his triumph, and his people would share in it.

The story is told of Lewis's store in Birmingham that it wanted to extend its already considerable premises over an adjoining piece of land on which stood a small Friends' Meeting House. A letter was sent: "Dear Sir, We are anxious to extend our premises and would like to purchase your site. Will you please name your price and we shall settle the matter as soon as possible. Signed: Lewis's". Some days later a reply came back: "Dear Sir, We have been here longer than you and would like to purchase *your* site. Will you please name your price and we shall settle the matter as soon as possible. Signed: CADBURY." What matters is not the size of the building (or the nation, or the Church) but who signs the letter—in this case a multi-millionaire! Behind the small and despised people of Israel, labouring under the yoke of foreign powers, lay the infinite resources of Almighty God. As in his mercy he had favoured Daniel, so he would look after them.

(ii) This was the very message Jesus was to give to his disciples as they in their turn were to face oppression and opposition: "Fear not, little flock, for it is your Father's good pleasure to give you the kingdom" (Luke 12:32). Or we think of Paul's words to the Romans: "In all things God works for good with those who love him" (Rom. 8:28). He does not say that "all things work together for good" (as the Authorised Version has it), for they obviously do not, but that, whatever the circumstances, God is in control and will realise his holy purpose for his people. The claim that "Jesus Christ is Lord" (Phil. 2:11) is not mere triumphalism; it is the calm and confident assurance of faith that God will be with his people always to bless them—not least in times of suffering and persecution.

(iii) For such assurance to be theirs men require the gift of "interpretation"—the ability to see beyond appearance to meaning, beyond semblance to reality, beyond shadow to substance. This ability, as Daniel reminds us, is not just an acquired skill or even an inspired guess; it is essentially a divine gift. Jesus had hard words to say about those who could discern the signs of the seasons but were incapable of interpreting "the signs of the times" and the working of God's hand in history (cf. Matt. 16:3). The gift of discernment is a gift of the Spirit (cf. 1 Cor. 2:14) who takes the things of Christ and reveals them—interprets them—to us (cf. John 15:13f.). This is true wisdom which comes, not from human learning or arduous training, but as a divine revelation and a gift from God himself.

PAGAN WISDOM

Daniel 2:1-13

In the second year of the reign of Nebuchadnezzar, Nebuchadnezzar had dreams; and his spirit was troubled, and his sleep left him. Then the king commanded that the magicians, the enchanters, the sorcerers, and the Chaldeans be summoned, to tell the king his dreams. So they came in and stood before the king. And the king said to them, "I had a dream, and my spirit is troubled to know the dream." Then the Chaldeans said to the king, "O king, live for ever! Tell your servants the dream, and we will show the interpretation." The king answered the Chaldeans, "The word from me is sure: if you do not make known to me the dream and its interpretation, you shall be torn limb from limb, and your houses shall be laid in ruins. But if you show the dream and its interpretation, you shall receive from me gifts and rewards and great honour. Therefore show me the dream and its interpretation." They answered a second time, "Let the king tell his servants the dream, and we will show its interpretation." The king answered, "I know with certainty that you are trying to gain time, because you see that the word from me is sure that if you do not make the dream known to me, there is but one sentence for you. You have agreed to speak lying and corrupt words before me till the times change. Therefore tell me the dream, and I shall know that you can show me its interpretation." The Chaldeans answered the king, "There is not a man on earth who can meet the king's demand; for no great and powerful king has asked such a thing of any magician or enchanter or Chaldean. The thing that the king asks is difficult, and none can show it to the king except the gods, whose dwelling is not with flesh."

Because of this the king was angry and very furious, and commanded that all the wise men of Babylon be destroyed. So the decree went forth that the wise men were to be slain, and they sought Daniel and his companions, to slay them.

(i)

Nebuchadnezzar, we are told, spent some sleepless nights because of certain dreams that sorely troubled him. His wise men are sent for and summoned into his presence. After courteous greetings they ask the king to tell them what he had dreamed. (The text indicates that they spoke "in Aramaic". It is likely, however, that these words have crept into the text from the margin where a scribe noted that at this point in the book the language used changes from Hebrew to Aramaic and continues to 7:28).

It soon becomes clear that the wise men have been given a hard task indeed. Not only are they to give the interpretation of the king's dream; they are to describe the dream itself! Failure to do so will result in their being torn limb from limb! The wise men protest that the king's request is beyond human wisdom. The exasperated king gives orders for them to be killed. Daniel and his companions are among those who come under threat of death.

The contemporaries of the author of Daniel would no doubt have a strong fellow-feeling for our four heroes in such circumstances as these. They themselves knew what it was to live under threat to their lives and property. They would read on eagerly to see how Daniel and his friends would react and how God would deal with them in their difficult predicament.

(ii)

The similarities between this story and that recorded in Genesis 41 concerning the young man Joseph and Pharaoh's dream of seven years' famine and seven years' plenty are too pronounced to be accidental. The Joseph story would, of course, be well known to the writer who saw in his hero of the exile yet another illustration of the same providence and goodness of God revealed in ancient times. He does not slavishly copy the Genesis story, for there are differences between them, but in a number of ways he lets the one mirror the other. In each account the king in question is troubled by a dream (2:1; Gen. 41:8); the magicians can do nothing to help (2:10f; Gen. 41:8); a Hebrew slave comes to the rescue and, with the help of God (2:30; Gen. 41:16), is able to give the dream's interpretation (2:36–45; Gen. 41:25–33); as a result he is promoted as chief minister of state and head of the sages (cf. 2:48; Gen. 41:40ff.).

In two respects, however, the Daniel story is distinctive. As we shall see, its chief lesson is not only that God is in control of the day by day affairs of men, which the Genesis story so graphically illustrates, but that the whole of history is in his hands and that he will bring it to a dramatic climax in the very near future. A second lesson is that, despite the vaunted wisdom of pagan philosophers, they can do nothing at all to interpret life's mysteries or to make known the secret things of the Most High. The subsequent story underlines the point made in these verses, that the lore of the pagan world, with its wonder-workers, astrologers, soothsayers, and exorcists, cannot even begin to compare with the wisdom possessed by the followers of the true God. The magicians and their fellow-prognosticators may consult their sacred book containing enchantments, pre-dictions and incantations, but they will fail to make any impression. They may try by bluff and blandishment, as with Nebuchadnezzar, to side-step the intractable problems life throws up or else play for time, but in the end it will be of no avail. With all their secret learning and all their accumulated esoteric lore, they cannot even tell the present, far less the future. They are utterly bankrupt.

(iii)

None of this would be lost on the readers of the book of Daniel from the time of Antiochus Epiphanes onwards, for theirs was a society in which the wisdom of their fathers was being challenged on every side by the wisdom of the pagan world with which they were surrounded.

Many years before, Alexander the Great had taken over the Persian Empire which in turn had absorbed the old Babylonian Empire with its teaching concerning astrology, occultism, cosmology, demonology, and angelology. When, a few years later, he made his forced march to India he broke the cultural barrier between East and West through which "there came flooding back the lore, magic, astrology, determinism, dualism and 'wisdom' of the east" (S. B. Frost). Information of a like kind is given by Josephus, Eusebius and others who refer to a certain Chaldean priest of the third century B.C. named Berossus who represents a strong Magian missionary movement of that time which forged its way throughout the countries of the Eastern Mediterranean "preaching a Greek-philosophized blend of Iranian esotericism with Chaldean astrology and determinism". The accumulated lore of the Greek West and the Magian East built up a highly syncretistic body of belief in which "wisdom", so unlike that of the ancient Hebrew writers, played a significant part, and with it a professional class of "wise men" who claimed the authority of sacred books and ancient tradition. The whole of Syria—a bridge between East and West—was wide open to these influences and came to show a widespread interest in the occult, magical incantations, astrological phenomena, demonology, angelology, and eschatological prognostications.

It is a moot point to what extent the Jews, and in particular the Jewish writers of the period, were affected by specifically Persian ideas, but there can be little doubt that they felt the impact of foreign influence, not just on their way of life, but on their religious beliefs as well. The book of Enoch, for example, dating from the first two centuries B.C., shows a keen interest in cosmology and astrology. Much attention is given to the movements of the heavenly bodies and their supposed influence on human destiny. Even such an exclusive sect as the Qumran Covenanters were apparently not exempt from such influence, for among their writings are fragments of a horoscope naming the signs of the Zodiac and giving predictions based on the roar of the thunder.

The Jews in the Dispersion had lived under the influence of this syncretistic culture for many years, not least in Babylonia itself. The Jews of Palestine were hardly any better off, surrounded as they were by the Hellenistic brand of paganism. It is just possible that the pressures on them were made even stronger in the years immediately following the writing of the book of Daniel, for with the establishment of a strong Jewish state under the Maccabees and their successors, many Jews may well have been attracted to return home, bringing with them inevitably an awareness and even an appreciation of that pagan culture in which they had grown up. The book of Daniel, then, was written at an opportune time, declaring that the wisdom of the pagan world, for all its display of learning and power, was of no avail and could not compare with that true wisdom which was the gift of God to his people. Divination, incantation, and magical formula were no match for that divine revelation vouchsafed to those who worship the true God and obey his laws.

GOD'S WISDOM

Daniel 2:1–13 *(cont'd)*

Throughout this book the name of Daniel is associated with the gift of wisdom—a wisdom, as these verses show, so very different from that of the Babylonian "wise men". Indeed, his name has remained a byword, together with that of Solomon, as the wise man *par excellence*. In "The Merchant of Venice", for example, in Act IV Scene I, the sagacity of Portia is recognised by Shylock in these celebrated words;

> "A Daniel come to judgment! Yea, a Daniel.
> O wise young judge! how I do honour thee!"

Such wisdom is not just technical know-how or professional skill or academic learning or native ability. It is that penetrating spiritual insight, God-given and God-inspired, that sees meaning in mysteries and light in darkness because it knows that God is there and that God is in control.

(i) Behind its use in Daniel lies a rich and varied ancient "wisdom tradition" illustrated in the canonical Scriptures by the books of Job, Proverbs, and Ecclesiastes, together with certain of the Psalms. Throughout these writings it takes many different forms and assumes a whole variety of expression—the witty saying, the pithy remark, the wise aphorism, the tantalising riddle, the profound observation, the weighty proverb. Here in Daniel it expresses itself rather in the form of stories from the past designed to preserve the tradition of the fathers and to strengthen the faith of God's people in times of tribulation. These "wisdom stories" show that there is a wisdom and a power which belong to God and which he gives as a gift to his faithful people. By this means they are able to outdo the wisdom of "the wise", who rely on chicanery and chance.

(ii) This "wisdom tradition" is continued and developed by writers of the intertestamental period along lines that are of no small importance for our understanding of God's revelation in Jesus Christ.

Thus, Ben Sira (c.180 B.C.) continues the line of thought introduced much earlier in Proverbs 8 and Job 28 where the figure of wisdom is personified as if having a life and being of its own. But he goes further. Wisdom, though active in the creation of the world, is herself (the word is feminine in Hebrew) created by God. But the writer goes further even than this, for wisdom is associated with God not only in the creation of the universe, but also in the revelation of his will and is to be identified with the eternal Law of God. It is an authoritative representative of the Most High which comes forth from the mouth of God, seeking a dwelling-place on earth and finding it eventually in Israel. In so doing Ben Sira goes some way beyond the personification to be found in either Job or Proverbs in the direction of "personalisation".

A further step still in this process is taken by the writer of the Wisdom of Solomon who attempts to bring the Old Testament teaching on wisdom into line with Greek speculation. He adopts the language of the Stoic philosophers who spoke in terms of a divine power immanent in the world and operative behind the many and diverse activities of creation. Here wisdom appears as an emanation, a reflection, an image of God. Though possessing many personal attributes, she is not to be regarded as a divine being alongside God. She is rather a divine principle or presence through which God is seen and known by men, which pervades and penetrates all things and is a perfect revelation of God (cf. Wisdom 7:22-8:1). This picture calls to mind the world-soul or world-principle of Stoic belief by which all things are held together—an idea which elsewhere is used also with reference to the Spirit (cf. Wisdom 1:7) or the Word of God (cf. Ecclesiasticus 43:26) and in the New Testament is related to the cosmic work of Christ (cf. Col. 1:17; Heb. 1:3).

(iii) Small wonder that the writers of the New Testament saw in these spiritual insights a rich seam to be mined in their search for the truth about Jesus Christ their Lord. In him they found the fulfilment, the embodiment of that divine wisdom made known by God from the beginning. Pagan wisdom could not begin to compare with what they found revealed in him: "Where is the wise man? Where is the scribe? Where is the debater of this age? Has not God made foolish the wisdom of this world?... Greeks seek after wisdom, but we preach Christ crucified... Christ the power of God and the wisdom of God" (1 Cor. 1:20ff.) With him the Spirit of God is vitally related (cf. Gal. 4:6); in him the Word of God fully dwells (cf. John 1:1ff.); through him is revealed "the manifold wisdom" of God (cf. Eph. 3:10). One greater than Solomon is here (cf. Luke 11:31).

PRAYER AND PRAISE

Daniel 2:14-23

Then Daniel replied with prudence and discretion to Ari-och, the captain of the king's guard, who had gone out to slay the wise men of Babylon; he said to Ari-och, the king's captain, "Why is the decree of the king so severe?" Then Ari-och made the matter known to Daniel. And Daniel went in and besought the king to appoint him a time, that he might show to the king the interpretation.

Then Daniel went to his house and made the matter known to Hananiah, Misha-el, and Azariah, his companions, and told them to seek mercy of the God of heaven concerning this mystery, so that Daniel and his companions might not perish with the rest of the wise men of Babylon. Then the mystery was revealed to Daniel in a vision of the night. Then Daniel blessed the God of heaven. Daniel said:

"Blessed be the name of God for ever and ever,
    to whom belong wisdom and might.
He changes times and seasons;
    he removes kings and sets up kings;
he gives wisdom to the wise
    and knowledge to those who have understanding;
he reveals deep and mysterious things;
    he knows what is in the darkness,
    and the light dwells with him.
To thee, O God of my fathers,
    I give thanks and praise,
for thou hast given me wisdom and strength,
    and hast now made known to me what we asked of thee,
    for thou hast made known to us the king's matter."

Faced with a dire situation Daniel acts with politeness and tact. He goes straight to the man who matters, Arioch captain of the king's guard, and asks the reason for the king's harsh decree. Then off to the king himself to ask for time to discover the required dream and its interpretation. The next port of call is his own house where he beseeches his three companions to pray for divine compassion in revealing the mystery of the dream. As a result the mystery is made known in a night-vision, though the reader is kept in suspense to know what it is whilst Daniel recites or sings a hymn of praise.

(i)

The reference here and elsewhere in the book to the efficacy of prayer and in particular of intercessory prayer is a reminder that religion to the Jew at that time was not confined to the Temple or even the synagogue worship. The period from the writing of the book of Daniel to New Testament times was marked by deep piety on the part of many in Israel. "Though the prophetic Psalms became crystallized as part of the temple liturgy,and though the synagogues developed a prayer liturgy, never did *ex tempore* prayer lose its prominent role in the religion of the Jew" (Norman B. Johnson). The books of the Apocrypha and Pseudepigrapha provide many examples of this, as indeed does the book of Daniel itself.

This is substantiated later in the book (cf. 6:10) where it is said that Daniel and his friends offered prayers three times daily to God in heaven. It is safe to assume that this reflects the attitude of the writer himself and his own practice of the presence of God. Such piety in the author is hardly surprising if, as is likely, the book reflects the outlook of the *Hasidim* or "Pious Ones" to whom reference is made in I Maccabees and elsewhere, and if he himself actually belonged to their number. For these, as their name indicates, were men of deep piety, devoted to prayer and the study of the Torah, who at the time of the Maccabean Revolt showed themselves to be powerful champions of Judaism over against the evil influences of Hellenism.

Daniel and his companions, in their reliance upon God in prayer, set an example to the faithful in the author's own generation—and indeed in every generation. "Only by the practice of the presence of God", writes Adam C. Welch, "could they, living in the alien world of heathenism with its lower ideals, keep the citadel of their inner life their own". By the power of intercessory prayer they were to prove that all might and wisdom belong to God.

(ii)

This indeed is the theme of the hymn of praise with which Daniel now blesses "the God of heaven". This particular expression occurs four times in the present chapter. It is the

Jewish equivalent of the Canaanite expression *Baal Shamen* and corresponds to the Greek title *Zeus Olympios* (see comments on 8: 13-14; 9:25-27 *(cont'd)*). It was the common title used by the Persians with reference to the God of the Jews, but by reason of its pagan associations, came to be suspect in the eyes of the faithful.

More important, however, is the hymn itself which is offered to the God who has graciously answered their prayers. In form it has much in common with the Psalms and other hymns which appear in a number of Old Testament books. It is written in verse and consists of four stanzas made up of alternating three-stress and four-stress lines. Its phraseology is reminiscent of other biblical hymns (cf. Ps. 41:13; Job 12:12f.; Neh. 9:5; Esth. 1:3), but it is no doubt an original composition whose mood fits the context admirably and which, in poetic praise rather than in prose, directs the reader's attention once more to God as the source of all wisdom and power.

During the post-exilic period and right up to New Testament times much use was made of Psalms and hymns, not least in the Temple worship. There is evidence that in the fourth century B.C., for example, at least some Psalms were being used for cultic and liturgical purposes by special "guilds" of singers and musicians (cf.I Chron. 16:8ff.; Ps. 105:1-15). In due course they came to hold an important place not only in the Temple worship, but also in the synagogue liturgy as in the Sabbath services and on the occasion of the great festivals.

But we are reminded by this Danielic hymn, as indeed by the many hymns or *Hodayot* found, for example, among the writings of the Qumran Convenanters, that such compositions are much more than mere "accompaniments of ritual". They are an expression of that personal piety to which reference has already been made and in their teaching concerning the nature and activity of God are an epitome of the Jewish faith. In a number of the biblical Psalms this piety expresses itself in a love for the law of God (cf. Ps. 19:7-10). The good life, which is the goal of true wisdom, is to be found in obedience to the law (cf. Pss. 1; 49; 112; 119). "Here", writes Sigmund Mowinckel, "we are face to face with a learned Psalmography which is not derived from the Temple singers, but is of a truly private nature and has no longer any direct relation to the cult." The resultant religion is that of a genuine legal piety characterised by a confidence in God's control over all exigencies and a trust in the divine wisdom which he imparts to his faithful worshippers. It is this piety and this theme that the hymn so clearly reveals.

(iii)

The hymn begins on a note of adoration with Daniel blessing the name of God. Blessings are God's gifts to men; in blessing him men acknowledge the source of such blessings and return to him what is already his. God's name, moreover, is not just the title or appellation by which he is known; it is the sum total of what he is in himself—the being of God who is known for what he is by what he does in the life of his people and in the life of the world at large. The very name by which he is known is holy because he himself is holy, and so we find in the intertestamental period especially—and not least among pious Jews today— a great reluctance even to pronounce his name but instead the practice of using circumlocutions which express but do not define the identity of the Almighty.

Two qualities in the being and character of God are singled out for special mention. These are his wisdom and his might. Nothing is hidden from his understanding and nothing is beyond his power to achieve. This is demonstrated in his control over creation and over the events of history—as illustrated in the dream about to be disclosed. Men may imagine that times and seasons are fixed by the movements of the heavenly bodies or else are in the hands of capricious celestial powers that are believed to control men's destinies. But this is not so. Times and seasons are in God's hands, and he changes them as he wills. And as in the wide universe beyond, so also in the affairs of nations and peoples around. Kings like Nebuchadnezzar or, for that matter, like Antiochus Epiphanes, may vainly imagine that their power and rule are in their own hands. But this is not so. It is God, and God alone, who sets them up and puts them down.

It is this God who is pleased to make known to the wise among his people his own divine wisdom and the knowledge of what is hidden from mortal man. As with the prophets of old times, Daniel is permitted to stand in the secret council of God—his heavenly Parliament, as it were, where God takes counsel with his minions who are sent forth to do his bidding (cf. Isa. 6:6ff.; Jer. 23:18ff.). There he is allowed to see for himself "deep and mysterious things" that are hidden from those uninitiated in the ways of the true God. To the wise they are mysteries no longer but clear indications of the working of God's hand. They are clear because where God is light is; the darkness holds no mysteries and the night no terrors. This figure of the light with reference to God is to be found, of course, earlier in the Old Testament and is prominent throughout the intertestamental period. To the Christian it recalls John's words: "God is light, and in him is no darkness at all" (1 John 1:5) and the testimony concerning that other John (the Baptist): "He was not that light; he came to bear witness to the light. The true light that enlightens every man was coming into the world" (John 1:8f.). Jesus who reveals what is hidden is himself the light of the world (cf. John 8:12; 12:35) and is declared to be the wisdom and the power of God (cf. 1 Cor. 1:24).

THE MYSTERY REVEALED

Daniel 2:24-30

> Therefore Daniel went in to Ari-och, whom the king had appointed to destroy the wise men of Babylon; he went and said thus to him, "Do not destroy the wise men of Babylon; bring me in before the king, and I will show the king the interpretation." Then Ari-och brought in Daniel before the king in haste, and said thus to him: "I have found among the exiles from Judah a man who can make known to the king the interpretation." The king said to Daniel, whose name was Belteshazzar, "Are you able to make known to me the dream that I have seen and its interpretation?" Daniel answered

the king, "No wise men, enchanters, magicians, or astrologers can show to the king the mystery which the king has asked, but there is a God in heaven who reveals mysteries, and he has made known to King Nebuchadnezzar what will be in the latter days. Your dream and the visions of your head as you lay in bed are these: To you, O king, as you lay in bed came thoughts of what would be hereafter, and he who reveals mysteries made known to you what is to be. But as for me, not because of any wisdom that I have more than all the living has this mystery been revealed to me, but in order that the interpretation may be made known to the king, and that you may know the thoughts of your mind."

(i)

On presenting himself again to Arioch with the claim that he is able to interpret the dream, Daniel is ushered into the king's presence. Addressing him by his Babylonian name the king enquires if he is able to do as he has asked, making known both the dream and its interpretation. Daniel then declares that no-one, himself included, has sufficient wisdom for these things. There is one alone who reveals mysteries and there is one alone who can give the desired interpretation. God himself has revealed these things to Daniel with the express purpose of informing him what will be "in the latter days" which, as he will show, are almost here.

This phrase "in the latter days" is to be found in the Old Testament prophets to describe the coming of the messianic age which God will bring in as the climax of history. It is the final period when God will bring in his kingdom and all history will reach its consummation. This seems to be the meaning here. Elsewhere in the Jewish apocalyptic writings the phrase is sometimes used to indicate a coming kingdom beyond history itself, a new world which will supersede the old. "This present age" with its sin and rebellion will give way to "the age to come" in which evil will be destroyed and all wrongs set right. The perspective, however, in Daniel is that of this present age, albeit at its "latter end" when God's kingdom will be revealed. The interpretation of the mystery is a message about this coming kingdom.

(ii)

The word "interpretation" which appears here occurs thirty times in the Aramaic section of Daniel and is found frequently also in other apocalyptic writings, including the Dead Sea Scrolls. In this chapter it is used with reference to the meaning of the king's dream; frequently elsewhere it refers to the making known of the inner meaning of Scripture which, it is believed, is not self-evident but is made plain to the seer or scribe to whom God imparts this secret knowledge by means of divine revelation. Thus, in the Scrolls, the Teacher of Righteousness is able to interpret the book of Habakkuk in a way undreamed of by the ordinary reader. It contains truths that even the prophet himself who wrote the book did not understand! The authors of Daniel and the other apocalyptic books believe they have been given this gift and in their writings unfold the divine mysteries as they have been revealed to them.

The word "mystery" (or "secret") occurs five times in Daniel, all of them again in the Aramaic section. It is a Persian loan-word and is translated in the Greek versions by the word *mysterion*. It does not designate any ordinary secret; it is the hidden mystery of God's eternal purpose for the universe and for the whole course of human history. In this chapter, as we shall see, the mystery to be unfolded has to do with God's dealings with the nations in preparation for the coming kingdom. This emphasis on eschatology, on what will happen at the end, is characteristic of these books. Some other apocalyptic writers, failing to find the meaning of life in the movements of history, look for it in pre-mundane "history" and in the order and governance of creation. Thus alongside eschatology we find a profound interest expressed in cosmology, with its related subject, astrology. According to such writers, among the mysteries to be revealed by God are the knowledge of the structure of the universe, the movement of the heavenly bodies and acquaintance with seasonal changes. We have hints of these developments in Daniel, but in the present context the mystery to be revealed concerns God's coming rule over the affairs of men.

(iii)

The revelation or disclosure of such "mysteries" is not made known by merely human wisdom, however; it requires the gift of divine wisdom for its interpretation: "There is a God in heaven who reveals mysteries . . . Not because of any wisdom that I have more than all the living has this mystery been revealed to me, but in order that the interpretation may be made known to the king" (verses 28,30).

What is more, such knowledge is given only to the select few of whom Daniel is presumably one. This small elite of "wise men", a spiritual aristocracy as it were, claim special insights into the divine purpose and a special understanding of God's way in the universe. The author of Daniel, who identifies himself with our hero, obviously believed that he was one of the chosen few.

Frequent reference is made in these apocalyptic writings to "the wise", whose task it is to interpret to "the many" the things which they themselves have been privileged to see and hear so that "the many" may in turn become wise. This close connection between esoteric knowledge and divine wisdom is found at least as early as the time of Ben Sira (c.180 B.C.) who tells us, in what must surely be an autobiographical passage, that it was the privilege and responsibility of the "wise man" to uncover the secrets of wisdom to those who sought her illumination: "He will seek out the wisdom of all the ancients and will be occupied with prophecies . . . He will seek out the hidden meanings of proverbs and be at home with the obscurities of parables" (Ecclesiasticus 39:1ff.).

(iv)

Such considerations are of importance for an understanding not only of Jewish apocalyptic writings but also of Christian origins as these are recorded in the New Testament, for there the word *mysterion* appears quite prominently with several shades of meaning, the most common of which is to signify an "open secret", i.e. a divine plan in the form of a mystery concealed by God from the general run of men but now revealed to those chosen to be the recipients of it. Thus, those who came to Jesus asking the meaning of his parables are told, "To you has been given the secret of the kingdom of God, but for those outside everything is in parables" (Mark 4:11). Jesus himself is the supreme interpreter of the divine mystery, not least in his interpretation of the sacred Scriptures where it remains hidden until, by divine revelation, it is disclosed. According to the Apostle Paul this was a mystery which "was kept secret for long ages but is now disclosed" (Rom. 16:25f.).

The association we have noted between "mystery" and "wisdom" is also evident in the New Testament. This is brought out clearly, for example, in such a passage as Rom. 11:25: "Lest you be wise in your own conceits, I want you to understand this mystery, brethren" (cf. Rom. 16:25f.). Its content is filled out in Eph. 3:3,9f., where Paul describes it as "the mystery made known to me by revelation... the plan of the mystery hidden for ages in God who created all things, that through the Church the manifold wisdom of God might now be made known to the principalities and powers in the heavenly places". In Col. 1:26f. he goes further still and asserts that this divine mystery, "hidden for ages and generations but now made manifest to his saints", is to be identified with "Christ in you, the hope of glory".

As in Jewish apocalyptic, moreover, so here, God's revealed mystery shows a redemption that involves not only the nations of the earth but also the whole created universe which "waits with eager longing for the revealing of the sons of God" (Rom. 8:19). In particular, the coming kingdom will remain a mystery until its secret is revealed (cf. Mark 4:11). This is part of the "messianic secret" of Jesus as the Son of Man.

(v)

Such revelations are made known in the apocalyptic writings in many different ways, but chiefly through the medium of an angel or, as in the present passage, by means of a vision or a dream or sometimes by an audition or by bodily translation to the courts of heaven where the seer enters into the "secret council" of God and listens to his divine word. Here the writer, through the mouth of the exile Daniel, takes his place in the ranks of those wise men who have been initiated into the hidden mysteries of God's purpose and have been chosen and endowed to make them known.

The writer of the book of Revelation has the same kind of experience and indicates the same means of revelation. Angels convey the divine message and through dreams and visions the divine mystery is made known. But such things are not confined to the apocalyptic books. In the Gospels, in the Acts of the Apostles and in the Epistles, God speaks by such chosen means to those who are wise with the wisdom of Christ. Even the hard-headed Paul can write these words, presumably of himself: "I know a man in Christ who fourteen years ago was caught up to the third heaven—whether in the body or out of the body I do not know, God knows. And I know that this man was caught up into Paradise...and he heard things that cannot be told, which man may not utter" (2 Cor. 12:2–4). By whatever means the interpretation is given, the mystery is made known by that wisdom which God alone imparts.

THE STATUE AND THE STONE

Daniel 2:31–45

"You saw, O king, and behold, a great image. This image, mighty and of exceeding brightness, stood before you, and its appearance was frightening. The head of this image was of fine gold, its breast and arms of silver, its belly and thighs of bronze, its legs of iron, its feet partly of iron and partly of clay. As you looked, a stone was cut out by no human hand, and it smote the image on its feet of iron and clay, and broke them in pieces; then the iron, the clay, the bronze, the silver, and the gold, all together were broken in pieces, and became like the chaff of the summer threshing floors; and the wind carried them away, so that not a trace of them could be found. But the stone that struck the image became a great mountain and filled the whole earth.

"This was the dream; now we will tell the king its interpretation. You, O king, the king of kings, to whom the God of heaven has given the kingdom, the power, and the might, and the glory, and into whose hand he has given, wherever they dwell, the sons of men, the beasts of the field, and the birds of the air, making you rule over them all—you are the head of gold. After you shall arise another kingdom inferior to you, and yet a third kingdom of bronze, which shall rule over all the earth. And there shall be a fourth kingdom, strong as iron, because iron breaks to pieces and shatters all things; and like iron which crushes, it shall break and crush all these. And as you saw the feet and toes partly of potter's clay and partly of iron, it shall be a divided kingdom; but some of the firmness of iron shall be in it, just as you saw iron mixed with the miry clay. And as the toes of the feet were partly iron and partly clay, so the kingdom shall be partly strong and partly brittle. As you saw the iron mixed with miry clay, so they will mix with one another in marriage, but they will not hold together, just as iron does not mix with clay. And in the days of those kings the God of heaven will set up a kingdom which shall never be destroyed, nor shall its sovereignty be left to another people. It shall break in pieces all these kingdoms and bring them to an end, and it shall stand for ever; just as you saw that a stone was cut from a mountain by no human hand, and that it broke in pieces the iron, the bronze, the clay, the silver, and the gold. A great God has made known to the king what shall be hereafter. The dream is certain, and its interpretation sure."

(i)

Daniel describes Nebuchadnezzar's dream. In it he sees a great statue made of different metals—the head of gold, the chest and arms of silver, the middle and upper legs of bronze, the lower legs of iron, and the feet of iron and clay together. These represent a descending order of worth, the feet perhaps being a check-work of iron and ceramic tiles. It is not an idol, but a colossus such as the dreamer may have seen in the art-form of the world of his time. The symbolism of metals to represent the several ages of world history was not uncommon in ancient times and, as the interpretation is to show, is used as such here.

Something happens to the statue which can happen only in dreams. A stone cut from a mountain "by no human hand" strikes the statue at its feet and smashes it into pieces that the wind blows away like chaff. The stone then grows and grows until at last it becomes a mountain and fills the whole earth! This reference to a mountain recalls the reference in Isa. 2:2–4 where the prophet foretells the time when all the nations will come streaming to "the mountain of the Lord's house" to receive instruction in Mount Zion. The centre of Yahweh's worship is to be the centre of the whole earth.

Daniel now proceeds to the dream's interpretation. The head of gold is Nebuchadnezzar himself, representing the neo-Babylonian empire. The sovereignty he enjoys over man and beast has been given him in trust by God. A second kingdom, symbolised by silver, will arise and take his place. This kingdom is not identified, but the sequence of the dream and other indications in the book point to a Median kingdom for which there is in fact no record in the history of the time. If this identification is correct then the third kingdom of bronze is that of Persia. The fourth of iron is that of Greece which came to be divided into two and like the iron and the ceramics, could not hold together. This unstable union is explained by reference to the fact that they "mix with one another in marriage". The allusion here may be one of two kinds. It may refer to the union of the dynasties of the Ptolemies ("the clay") and the Seleucids ("the iron"), the successors to Alexander's kingdom, or it may refer to the intermarriage of different races and cultures encouraged by Alexander and his successors throughout the East, a practice abhorrent to the Jews.

The writer dwells on this fourth kingdom more than on those that have gone before because this, as he will show, is the point of contact with the coming kingdom of mystery and might symbolised by the stone whose origins owe nothing to man. Moreover, it is a kingdom contemporary with himself "whose doom is writ". The kingdom of God—for this is the symbolism of the rolling stone—is about to be revealed and the people of the Jews are about to experience a great deliverance from the hand of their enemies and have a share in the rule of God. Several things, then, are said about this coming kingdom that are worthy of note. It is, as we have seen, not man-made at all, but God-given—a mysterious kingdom created and controlled by God. It is an eternal kingdom for "it shall stand for ever"—in contrast to the kingdoms of this world which, for all their glory and strength, will speedily pass away. The sovereignty of this kingdom, moreover, will not be left to any other people—an allusion perhaps to the conviction elsewhere expressed that the people of Israel will themselves inherit the kingdom and will rule in it for ever. All this implies—and again this is made plain later—that it is an earthly kingdom in which all evil will be destroyed. And finally, its coming will be soon and with devastating force. The proud kingdoms that have trampled Israel underfoot will then be shattered into small pieces and be scattered by the wind. Popular hopes that some other great power would arise to take the place of the great kingdoms would come to nothing. The climax of history is at hand. The kingdom of God is about to be ushered in.

(ii)

Much strained and fanciful exegesis of the book of Daniel might have been avoided if this fact had been recognised, that the writer's declaration concerning the kingdom of God is not intended to point forward to some far-off date in the future; it is addressed essentially to the there-and-then of the second century B.C. and to Jews awaiting deliverance from the hands of their enemies by the supernatural intervention of God.

In this literal sense the hopes of the writer fell short of realisation, and the kingdom did not come in the way that he and others had hoped and prayed it might. And yet there is a sense in which these hopes and prayers still await fulfilment in ways other than the writer could appreciate at that time. For there is a sense in which every succeeding generation—past, present and future—is vitally related to "the end" and so to the coming kingdom. To the writer of Daniel and the apocalyptic writers who followed him, the end is a denouement, a climax, in which the whole of history, and not just its final expression, is taken up into the purpose of God. It may be the feet of the statue that are smitten, but it is the whole image that is broken and falls to the ground. The coming kingdom is "eternal" in retrospect as well as in prospect, sweeping up all history into its purview.

Such teaching is relevant to the teaching of Jesus in the New Testament. There will come a day, he says, when the kingdom will come "in power" (cf. Mark 9:1; Rom: 1:4). That coming will mark the end of history and indeed the consummation of all things. This denouement is still in the future, awaiting the revelation of God's purpose when his judgment will be made known on men and nations. And yet it is also near at hand; indeed it has already appeared in his coming—in his miracles and life of service and in his death and resurrection. It is a divine new order in which those who believe in him may share now and in which the judgment and the mercy of God are being revealed. It is a long way from Daniel to Jesus, but in the providence of God, Daniel's prophecy has come to be fulfilled in him.

(iii)

Nebuchadnezzar's dream, as interpreted by Daniel, is a declaration that all nations which exalt themselves vaingloriously and trust in human might are subject to the judgment of God and must in the end submit to the power of the kingdom. It demonstrates their vulnerability and declares that the vindication of God's people is at hand. He is in control and will accomplish his eternal purpose in spite of all the machinations of men. It is a timely reminder to the nations of the world which play the game of power-politics, which wear the iron glove and act as if might is right. The book of Daniel would have us know that there is a judgment in history and that God rules even now in the affairs of men. The Church may appear in the eyes of this world weak and insignificant and altogether irrelevant, a puny figure alongside the colossus of the nation or the state. But it has the confidence to believe that God's kingdom will prevail, that in the providence and goodness of God it will grow and "fill the whole earth".

(iv)

It is perhaps not altogether without significance that *all* the nations from Babylon to Greece are here seen together at a glance. Following the great prophets of the Old Testament and going beyond them the writer views the course of history as forming a unity in terms of the coming kingdom. All nations and all peoples, of whatever age or culture, are affected by its coming. Later apocalyptic writers go further than this and assert that not only the course of history but the very cosmos itself is involved and will in the end be transformed by the powers of the kingdom. Every event and every creature will find its meaning and its judgment or fulfilment in terms of that kingdom which is inevitable and final. The unity of history and the unity of creation are corollaries of the unity of God himself who will bring both to their completion in the coming of that kingdom which will have no end.

A JOB WELL DONE

Daniel 2:46-49

> Then King Nebuchadnezzar fell upon his face, and did homage to Daniel, and commanded that an offering and incense be offered up to him. The king said to Daniel, "Truly, your God is God of gods and Lord of kings, and a revealer of mysteries, for you have been able to reveal this mystery." Then the king gave Daniel high honours and many great gifts, and made him ruler over the whole province of Babylon, and chief prefect over all the wise men of Babylon. Daniel made request of the king, and he appointed Shadrach, Meshach, and Abednego over the affairs of the province of Babylon; but Daniel remained at the king's court.

(i)

The writer adds a tail-piece to his story that would warm the hearts of his readers. The mighty monarch, the haughty ruler, the king whose word means life or death to his subjects, falls down in homage before Daniel. Not content with this he actually worships him, commanding that an offering and

incense be offered up to him. The purist might object that
Daniel should allow such a thing to be done to him. But we are
surely not to press the details of the story but rather to enter into
its spirit. As a representative of God's faithful people Daniel
sees in the king's obeisance a fulfilment of the promise of
Scripture that "kings shall see and arise: princes, and they shall
prostrate themselves... with their faces to the ground they shall
bow down to you, and lick the dust of your feet" (Isa. 49:7,23;
cf. 52:15; 60:14). An interesting parallel to this story is given
by the first century Jewish writer Josephus. Alexander the
Great, in a supposed visit to Jerusalem, fell down before the
High Priest, acknowledging by so doing the God whose priest
he was (cf. *Antiquities* XI,8,5). So also here. It is Daniel's God
whom Nebuchadnezzar is worshipping. He is the greatest of the
gods whom kings must acknowledge as Lord, for he is a
revealer of mysteries beyond all other gods.

(ii)

Having paid his homage, the king now distributes his rewards.
It is promotion all round! Daniel is given the chief place of
authority in the whole province of Babylon and is established as
a member of the king's court, just as Joseph had been rewarded
by Pharaoh (cf. Gen. 41:39ff.) and Mordecai had been treated
by a Persian king (cf. Esth. 6:3ff.). What is more he is put in
charge of the *élite* corps of soothsayers and astrologers and
other wise men who advised the king in all matters of state.
Mindful of those who had stood by him in days of testing, he
requests that his three friends be given positions of responsibility also. His request is granted and they are appointed "over the
affairs of the province of Babylon". Such tales of promotion
and reward are to be found elsewhere in Jewish writings of this
period and later, reflecting not only the superiority of the God
of Israel but also the ultimate triumph of his people.

(iii)

Not every encounter with alien powers and heathen rulers ends
on such a happy note. The villain does not always "see the light"

and turn in repentance to God. The faithful God-fearing man is seldom rewarded by wordly masters with promotion and a position of responsibility.

And yet the truth behind the dream remains—the ultimate victory of God is assured in which his people will share and with it the recognition of him by all men as Lord and King. And so the Apostle Paul can assert with complete confidence that "at the name of Jesus every knee shall bow, in heaven and on earth, and every tongue confess that Jesus Christ is Lord, to the glory of God the Father" (Phil. 2:10f.). This is a hope, born of faith, that strengthens devotion and engenders praise.

WORSHIP THIS IMAGE

Daniel 3:1-7

King Nebuchadnezzar made an image of gold, whose height was sixty cubits and its breadth six cubits. He set it up on the plain of Dura, in the province of Babylon. Then King Nebuchadnezzar sent to assemble the satraps, the prefects, and the governors, the counsellors, the treasurers, the justices, the magistrates, and all the officials of the provinces to come to the dedication of the image which King Nebuchadezzar had set up. Then the satraps, the prefects, and the governors, the counsellors, the treasurers, the justices, the magistrates, and all the officials of the provinces, were assembled for the dedication of the image that King Nebuchadnezzar had set up; and they stood before the image that Nebuchadnezzar had set up. And the herald proclaimed aloud, "You are commanded, O peoples, nations, and languages, that when you hear the sound of the horn, pipe, lyre, trigon, harp, bagpipe, and every kind of music, you are to fall down and worship the golden image that King Nebuchadnezzar has set up; and whoever does not fall down and worship shall immediately be cast into a burning fiery furnace." Therefore, as soon as all the peoples heard the sound of the horn, pipe, lyre, trigon, harp, bagpipe, and every kind of music, all the peoples, nations, and languages fell down and worshipped the golden image which King Nebuchadnezzar had set up.

(i)

The story told in these verses and throughout the rest of this chapter is powerful in its impact and moving in its appeal. It is a typical "martyr story" in which God miraculously comes to the rescue of his faithful people and delivers them out of all their trouble. Its language is intentionally stilted and its tone pompous. With mock seriousness the writer identifies the officials with their high sounding names, summoned by the king to the plain of Dura to witness the dedication of the golden image he had set up. With equal "seriousness" he lists in sonorous tone the motley array of musical instuments to be blown, banged or twanged as a signal to all peoples, nations, and languages to bow down and worship. Failure to obey would seal their fate in a burning fiery furnace.

The mocking tone of the passage recalls the more obvious jibes of the prophet of the exile who, with devastating sarcasm, denounces the idols of his day as nothing and less than nothing before the greatness and majesty of the living God whom Israel worshipped and served (cf. Isa. 40:18ff.; 44:9ff.). The image in the plain of Dura is only a piffling idol in stark contrast to the greatness of the mighty God.

(ii)

The story, as subsequent verses show, is about Daniel's three companions and makes no mention of Daniel himself. This may well indicate its independent origin and its incorporation at this point into the writer's material.

King Nebuchadnezzar sets up an enormous statue measuring 96 feet tall and 9 feet wide. Its dimensions and symmetry are not to be pressed; they are simply intended to impress. The statue was huge, towering over puny men. Such images were to be found not infrequently in that part of the world at that time. Herodotus, for example, refers to two great statues of gold in Babylon, one of them a representation of the god Zeus and the other in human form. It has been suggested that the golden statue erected by Nebuchadnezzar may have been a representation of himself; the references in verses 12, 14 and 18, however, suggest that we are to see in it a representation rather of the king's favourite god.

(iii)

The warning given in this passage against idolatry and apostasy, and its plea for loyalty to the only true and living God, had a particularly sharp cutting edge to it in the time when this book was first written, the time of Antiochus Epiphanes. It would appear from such a passage as Judith 3:8, to be dated some little time later in the Maccabean period, that Nebuchadnezzar had the reputation of trying to destroy all other gods "so that all nations should worship Nebuchadnezzar alone, and all their tongues and tribes should call upon him as god". It may well be that the writer of Daniel, together with his readers, were meant to see in Antiochus a reflection of the king of Babylon. As we have seen, in the year 168 B.C. Antiochus set about wiping out the Jewish faith and set up an altar to the god Zeus, of whom he claimed to be a manifestation, on the site of the sacred altar in Jerusalem. Already he had declared himself to be "God Manifest" and, on pain of death, demanded the Jews' total allegiance and required that they bow down and worship other gods.

(iv)

There is no other sin more seriously trounced in the Bible than the sin of idolatry, for idolatry is apostasy and apostasy is a betrayal of the true God.

Broadly speaking it may be said to fall into two categories: the misrepresentation of God where, for example, he is worshipped by his own name but has the attributes of the Baal or some other deity superimposed upon him; and the replacement of God by someone or something else as in the case of the Babylonian god Marduk whom many Jews in Babylon were no doubt tempted to worship as "the god of the land".

Both categories have been common throughout the Christian era too and are with us still. To some God is misrepresented as an abstract figure—the power of nature, the first principle, the evolutionary process—hardly to be worshipped, and to whom prayer would be of no avail; to others he is a mythical figure, important but only in terms of art and culture and the history of civilisation; to others again he is the stern Father-figure, the

Judge who will make sure we receive our deserts, a Big Brother figure who notes down meticulously everything we do. The New Testament claims that if we are to know what God is like we have to look into the face of Jesus Christ. God the Father is to be recognised through God the Son. Or, as the writer of Hebrews puts it, "He [i.e. Jesus] reflects the glory of God and bears the very stamp of his nature" (1:3). He is the reflection as in a mirror of God himself; he is the representation of God as the imprint in wax is to the seal that made it. Or, as Paul puts it, "He is the image of the invisible God" (Col. 1:15). This is no image of wood or stone or metal. It is an image of flesh and blood.

But very often the expression of idolatry has been of the other kind—the ousting of God by an idol of man's making. In the days of the early Church this, for a while, took the form of emperor-worship. Christians were forced to comply under threat of banishment or death. The Emperor claimed to be divine and so demanded the allegiance and worship of all his subjects. We recall the story of one tolerant emperor who thought he would please the Christians by setting up a little figurine of "the Jesus-God" in his private shrine alongside the statues of the other gods and goddesses. He could not understand when he found he had a near-rebellion on his hands! The Christians refused to share their worship of Jesus with any other. There was only one name under heaven given among men by which they must be saved (cf. Acts 4:12). There are many Christians today who would argue from experience that this is a very modern phenomenon and that there is little to choose, for example, between emperor-worship then and the claims now of the all-powerful, totalitarian state.

WORSHIP THIS IMAGE—OR ELSE!

Daniel 3:1–7 *(cont'd)*

(i)

The procedure outlined here for the dedication of the image is familiar to us from other extra-biblical sources also.

Various officials with high-sounding names are summoned
to the ceremony. They are clearly leaders and influential men,
representing many peoples, nations, and languages throughout
the king's wide domain. The offices and titles given here reflect
Persian influence and were possibly borrowed by our author
from lists known to him, although the form of some of them
seems to have been "damaged in transit".

Music played an important part in such ceremonies. Six
instruments are mentioned here—the horn, the pipe, the lyre,
the trigon (a small stringed instrument, triangular in shape), the
harp, and the bagpipe. The last named instrument, *sumponyah*
is the Greek *symphonia* and is not found in Greek literature in
this sense before the second century B.C. (This is one indication
among others of the late date of this passage in its present form,
or at least of late influence upon it). It is of interest to note in
this connection that the contemporary writer, Polybius, tells
how Antiochus, at his drunken orgies, used to dance to the
accompaniment of the bagpipe.

Failure to worship the golden image at the sound of the
musical instruments would result in death by burning in a fiery
furnace. Norman Porteous suggests that "the sounding of
musical instruments may be intended as a blasphemous parody
of the blaring of trumpets on the Jewish New Year's Day. The
martyrs were thus expected on this view to take part in a kind of
black mass or witches' sabbath". The method of punishment
here described—by burning—was known from earlier Old
Testament times (cf. Jer: 29.22). Herodotus refers to its use by
Cyrus and by the Scythians, whilst its continuing use in the
second century B.C. is documented in such a passage as 2
Maccabees 7:3ff. There we are told how Antiochus gave orders
for the death of one of seven brothers who were subjected to
terrible torture, and commanded "that pans and cauldrons be
heated", and "when he was utterly helpless, the king ordered
them to take him to the fire, still breathing, and to fry him in a
pan".

The furnace referred to in this Daniel passage is presumably
the "beehive" variety of which there is ample evidence elsewhere,

the fuel being fed in from the top and the cinders raked out through an opening in the side.

(ii)

Nebuchadnezzar would have them know he was a powerful man and would brook no rival to his absolute rule. Having marshalled his monster parade he orders them to take part in the dedication of the image.

It is not enough that they should just stand passively by, admiring the ceremony and enjoying the music. They must fall down and worship. "Here is the culmination of the ceremony—not when backs are curved and necks are strained, but when knees are bent and hands begin to fold in prayer. Strange! In all ages Nebuchadnezzar can only maintain his throne if an altar stands near the throne and lends him the security and strength which he lacks" (Walter Lüthi).

Adam C. Welch views these verses in terms of the relationship between Church and state in the 20th century and comments thus: "Some day it [the state] may demand an obedience which will make it impossible for certain men to save their souls alive. Then the opposite ends for life will come into open collision and men will have to choose whom they mean to serve. Are they only citizens of Babylon, finding their complete life in it and drawing their final sanctions from it; or are they *gerim* (aliens) in Babylon, seekers after a better kingdom and subject to a higher law?" The question is a pertinent one today, if ever it was. There must be a limit to the demands the state can make. It can claim loyalty and sacrifice on the part of its subjects. But it cannot demand worship and love. This is to commit sacrilege, to replace the Creator with the creature and to bow down before the work of men's hands. It matters not whether the idol is a potentate or an institution. When it goes beyond its God-given sanction and claims from its subjects what God alone can claim, it must stand condemned.

The driving force behind Nebuchadnezzar's command is plain to see. It is fear—fear of the fiery furnace. And human nature being what it is, "All the peoples, nations and languages fell down and worshipped the golden image which king Nebuchadnezzar had set up". Subsequent verses show a different reaction on the part of the three Jewish youths, but they too were subjected to the same threat and, no doubt, experienced the same fear.

The New Testament suggests the only adequate antidote: "Perfect love casts out fear" (1 John 4:18). Nebuchadnezzar does not know the meaning of love and so cannot understand its readiness to resist evil, its willingness to suffer and its power to overcome. Fear is still the motivating power behind so much of the world's commands—fear of imprisonment, of torture, of banishment, of separation. "Behold", says Jesus to his disciples, "I send you out as sheep in the midst of wolves...you will be hated by all for my name's sake...Do not fear those who kill the body but cannot kill the soul; rather fear him who can destroy both soul and body in hell" (Matt. 10:16,22,28). "Fear not, little flock, for it is your Father's good pleasure to give you the kingdom" (Luke 12:32).

INFORMERS AND CONFESSORS

Daniel 3:8–18

Therefore at that time certain Chaldeans came forward and maliciously accused the Jews. They said to King Nebuchadnezzar, "O king, live for ever! You, O king, have made a decree, that every man who hears the sound of the horn, pipe, lyre, trigon, harp, bagpipe, and every kind of music, shall fall down and worship the golden image; and whoever does not fall down and worship shall be cast into a burning fiery furnace. There are certain Jews whom you have appointed over the affairs of the province of Babylon: Shadrach, Meshach, and Abednego. These men, O king, pay no heed to you; they do not serve your gods or worship the golden image which you have set up."

Then Nebuchadnezzar in furious rage commanded that Shadrach, Meshach, and Abednego be brought. Then they brought these men before the king. Nebuchadnezzar said to them, "Is it true, O Shadrach, Meshach, and Abednego, that you do not serve my gods or worship the golden image which I have set up? Now if you are ready when you hear the sound of the horn, pipe, lyre, trigon, harp, bagpipe, and every kind of music, to fall down and worship the image which I have made, well and good; but if you do not worship, you shall immediately be cast into a burning fiery furnace; and who is the god that will deliver you out of my hands?"

Shadrach, Meshach, and Abednego answered the king, "O Nebuchadnezzar, we have no need to answer you in this matter. If it be so, our God whom we serve is able to deliver us from the burning fiery furnace; and he will deliver us out of your hand, O king. But if not, be it known to you, O king, that we will not serve your gods or worship the golden image which you have set up."

(i)

The three young men, in their refusal to conform, stood out like the proverbial sore thumb. They were, according to the story, men of standing in the community and might be expected to set an example to others. No doubt they had given the matter careful thought and had decided to pay whatever price might be demanded of them. Where idolatry was concerned they would not conform. Certain of their colleagues among the Chaldean "wise men", out of malice, made accusations against them to the king in person. The word used here for "accused" is a particularly graphic one. It is literally "ate their pieces" or, as we might say, they made mincemeat out of them! The appearance of the informer is a fairly common feature of the oriental tale and runs true to form in this passage. The fact that the accusation is itself true does not conceal the malicious intent, perhaps with a view to preferment over the Jewish interlopers.

Informers and the totalitarian state go hand in hand. Stories are legion of men and women in Hitler's Germany, for example, being betrayed by their business associates or even by members of their own families. Sometimes resistance to the regime was kept a close secret until the moment of betrayal; at other times no attempt was made at concealment and betrayal was easy. We think in this connection of Dietrich Bonhoeffer and members of his family who, with others, were implicated in the attempted killing of Hitler. Here is an excerpt from one of his letters written from prison:

There is hardly one of us who has not known what it is to be
betrayed. The figure of Judas, which we used to find so difficult to
understand, is now fairly familiar to us. The air that we breathe is so
polluted by mistrust that it almost chokes us...Our duty is to foster
and strengthen confidence wherever we can. Trust will always be
one of the greatest, rarest, and happiest blessings of our life in
community, though it can emerge only on the dark background of a
necessary mistrust. We have learnt never to trust a scoundrel an
inch, but to give ourselves to the trustworthy without reserve.

(ii)

The king, we are told, breaks into a furious rage—yet another
typical feature of such oriental stories. He gives the young men
another chance to "see the error of their ways" and to fall down
in worship before the golden image. In so doing he makes the
blasphemous assertion that there is no god who will be able to
deliver them from his hands. Here we see a picture of what the
Old Testament would consider to be the ultimate sin—rulers or
nations setting themselves up in place of God, claiming that
sovereignty that belongs to him alone, ousting him from his
rightful place of authority. "Ye shall be as gods" (Gen. 3:5) is a
temptation as old as Eden for which mighty monarchs and tin-
pot dictators have fallen time without number.

The response made by the young confessors is clear, even
though the text before us is somewhat difficult and may be in
need of emendation. With supreme confidence they remark
that they have no need to say a thing to the king, implying no
doubt that deeds will speak louder than words. Then come
some memorable words: "If it be so [i.e. if things plan out as you
suggest] our God whom we serve is able to deliver us from the
burning fiery furnace; and he will deliver us out of your hand.
But if [he does] not [choose to do so], be it known to you, O
king, that we will not serve your gods or worship the golden
image which you have set up." The calm confidence of the three
youths is presented in dramatic contrast to the raging fury of
the king. Come what may, the young men will trust in God and
refuse to deny his name. Later on, in chapter 12, we are given
some hints concerning the ground of this trust—their belief that

God will give them their reward beyond death. But here no explanations are given. Later in the chapter we are told of their vindication. But at this point in the story it is enough that, like God's servant Job, they accept faithfully the outcome of any trial that may befall them.

The life—and death—of Dietrich Bonhoeffer, to whom reference has just been made, again supplies a vivid commentary on the brave response of the three Jewish youths. In his prison cell and awaiting the outcome of his trial which, almost certainly, must mean death, he showed a tranquillity and trust that put many of us to shame. Let these excerpts from his notes and letters speak for themselves:

> We still love life, but I do not think that death can take us by surprise now...It is we ourselves, and not outward circumstances, who make death what it can be, a death freely and voluntarily accepted.

> Faithless vacillation, endless deliberation without action, refusal to take any risks—that is a real danger. I must be able to know for certain that I am in God's hands, not in men's. Then everything becomes easy, even the severest privation.

> No earthly power can touch us without his will, and danger and distress can only drive us closer to him...We are often told in the New Testament to "be strong" (1 Cor. 16:13; Eph. 6:10; 2 Tim 2:1; 1 John 2:14). Is not people's weakness (stupidity, lack of independence, forgetfulness, cowardice, vanity, corruptibility, temptability, etc.) a greater danger than evil? Christ not only makes people "good", he makes them strong, too. The sins of weakness are the really human sins, whereas the wilful sins are diabolical (and no doubt "strong", too!).

> Whether I live or die, I am with thee,
> and thou, my God, art with me.
> Lord I wait for thy salvation
> and for thy kingdom. Amen.

THE ORDEAL AND ITS OUTCOME

Daniel 3:19–30

Then Nebuchadnezzar was full of fury, and the expression of his face was changed against Shadrach, Meshach, and Abednego. He ordered the furnace heated seven times more than it was wont to be heated. And he ordered certain mighty men of his army to bind Shadrach, Meshach, and Abednego, and to cast them into the burning fiery furnace. Then these men were bound in their mantles, their tunics, their hats, and their other garments, and they were cast into the burning fiery furnace. Because the king's order was strict and the furnace very hot, the flame of the fire slew those men who took up Shadrach, Meshach, and Abednego. And these three men, Shadrach, Meshach, and Abednego, fell bound into the burning fiery furnace. Then King Nebuchadnezzar was astonished and rose up in haste. He said to his counsellors, "Did we not cast three men bound into the fire?" They answered the king, "True, O king." He answered, "But I see four men loose, walking in the midst of the fire, and they are not hurt; and the appearance of the fourth is like a son of the gods."

Then Nebuchadnezzar came near to the door of the burning fiery furnace and said, "Shadrach, Meshach, and Abednego, servants of the Most High God, come forth, and come here!" Then Shadrach, Meshach, and Abednego came out from the fire. And the satraps, the prefects, the governors, and the king's counsellors gathered together and saw that the fire had not had any power over the bodies of those men; the hair of their heads was not singed, their mantles were not harmed, and no smell of fire had come upon them.

Nebuchadnezzar said, "Blessed be the God of Shadrach, Meshach, and Abednego, who has sent his angel and delivered his servants, who trusted in him, and set at naught the king's command, and yielded up their bodies rather than serve and worship any god except their own God. Therefore I make a decree: Any people, nation, or language that speaks anything against the God of Shadrach, Meshach, and Abednego shall be torn limb from limb, and their houses laid in ruins; for there is no other god who is able to deliver in this way." Then the king promoted Shadrach, Meshach, and Abednego in the province of Babylon.

(i)

The defiance of the three young men infuriated the king. Losing his calm demeanour he dropped his kingly control and fell into a rage so that his very visage was contorted. Without more delay he gave orders that the furnace, to whose flames they would be consigned, be heated seven times beyond its accustomed temperature—a nice touch on the part of the story-teller which heightens the sense of drama. This emphasis is continued in the king's order that the heftiest men in his army bind the culprits and carry out the execution, and also in the reference to their remaining fully clothed in their mantles, tunics, and hats which, as we are to see, remained unsinged throughout! The mixture of mockery and miracle continues, for as the three young men were being thrown into the furnace, the flames licked round the opening and killed the men who threw them in. At this point a later writer has interpolated after verse 23 a graphic passage, usually referred to as "The Prayer of Azariah and the Song of the Three Young Men", which appears in the Apocrypha. It tells how Azariah (or Abednego) walks in the furnace singing hymns to God. The furnace, which was fed with "naphtha, pitch, tow and brush", shot out flames 73 feet high. But the presence of "the angel of the Lord" made the midst of the furnace "like a moist whistling wind" so that the fire did not touch the young men at all. Together they praised and glorified God.

The miracle now reaches its height for, as the king watches, to his utter astonishment he sees the three young men who had been thrown in bound with ropes walking about in the midst of the flames—and they are completely unharmed. But, more astonishing still, with them he sees a fourth figure whose appearance is "like a son of the gods" and who is identified in verse 28 by the king himself as "an angel". This *motif* of divine deliverance through God's special angelic messenger is to be found fairly frequently in such martyr stories and has precedents in the Old Testament narratives concerning Hagar (cf. Gen. 31:17ff.) and Isaac (cf. Gen. 22:1) and occurs again in Dan. 6:22. The phrase "son of the gods" recalls "the sons of God" in Job 1:6 who "presented themselves before the Lord" or the angelic beings of that same name who in Gen. 6:2ff. cohabited with "the daughters of men". Here in Daniel, then, one of God's angelic messengers is sent to preserve the young men and to deliver them out of their trouble.

On the king's command they come out of the furnace—no doubt by the side door through which he is watching—and, wonder of wonders, not a hair of their heads is singed, their clothing remains intact, there is not even a smell of burning about them! Nebuchadnezzar recognises them as "servants of the Most High God"—an acknowledgment from the pagan king that the one they worship is the only true God.

This recognition is brought out more clearly in the doxology which follows, in verse 28, where Nebuchadnezzar blesses the God of Israel and praises the three young men, commending them for putting their trust in him alone. The story ends on a happy note. The king recognises not only the God of Israel, but also the religion of Israel. He himself is presumably not a convert, but he gives his royal protection to all who are and who follow the religion of the three young men. Preserved instead of persecuted, they can rest assured their persecutors will be destroyed. With this guarantee of royal protection they are promoted yet again to positions of authority in the land.

(ii)

A reading of this story calls to mind those magnificent words of the prophet of the Exile which may, indeed, have been the inspiration behind the writing of this third chapter of the book of Daniel: "Fear not, for I have redeemed you; I have called you by name, you are mine. When you pass through the waters I will be with you; and through the rivers, they shall not overwhelm you; when you walk through fire you shall not be burned, and the flames shall not consume you" (Isa. 43:1f.)

The writer of Daniel, having in mind the temptations to apostasy that faced his fellow-Jews and knowing the pressures now being brought to bear upon them in the practice of their religion, urges them to trust in God in the sure belief that he will not forsake them. It is true that he paints an all-too-rosy picture of the miraculous outcome of all their troubles. But the conviction of the story is grounded in the hard fact of verse 18 which asserts that, come what may, they will not apostasise but will trust in God to the point of death.

But the writer's own faith and trust go beyond even this. He declares, against all appearances to the contrary, that the time will speedily come when the pagan world, in the person here of the king, will be forced to recognise the God of Israel for what he is, the Most High God, the God of the ends of the earth. This is a theme to be found in the writings of some of the post-exilic prophets (cf. Isa. 60:3; 62:2; 66:12,19; Mal. 1:11) and runs through much of the intertestamental literature. The Gentiles will, in the end, acknowledge him and bow before him with the coming of his kingdom (Sibylline Oracles III, 740; Testament of Benjamin 9:2; Testament of Levi 14:4ff.; Rev. 21:24ff.). This message was particularly appropriate just at this time, when Antiochus had banned the practice of the Jewish religion in Jerusalem and declared it illegal on pain of death. God's people, it seems to say, will prevail and will live to see the Gentile world—with Antiochus himself at its heart—fall down and worship him. This, as we have seen, was a hope kept alive in the Christian Church also where it was confidently asserted that "at the name of Jesus every knee should bow" (Phil. 2:10f.).

God's triumph and his people's deliverance are symbolised by the presence of the mysterious divine figure in the midst of the flames. This is not a figure of the Messiah, nor did the writer intend that it should be taken as such. It is hardly surprising, however, that in Christian devotion and in Christian theology throughout the ages it has in fact been taken as a representation of Jesus, the Christ, the Son of God. It is out of apparent defeat that victory comes; in the midst of affliction is one who was himself afflicted more than any man. Just as the mysterious figure remains in the centre of the fire so God continues to be identified with the sufferings of his people.

BEHOLD, A TREE

Daniel 4:1-18

King Nebuchadnezzar to all peoples, nations, and languages, that dwell in all the earth: Peace be multiplied to you! It has seemed good to me to show the signs and wonders that the Most High God has wrought toward me.

How great are his signs,
how mighty his wonders!
His kingdom is an everlasting kingdom,
and his dominion is from generation to generation.

I, Nebuchadnezzar, was at ease in my house and prospering in my palace. I had a dream which made me afraid; as I lay in bed the fancies and the visions of my head alarmed me. Therefore I made a decree that all the wise men of Babylon should be brought before me, that they might make known to me the interpretation of the dream. Then the magicians, the enchanters, the Chaldeans, and the astrologers came in; and I told them the dream, but they could not make known to me its interpretation. At last Daniel came in before me—he who was named Belteshazzar after the name of my god, and in whom is the spirit of the holy gods—and I told him the dream, saying, "O Belteshazzar, chief of the magicians, because I know that the spirit of the holy gods is in you and that no mystery is difficult for you, here is the dream which I saw; tell me its interpretation. The visions of my head as I lay in bed were these: I saw, and behold, a tree in the midst of the earth; and its height was great. The tree grew and became strong, and its top reached to heaven, and it was visible to the end of the whole earth. Its leaves were fair and its fruit abundant, and in it was food for all. The beasts of the field found shade under it, and the birds of the air dwelt in its branches, and all flesh was fed from it.

"I saw in the visions of my head as I lay in bed, and behold, a watcher, a holy one, came down from heaven. He cried aloud and said thus, 'Hew down the tree and cut off its branches, strip off its leaves and scatter its fruit; let the beasts flee from under it and the birds from its branches. But leave the stump of its roots in the earth, bound with a band of iron and bronze, amid the tender grass of the field. Let him be wet with the dew of heaven; let his lot be with the beasts in the grass of the earth; let his mind be changed from a man's, and let a beast's mind be given to him; and let seven times pass over him. The sentence is by the decree of the watchers, the decision by the word of the holy ones, to the end that the living may know that the Most High rules the kingdom of men, and gives it to whom he will, and sets over it the lowliest of men.' This dream I, King Nebuchadnezzar, saw. And you, O Belteshazzar, declare the interpretation, because all the wise men of my kingdom are not able to make known to me the interpretation, but you are able, for the spirit of the holy gods is in you."

(i)

The story told in this chapter takes the form of an epistle sent by Nebuchadnezzar to "all peoples, nations and languages". Like the decree drafted and despatched by Cyrus and recorded in 6:25ff., it incorporates, in verse form, an acknowledgment of the greatness of God and his everlasting kingdom and dominion. The opening doxology and the subsequent dream-account may well be drawing on an independent traditional tale which the writer adapts to serve the purpose he has in mind, namely, to show that the pride of great rulers—be they Nebuchadnezzar or Antiochus—will be brought low and God and his kingdom will be exalted. If this assumption is correct, it helps to explain the king's change of mood from critical to conciliatory when compared with the earlier part of the previous chapter and is supported by the fact that although the letter is written in the first person, the text slips over into the third person in verses 28–33.

(ii)

The situation here described is different from that in chapter 2, and Daniel's task somewhat easier. This time the king remembers his dream and asks only that its interpretation be made known to him. He goes through the same rigmarole of interviews as that described in the earlier chapter. The "plot" of the story is beautifully laid out—the king was at peace with the world when he had a dream that haunted and alarmed him greatly. Building on past experience he might have been expected forthwith to call upon the services of Daniel. But, as we have seen, this was probably an independent story in origin and in any case the impact stylistically is much greater when our hero at last makes his appearance. First the king enquires of the Chaldean magicians, but all to no avail. Then at last—Daniel appears! The timing is just right! He is addressed by his Babylonian name "Belteshazzar", which the writer assumes contains the name of the Babylonian god "Bel", though this is in fact not the case etymologically (see comment on 1:7). The king recognises "the spirit" in Daniel, the same spirit which had inspired the wisdom of Joseph (cf. Gen. 41:38) and was the source of the prophets' inspiration (cf. Num. 24:28; Ezek. 11:5). Here it is identified as "the spirit of the holy gods". The plural, however, is not to be stressed. The reference to "the Most High" in verse 34 indicates that the king is using the expression with a singular connotation. Daniel's reputation for wisdom and his ability to solve "mysteries" and provide interpretations (see comment on 2:24-30) is now well known. The king is ready to tell the dream; Daniel is ready to give its inspired interpretation.

(iii)

The dream described by the king is a graphic one. It concerns a great tree reaching to heaven and visible to the whole earth which provided food and shelter for man and beast. A heavenly messenger appears and commands that its branches be lopped and its fruits scattered and that the tree itself be felled, leaving only a stump behind bound with a band of iron and brass. The one who is represented by the tree—his identity will be made clear in the interpretation—will share the lot of the brute beast until such time as he and his fellows learn that the Most High rules and gives the authority to whomsoever he will, even the lowliest of men.

This reference to a ruler under the symbol of a tree was familiar in the ancient world. Thus, Herodotus refers to the rules of Xerxes and of Astyages the Mede under the figure of a spreading tree. The same language is used with regard to the grandiose building schemes of Nebuchadnezzar himself in one of his inscriptions, the tree symbolising the Babylonian empire which protects and preserves many peoples. The primary influence on this Daniel passage, however, is probably to be found in Ezek. 31:1ff., which is itself closely associated with the oracle in Ezek. 28 where, as we have seen, the name "Dan'el" is referred to. In the former passage, in an oracle against Egypt, Pharaoh is likened to a great cedar in a well-watered place which gave shelter to beast and fowl and was the envy of "all the trees of Eden". The tree is felled as a warning to all who lift themselves up in pride. Its fall has repercussions even in Sheol!

This reference recalls the taunt-song in Isa. 14:4–20 which tells how the king of Babylon sought to "exalt his throne above the stars of God" and, because of his overweening pride, is brought down to Sheol "to the uttermost parts of the pit". It seems clear that, whether the writer of Daniel was aware of it or not, there lies behind this figure of the tree and these stories about it, a long mythological tradition reflecting, perhaps, the oriental notion of the "world tree" which is thought of as growing at the very centre of the earth and whose branches reach up to the dome of heaven spanning a flat disc-like earth. Whether influenced by such a notion or not, the writer takes the material ready to hand and conveys through it his own powerful message not only that proud rulers will be brought low but also that God alone rules in the affairs of men.

The command that the tree be felled is given by "a watcher, a holy one". The word "watcher" is found here in verses 13 and 17 (also verse 23) and in many places throughout the Jewish apocalyptic writings. It is used for a class of heavenly beings known as "watchful ones" who serve God and intercede on behalf of men. In I Enoch 6 it is they who are said to mingle with "the daughters of men" (cf. Gen. 6:1–4) and whose evil progeny, in the form of demons and evil spirits, frequent the earth. This, however, is a somewhat later use of the word. In Daniel (the name occurs in no other biblical book) it simply alludes to "an angel" as does the expression "holy one" which is also commonly found throughout this literature. These "watchers" or "holy ones" form a heavenly council whose members listen to God's word and go forth to carry out his command. Their decree is God's decree (cf. verse 17).

Urgently the watcher bids the birds and beasts which shelter in the branches or under the shadow of the tree to flee. The tree itself is felled, lopped and stripped. Only a bound stump remains—like the king himself (for already we can guess who is meant), fettered in his madness. He will lose his human reason and be given the mind of an animal for seven "times" (probably meaning "years"). Already, even without the interpretation, the message is coming through loud and clear. Soon the interpretation will focus the message of the dream on Nebuchadnezzar himself—man proposes, but God disposes. God alone is sovereign. He will humble the proud and exalt those of low degree.

(iv)

The lesson of the dream is a familiar one throughout the Scriptures. Human pride forgets too readily that God is Creator and that man is creature, utterly dependent on him for all life's provision and even for life itself. In the beginning God gave man dominion over the fish of the sea, over the fowl of the air, over the beasts of the field (cf. Gen. 1:26) and (we may add) over all the raw materials of the earth. But dominion easily becomes domination. All things have been made subservient to man (cf. Ps. 8:6ff.; Heb. 2:8) and are at his service. But use readily develops into abuse. Creation and authority over creation are given in trust, but human pride creates mistrust and claims for itself prerogatives which belong to God alone.

If this is true of man in general, it is even more true of rulers in particular who, by abusing their trust, set themselves up as gods, whether they claim that title or not. Nebuchadnezzar is a case in point. So also is Antiochus. In the New Testament the Magnificat is an admirable commentary on this very theme: "He has shown strength with his arm; he has scattered the proud in the imagination of their hearts, he has put down the mighty from their thrones and exalted those of low degree" (Luke 1:51f.). Rulers and leaders—in state or in Church—who occupy exalted positions have further to fall than most. They forget at their peril that "the Most High rules in the kingdom of men, and gives it to whom he will, and sets over it the lowliest of men".

THE TREE AND ITS INTERPRETATION

Daniel 4:19–27

Then Daniel, whose name was Belteshazzar, was dismayed for a moment, and his thoughts alarmed him. The king said, "Belteshaz-

zar, let not the dream or the interpretation alarm you." Belteshazzar
answered, "My lord, may the dream be for those who hate you and
its interpretation for your enemies! The tree you saw, which grew
and became strong, so that its top reached to heaven, and it was
visible to the end of the whole earth; whose leaves were fair and its
fruit abundant, and in which was food for all; under which beasts of
the field found shade, and in whose branches the birds of the air
dwelt—it is you, O king, who have grown and become strong. Your
greatness has grown and reaches to heaven, and your dominion to
the ends of the earth. And whereas the king saw a watcher, a holy
one, coming down from heaven and saying, 'Hew down the tree and
destroy it, but leave the stump of its roots in the earth, bound with a
band of iron and bronze, in the tender grass of the field; and let him
be wet with the dew of heaven; and let his lot be with the beasts of the
field, till seven times pass over him'; this is the interpretation, O
king: It is a decree of the Most High, which has come upon my lord
the king, that you shall be driven from among men, and your
dwelling shall be with the beasts of the field; you shall be made to eat
grass like an ox, and you shall be wet with the dew of heaven, and
seven times shall pass over you, till you know that the Most High
rules the kingdom of men, and gives it to whom he will. And as it was
commanded to leave the stump of the roots of the tree, your
kingdom shall be sure for you from the time that you know that
Heaven rules. Therefore, O king, let my counsel be acceptable to
you; break off your sins by practising righteousness, and your
iniquities by showing mercy to the oppressed, that there may
perhaps be a lengthening of your tranquillity."

(i)

Now comes the interpretation of the king's dream. Knowing
how momentous his pronouncement is to be, Daniel is alarmed
but is encouraged by the king to speak out. Before doing so
Daniel expresses the respectful wish that the dream might have
been about the king's enemies. But this is not so. It is about the
king himself. He is the tree. He will be hewn down so that only a
stump remains, indicating perhaps that all is not lost and that
there is still some hope even for a proud king like Nebuchadnezzar. He will be stricken by madness; he will be driven out to
dwell with the wild beasts; he will eat grass like an ox. After
seven years his reason will return and he will recognise that

"heaven rules". (This is the one instance in the Old Testament where the word "heaven" is used as a periphrasis for "God"—a usage which became quite common in later Jewish writings and in the New Testament as in the Gospel of Matthew where the expression "Kingdom of Heaven" is used for the more customary "Kingdom of God". Such language reflects the tendency among Jews of that time to avoid even mentioning the divine name.)

(ii)

Daniel concludes his interpretation of the dream with an appeal to the king to break off his sins by practising righteousness which will be evidenced by his showing mercy to the oppressed. In this way the "tranquillity" that had previously marked his reign would be restored and increased.

Two expressions in verse 27 are of particular interest. One is the word translated "break off", which may also be translated "redeem" and is used in this sense twice in the Old Testament (cf. Lam. 5:8; Ps. 136:24) and frequently in later Jewish writings. This is the meaning given to it in the Septuagint here in the Daniel text. The other expression is "by practising righteousness" where "righteousness" signifies righteous deeds and so good works. Again it is of interest to observe that the Septuagint renders the phrase "by almsgiving", reflecting a late Hebrew usage of the word "righteousness". In Ben Sira, for example, we find the phrase, "Almsgiving will make atonement for sins" (Ecclesiasticus 3:30; cf. 7:10). It is unlikely that this is the meaning in our present passage, but we have here more than a suggestion that the offering of good works plays its part in man's relationship with God.

We are not, however, to find in this verse a happy hunting ground for the doctrinal debate "justification by faith" *versus* "justification by works". The Aramaic word here translated "righteous", like its Hebrew equivalent, expresses not just a right relationship with God in which one is accepted and "justified", but also a right attitude towards one's neighbour which expresses itself in righteous and just acts. Attitudes and acts together are acceptable to God, though neither can atone for sin or effect reconciliation with him. It is true that during the intertestamental period and beyond, "righteousness" comes increasingly to signify "right acts" in the sense of benevolent deeds and that the need to comply with the ceremonial law developed the notion of meritorious works. It was against the notion that God's favour can be won by the offering of such works that Paul, for example, elaborated his teaching concerning justification by grace through faith. But Paul no less than James makes it clear that "faith without works is dead" (Jas. 2:20). A right relationship with God must express itself in right relationship with others, in just acts, and in deeds of loving kindness.

THE KING'S MADNESS AND RESTORATION

Daniel 4:28–37

All this came upon King Nebuchadnezzar. At the end of twelve months he was walking on the roof of the royal palace of Babylon, and the king said, "Is not this great Babylon, which I have built by my mighty power as a royal residence and for the glory of my majesty?" While the words were still in the king's mouth, there fell a voice from heaven, "O King Nebuchadnezzar, to you it is spoken: The kingdom has departed from you, and you shall be driven from among men, and your dwelling shall be with the beasts of the field; and you shall be made to eat grass like an ox; and seven times shall pass over you, until you have learned that the Most High rules the kingdom of men and gives it to whom he will." Immediately the word was fulfilled upon Nebuchadnezzar. He was driven from among men, and ate grass like an ox, and his body was wet with the dew of heaven till his hair grew as long as eagles' feathers, and his nails were like birds' claws.

At the end of the days I, Nebuchadnezzar, lifted my eyes to heaven, and my reason returned to me, and I blessed the Most High, and praised and honoured him who lives forever;

> for his dominion is an everlasting dominion,
>   and his kingdom endures from generation to generation;
> all the inhabitants of the earth are accounted as nothing;
>   and he does according to his will in the host of heaven
>   and among the inhabitants of the earth;
> and none can stay his hand
>   or say to him, "What doest thou?"

At the same time my reason returned to me; and for the glory of my kingdom, my majesty and splendour returned to me. My counsellors and my lords sought me, and I was established in my kingdom, and still more greatness was added to me. Now I, Nebuchadnezzar, praise and extol and honour the King of heaven; for all his works are right and his ways are just; and those who walk in pride he is able to abase.

(i)

The warning apparently goes unheeded for the space of twelve months. Once more the king appears (verse 29) walking on the flat roof of his palace cogitating on the greatness of his achievements and glorying in the magnificence of the great building projects that had marked his distinguished reign. Besides many temples and the palace of Nabopolassor which he had built or rebuilt, he had been responsible for the famous hanging gardens of Babylon, to be prized as one of the wonders of the world. He felt proud of his great achievements—and ascribed glory to himself! Just then there came a voice from heaven—a phenomenon recorded in the New Testament (cf. Mark 1:11) and known in the apocalyptic and rabbinic traditions as the *bath qol,* or divine voice. The voice re-asserts his threatened doom and immediately the word is fulfilled. He is forthwith stricken with madness as predicted and to the dire pronouncements already declared is added the further detail that "his hair grew as long as eagles' feathers, and his nails were like birds' claws." The form the madness took was that he acted and behaved as if he were himself a wild animal, bereft of human dignity and deprived of human reason. It is in the providence of God that men should be "fully human". This is a mark of their place and their pre-eminence in creation. Nebuchadnezzar's reduction to the level of the beast suggests that his renouncement of the sovereignty of God was at the same time a renouncement of his own humanity.

(ii)

The allusion in this chapter to Nebuchadnezzar's madness is a puzzling one, for there is no independent historical evidence to corroborate what is said here. "Argument from silence" is, of course, not to be relied upon, but there are other fairly substantial indications that here, as elsewhere in the book, Nebuchadnezzar, perhaps the greatest of the Babylonian kings, has attracted to himself traits and descriptions which at one time belonged to the last Babylonian king, Nabonidus. If this is so, and if the madness described here is to be ascribed to Nabonidus, we may find in this episode a reason for that king's rather lengthy retirement to Tema in Arabia at a most critical period in his reign, as recorded in extra-biblical sources (see comment on 1:1-2, *cont'd*).

One important piece of evidence is provided by the "Prayer of Nabonidus", a document found among the Dead Sea Scrolls, which tells how Nabonidus, whilst in Tema, was "smitten with a malignant inflammation" and for a period of seven years had to live an isolated life. At the close of this time he was cured by a Jewish exorcist who called upon him to repent, counselled him to renounce his idolatries and brought him to acknowledge the Most High God. The document is somewhat later than the book of Daniel, but the evidence suggests that the name of Nabonidus and not that of Nebuchadnezzar appeared in the original tradition reflected here in Daniel. Additional support may be found in an older text—"The Verse Account of Nabonidus"—where the assertion is made, "the king is mad".

If this identification of Nabonidus is correct it may provide an acceptable explanation of the puzzle in Daniel 5 where, as we shall see, Belshazzar the son of Nabonidus is taken to be the son of Nebuchadnezzar. It is highly likely that if there is indeed this confusion between the names of these two monarchs, it was already an established fact before the time of the writing of Daniel and was taken over and made to serve the writer's purpose in the form in which it stood.

If this story and the figure of the mad king had been specially prepared and "tailor-made" by our author to fit the situation faced by the Jewish community in the second century B.C., it no doubt would have been presented rather differently and have carried different emphases. But "tailor-made" or "off the peg", the readers would have little difficulty in recognising an allusion to their own arrogant and autocratic ruler Antiochus, whose escapades and strange behaviour were "the talk of the town". It was well known among them that, although he had dubbed himself "Epiphanes" meaning "[God] manifest", he was popularly known as "Epimanes" meaning "madman"! Like the proud Nebuchadnezzar he, too, would be humbled to the dust.

(iii)

The sequel to the story is given in verses 34–37. Nebuchadnezzar, we are told, lifted his eyes to heaven, presumably in repentance for his pride and in recognition of the sovereignty of the Most High God. The experience had taught him that "the Most High rules the kingdom of men" (verse 25). Thus this theme of the pride of man's achievement (more especially of the monarch), and the sovereign rule of God, opens and closes this chapter and is the message of the whole dream and its interpretation. The accomplishments of the angel hosts and the exploits of humankind are as nothing and none can say him nay. Failure to recognise God's rule will bring its own judgment. Let the mighty empires and their proud rulers take heed and beware!

The result of Nebuchadnezzar's enlightenment is that his reason is restored, his kingdom regains its glory and splendour, his counsellors rally round him and he extols the King of heaven who brings low those who are exalted in pride. As soon as he recognises God's sovereignty and rule, his own life as king falls into place. He sees things reasonably and in perspective and is able to carry out his God-given responsibilities as king. This restoration to sanity and security probably explains the earlier allusion to the "stump". The judgment of God is swift and terrible. But it is not an uprooting. The stump gives hope for the possibility of a new beginning by the goodness of God.

BELSHAZZAR'S FEAST

Daniel 5:1–4

King Belshazzar made a great feast for a thousand of his lords, and drank wine in front of the thousand. Belshazzar, when he tasted the wine, commanded that the vessels of gold and silver which Nebuchadnezzar his father had taken out of the temple in Jerusalem be brought, that the king and his lords, his wives, and his concubines might drink from them. Then they brought in the golden and silver vessels which had been taken out of the temple, the house of God in Jerusalem; and the king and his lords, his wives, and his concubines drank from them. They drank wine, and praised the gods of gold and silver, bronze, iron, wood, and stone.

(i)

In these verses the writer follows up the account in chapter 4 concerning the arrogance of Nebuchadnezzar with a graphic portrayal of the insolence of his "son" Belshazzar. The historicity of this passage has led to much debate (see *Note* 4). Extrabiblical sources indicate that he was in fact never recognised as "king" nor was he the son of Nebuchadnezzar; he was in fact the son of Nabonidus, the last king of Babylon. Whatever the truth may be, he is represented here as acting beyond his station and behaving with insolence and flippancy in a manner unbefitting a royal personage.

(ii)

But Belshazzar's insolence was not the chief thing that troubled our author. Far worse was his appalling act of sacrilege in using at his drunken banquet the sacred Temple vessels plundered from Jerusalem by Nebuchadnezzar and which, according to Ezra 1:9ff., consisted of no fewer than 5,400 articles, chiefly goblets and basins of silver and gold.

Similar banquets are amply attested throughout the oriental world of that time to which the women-folk—as here—were sometimes invited. We are not told the exact nature of this particular feast or what it was supposed to celebrate. It may have had cultic associations in honour of the god Marduk or it may have been simply a state banquet. But even in this latter case it would still have a distinctly religious content, with libations being poured to the gods. In any case, the revellers "praised the gods of gold and silver, bronze, iron, wood and stone". This intrusion of religious ceremony into "secular" events was familiar to the reader of the second century B.C. and caused no little anxiety to faithful Jews in Jerusalem, where Jewish youths strove with Gentile youths in athletic prowess. Such contests were invariably accompanied by a religious ceremony in which votive offerings were made to pagan deities and libations poured out in their honour.

Even to take part in such revelries was bad enough. But to do what Belshazzar was about to do was to profane the holy God! The feast was a grand affair, attended by a thousand of his lords and ladies. When the drink began to be passed round and Belshazzar was feeling merry he called for the sacred vessels from the holy Temple and used them as wine bowls and goblets for himself and his guests. This incident would have a very special poignancy for those in Antiochus' day who first read the book, for they would no doubt recall that only a short time before, Heliodorus, the chief minister of Seleucus IV, had attempted to plunder the same Temple and make off with its treasures (cf. 2 Maccabees 3:10ff.). And more recently still Antiochus himself had desecrated the holy place and had removed the silver and gold vessels that still remained there, together with other sacred treasures (cf. 1 Maccabees 1:20–28; 2 Maccabees 5:15f.).

To the writer of Daniel this action of Belshazzar was sheer sacrilege. Not only was it a profanation of sacred objects, it was an insult to God himself and an arrogant assertion that, as the God of a vanquished people, he could be discounted and mocked with impunity. It has been an all-too-common assumption that God is on the side of "the big battalions" and that when a nation is defeated its god is discredited. Israel's experience of exile did much to change that judgment. God, they learned, was more often than not on the side of the defeated, the oppressed, the enslaved. This too was the experience of the Christian Church in following the way of the crucified Lord. It is in the cross that the power of God is seen at its greatest (cf. 1 Cor. 1:24), for his strength is made perfect in weakness (cf. 2 Cor. 12:9).

(iii)

Belshazzar's insolence and act of sacrilege, we are told, had a sudden and dramatic sequel—that very night the "king" was slain and the kingdom passed to another (cf. 5:30f.). The allusion here is to the capture of Babylon by Cyrus in 539 B.C. According to the so-called "Nabonidus Chronicle" this took place in the seventeenth year of Nabonidus, the king having returned from Tema just prior to that fateful event. We shall look later at some of the historical problems involved at this point. Here we simply note that, in the belief of our author, Israel may be a defeated nation—be it in the time of Nabonidus or in the time of Antiochus—but the God of Israel is still in control, not only over their own affairs but over the affairs of their conquerors as well. To mock his majesty and to flout his authority will bring its own judgment which will be swift and sure.

In expressing this conviction the writer of Daniel is in line with the prophetic tradition of the Old Testament. Rulers and nations, whether they recognise him or not, are under his control and will in due course receive their recompense.

Before Jehovah's awful throne,
Ye nations, bow with sacred joy;
Know that the Lord is God alone;
He can create, and He destroy.
(Isaac Watts)

THE WRITING ON THE WALL

Daniel 5:5-9

> Immediately the fingers of a man's hand appeared and wrote on the plaster of the wall of the king's palace, opposite the lampstand; and the king saw the hand as it wrote. Then the king's colour changed, and his thoughts alarmed him; his limbs gave way, and his knees knocked together. The king cried aloud to bring in the enchanters, the Chaldeans, and the astrologers. The king said to the wise men of Babylon, "Whoever reads this writing, and shows me its interpretation, shall be clothed with purple, and have a chain of gold about his neck, and shall be the third ruler in the kingdom." When all the king's wise men came in, but they could not read the writing or make known to the king the interpretation. Then King Belshazzar was greatly alarmed, and his colour changed; and his lords were perplexed.

(i)

The account that follows is in the true tradition of the mystery thriller! Suddenly, out of thin air as it were, in the light of the lampstand there appears a solitary ghostly hand which begins to write on the white plaster of the wall. Belshazzar is completely unnerved and quakes in his shoes. We are not yet told what it is he sees written there, but it is obviously something mysterious and frightening. He calls for his wise men who hurry into his presence.

Their task, as in the earlier account of Nebuchadnezzar's dream in chapter 2, is two-fold. There they had to describe the dream itself and then give its interpretation. Here they have to spell out what the writing says and then explain its meaning. The reader is kept in suspense on both counts until later in the chapter.

(ii)

Belshazzar, in the rather grandiose manner of such stories, now makes extravagant offers to anyone who is able to cast light on the mystery before them. He will be clad in royal purple (as Mordecai was in the book of Esther, cf. Esth. 8:15) and have a golden chain around his neck (like Joseph of old, cf. Gen. 41:42). More than this, he will be made "the third ruler in the kingdom"—an obscure expression referring perhaps to an office of state third in importance after Belshazzar and the queen-mother who is about to appear on the scene, or to the third of three presidents said later (cf. 6:2) to be appointed by Darius. Other suggestions are that it may reflect a Babylonian title given by the king to his army third-in-command, or it may originally have alluded to "the squire" in a chariot along with the warrior and the driver. Subsequently the numerical sense was lost and it came to signify simply a high ranking official. Whatever interpretation is taken, the sense is clear.

Belshazzar soon learns that there are things money and promotion cannot buy. The wisdom he looks for in his professional wise men is one of these. They are faced with a problem much too big for them. Learning and training are good, but they are not good enough to solve the mystery of divine intervention, for such it is. What is needed is insight and inspiration, gifts which God alone can impart. The scene is now set for God's man Daniel to appear again.

(iii)

The message on the wall, as Daniel's interpretation is to show, is one of judgment. Belshazzar had acted in a high-handed manner in his dealings with God and the vessels of God's temple. He had presumed to judge God; God would judge him.

This is what Pilate found when confronted by Jesus. In judging, he himself was judged. God and the Son of God may be abused and derided and denied, but the accuser stands before him as the accused. Victor Sparre, in his book *The Flame in the Darkness* , points out that icon painters, as distinct from other kinds of artists, use reversed perspective and ventures this explanation: "Uccello's introduction of perspective in the 14th century enabled an artist to create an illusion of space by making his lines converge at a vanishing point. The viewer judges the world. But the painters of icons turn perspective in the opposite direction. All their lines meet in front of the picture, where the viewer stands. Now it is the picture which contemplates the viewer. The picture is not weighed in the balance, but the viewer." This was to be Belshazzar's experience as it has been the experience of multitudes since when confronted by the Great God. The lines of judgment point unerringly from God to men.

> The Moving Finger writes; and having writ
> Moves on: nor all thy Piety or Wit
> Shall have it back to cancel half a line
> Nor all thy Tears wash out a Word of it.
> (Edward Fitzgerald, *Omar Khayyam*)

DANIEL BEFORE THE KING

Daniel 5:10–23

The queen, because of the words of the king and his lords, came into the banqueting hall; and the queen said, "O king, live for ever! Let not your thoughts alarm you or your colour change. There is in your kingdom a man in whom is the spirit of the holy gods. In the days of your father light and understanding and wisdom, like the wisdom of the gods, were found in him, and King Nebuchadnezzar, your father, made him chief of the magicians, enchanters, Chaldeans, and astrologers, because an excellent spirit, knowledge, and understanding to interpret dreams, explain riddles, and solve problems were found in this Daniel, whom the king named Belteshazzar. Now let Daniel be called, and he will show the interpretation."

Then Daniel was brought in before the king. The king said to Daniel, "You are that Daniel, one of the exiles of Judah, whom the king my father brought from Judah. I have heard of you that the spirit of the holy gods is in you, and that light and understanding and excellent wisdom are found in you. Now the wise men, the enchanters, have been brought in before me to read this writing and make known to me its interpretation; but they could not show the interpretation of the matter. But I have heard that you can give interpretations and solve problems. Now if you can read the writing and make known to me its interpretation, you shall be clothed with purple, and have a chain of gold about your neck, and shall be the third ruler in the kingdom."

Then Daniel answered before the king, "Let your gifts be for yourself, and give your rewards to another; nevertheless I will read the writing to the king and make known to him the interpretation. O king, the Most High God gave Nebuchadnezzar your father kingship and greatness and glory and majesty; and because of the greatness that he gave him, all peoples, nations, and languages trembled and feared before him; whom he would he slew, and whom he would he kept alive; whom he would he raised up, and whom he would he put down. But when his heart was lifted up and his spirit was hardened so that he dealt proudly, he was deposed from his kingly throne, and his glory was taken from him; he was driven from among men, and his mind was made like that of a beast, and his dwelling was with the wild asses; he was fed grass like an ox, and his body was wet with the dew of heaven, until he knew that the Most High God rules the kingdom of men, and sets over it whom he will. And you his son, Belshazzar, have not humbled your heart, though you knew all this, but you have lifted up yourself against the Lord of heaven; and the vessels of his house have been brought in before you, and you and your lords, your wives, and your concubines have drunk wine from them; and you have praised the gods of silver and gold, of bronze, iron, wood, and stone, which do not see or hear or know, but the God in whose hand is your breath, and whose are all your ways, you have not honoured."

(i)

The reader is now introduced to "the queen", or perhaps better "the queen-mother", a woman obviously of some standing at court for she has right of access to the banquet, her voice is readily heard and her advice readily followed. In support of the suggestion that it is the queen-mother who is referred to, it is pointed out that the king's wives are already present in the banquet room (cf. verse 3) and that her bearing and manner of address in speaking to Belshazzar are more "motherly" than "wifely"! This comes out especially in her speaking of his father who is here identified as Nebuchadnezzar. On this count, then, she would be the widow of Nebuchadnezzar and so, in her old age, would be treated with respect and listened to with proper attention. The honoured place often given to a queen-mother is amply attested in the Old Testament as well as in extra-biblical sources.

(ii)

Having overheard or been told of the mysterious event in the banqueting hall and the obvious lack of success on the part of the professional wise men, she counsels Belshazzar not to be alarmed and goes on to tell him of a man, Daniel, who in the days of Nebuchadnezzar had more than proved his worth. She describes him in terms which had previously been used by Nebuchadnezzar himself concerning him. Because of his obvious gifts of inspiration, intelligence and wisdom he had been promoted as chief of the wise men. Three special abilities or skills are then mentioned—the interpretation of dreams, the explaining of riddles and the solving of problems. The first of these is self-explanatory and is amply illustrated in chapters 2 and 4. The second refers to "riddles" or "hard sayings" consisting of obscure or enigmatic sentences, perhaps concerning life generally or some person or event, which the "wise man" is able to make plain. This is well illustrated by Ben Sira, writing not long before the appearance of the book of Daniel, who describes the "wise scribe" in these words:

> [He] will penetrate the subtleties of parables;
> He will seek out the hidden meanings of proverbs
> And be at home with the obscurities of parables.
> (Ecclesiasticus 39:2f.)

The third skill is literally "the loosening of knots". It has been suggested that, since the word "knots" is elsewhere used to identify magic spells, which "bind" the victim, Daniel's gift here may refer to his power to break the power of such spells and set the victim free. On the other hand the phrase may simply signify the untying of "knotty" problems—as in the case of the writing on the wall soon to be disclosed.

As on previous occasions the entrance of Daniel is delayed until the "psychological moment". At last he is ushered into the presence of the king who speaks as if he were not too well acquainted with him, though he had heard of his reputation. His friendly approach and his offer of reward, however, meet with a peremptory response on the part of Daniel who tells him to keep his gifts—an injunction he apparently did not want the king to take too seriously in view of his later acceptance of reward! But his point was made and would come over clearly to the readers of the book—the man of God will not "kowtow" to a heathen king, however powerful he may be, nor will he be in his debt for any favours given. What had to be said had to be said. This is a word from the Lord!

(iii)

And so Daniel lectures the king! God had given his "father" Nebuchadnezzar greatness and glory and majesty so that all peoples trembled before him. As absolute monarch he had the power of life and of death over his subjects. But he had acted with presumption and pride and had behaved as if he were God! God had shown him that, far from being divine, he was less than human. Instead of humbling himself Nebuchadnezzar had hardened his heart. The judgment recorded in the previous chapter is here repeated. It continued until at last he recognised the sovereignty of the Most High God.

How different was the case of Belshazzar! God had not exalted him; he had exalted himself (verse 23). What is more, he had failed to learn the lesson from the past and take note of what had happened to Nebuchadnezzar. Not only had he

exalted himself, as his "father" had done before him, he had
been guilty of sacrilege in his misuse of the sacred vessels, he
had worshipped idols which could make no response (cf. Deut.
4:28; 28:36, 64; Pss. 115:4–8; 135:15ff.) and he had dishonoured
God to whom he owed everything he was.

The scene is now set for the mysterious message to be made
known.

THE WRITING AND ITS INTERPRETATION

Daniel 5:24–28

"Then from his presence the hand was sent, and this writing was
inscribed. And this is the writing that was inscribed: MENE,
MENE, TEKEL, and PARSIN. This is the interpretation of the
matter: MENE, God has numbered the days of your kingdom and
brought it to an end; TEKEL, you have been weighed in the balances
and found wanting; PERES, your kingdom is divided and given to
the Medes and Persians."

Having castigated Belshazzar, Daniel now turns his attention
to the writing itself and the mysterious hand that inscribed it.
His explanation of the hand at least is clear—it was sent from
the presence of God. It discloses his judgment and pronounces
sentence on the king. It is this same hand that controls all his
ways (see verse 23).

(i)

Daniel then proceeds to read what is written on the wall,
something that the professional wise men had been unable to
do. Commentators have tried to explain their difficulty in a
number of ways, e.g. it was an ideogram, a cryptogram, a
strange script. We cannot say for certain what the reason for
their failure was, but possibly it had something to do with the
fact that the Aramaic script was "unpointed", i.e. it indicated
consonants only and did not include markings representing

vowel sounds. This is customary still today in, say, Hebrew and
Arabic newspapers. Normally no indication of vowel sounds is
needed. Only occasionally are they written in, at points where
there might be a doubtful meaning. Besides this, the writing on
the wall would have no space between the words and would be
written, as far as the Babylonian wise men were concerned, in a
foreign tongue. Daniel is able to break the writing up and to
distinguish recognisable and pronounceable words. These are
mn' mn' tql and *prsn* and may be pronounced *mene mene tekel*
and *parsin* (the *u* before this last word in the AV represents the
word "and").

So much for the form and pronunciation of the writing. But
what does it mean? It seems fairly certain that, as it stands, it
indicates three different weights or coins, *mn'* being the mina,
tql the shekel (one sixtieth of a mina) and *prs* (the singular form
of *prsn*) a half-mina. In our text the word *mn'* is written twice,
though in the interpretation that follows (also in Josephus and
certain other versions) it appears once only. It has been
suggested that the first occurrence should be vocalised, not as a
noun meaning "mina" but as a verb meaning "reckoned" or
"counted". And so the words would read: "Counted: a mina, a
shekel and a couple of half minas" (*parsin* having a dual form).

But what, we may ask, is the point of such words? What do
they signify? It has been suggested that they have a symbolic
meaning and that they represent certain rulers and certain
empires. Support for this may be found in the Talmud where
weights are used to indicate the value or worth of *people*. Thus a
man who is reckoned to be twice as good as his father is
described as "a mina, son of half a mina". On this reckoning the
writing on the wall may suggest that Nebuchadnezzar, for
example, is worth a mina compared with Belshazzar who is
worth a mere shekel, and the Medes and Persians who may be
valued at half a mina each. Many permutations of names have
been suggested which need not concern us here. The real point
of the story lies, not in this·(popular?) tag or jingle about
weights, but rather in the interpretation Daniel is now to place
upon them.

(ii)

Here again, in considering the interpretation, the key to understanding lies in the fact that Aramaic (like Hebrew) is able to change the meaning of a word by giving to the written consonants a different vocalisation. Here Daniel interprets each of the nouns as verbs. *Mn'* now becomes "counted" or "numbered"—and the interpretation is that God has numbered Belshazzar's kingdom and is bringing it to an end. *Tql* becomes "weighed"—and the interpretation is that Belshazzar has been weighed by God in the balances and found wanting. *Prs* becomes "divided"—and the interpretation is that God has divided up his kingdom. In this last connection there is a double play on words, for *prs* can be vocalised differently again to mean "Persian". The interpretation then of the word in its dual form *prsn* would be that the kingdom is not only to be "divided" but is to be given to the Persians and to the Medes with whom the Persians were closely associated.

(iii)

The lesson of this "parable"—for such it is—is the same as that already given in Daniel's "lecture" to Belshazzar. The judgment of God is sure. The mills of God grind slowly, but they grind exceeding small. Retribution will catch up with those who, like the king, act with total disregard for the God who holds their life and destiny in his hands. Kings and rulers are not exempt. On the contrary "to whom much is given, of him will much be required" (Luke 12:48). The Most High God is in control. The pagan religions, as for example in Egypt, may depict the souls of men being weighed in the balance. But God weighs the nations too; he counts them as nothing when they flout his will; he divides them asunder and gives them as a prey to others.

All this must have been strong meat for the Jews under Antiochus when, in their distress, they read these reassuring words. For Antiochus, too, and all his tribe, the writing was well and truly on the wall! His time would speedily come. His kingdom, despite its appearance of strength and endurance, would be "counted", "weighed" and "divided". The hand of the Lord would do this thing!

In his book *Christianity and History* Herbert Butterfield has a chapter entitled "Judgment in History". There he declares that "the whole of our existing order and the very fabric of our civilisation" are under the judgment of God. But although it is these orders and systems that are condemned, "at bottom it is an inadequacy in human nature itself which comes under judgment; for in the course of time it is human nature which finds out the holes in the structure, and turns the good thing into an abuse." He goes on: "Judgment in history falls heaviest on those who come to think themselves gods, who fly in the face of providence and history, who put their trust in man-made systems and worship the work of their own hands, and who say that the strength of their own right arm gave them the victory."

DANIEL AND DARIUS THE MEDE

Daniel 5:29-31

> Then Belshazzar commanded, and Daniel was clothed with purple, a chain of gold was put about his neck, and proclamation was made concerning him, that he should be the third ruler in the kingdom. That very night Belshazzar the Chaldean king was slain. And Darius the Mede received the kingdom, being about sixty-two years old.

(i)

His superior wisdom and understanding having been vindicated, Daniel receives his promised reward and is given a high place of honour in the kingdom. But though kings have control over their subjects to do with them as they please, God has control over kings to do with them as he wills. They may claim the powers of life and death, but they in turn are subject to the power of God. The command of Belshazzar is carried out and Daniel is rewarded. The command of God is carried out and Belshazzar is slain—"that very night". To the very end, it seems, he remains unperturbed about his actions, unmoved by the whip-lash of Daniel's tongue and unrepentant of his sins. In these words we hear an echo of another: "Fool! This night your soul is required of you" (cf. Luke 12:20).

The reference here to Belshazzar's death occurring at night finds an echo in Herodotus and Xenophon who, though they make no specific reference to this monarch or his death, observe that Babylon fell as a result of a night attack. The tradition that this took place at a time of revelry and feasting may find substance in the prophetic oracles against Babylon contained in Isa. 21:1–10 and Jer. 51:39 and 57.

The judgment, then, pronounced by Daniel in his address to Belshazzar, is given visible expression. The death of Belshazzar is a warning to all rulers and kings that no-one who challenges the authority of God or behaves with insolent disregard of his sovereignty can hope to do so with impunity. The judgments of God are sure. Let Antiochus, and all who follow in his train, take note!

(ii)

The cryptic footnote in verse 31 introduces a new character and at the same time introduces a major historical problem: who is this Darius the Mede and how does he fit into the historical scene (see *Note* 5)?

No king of this name is known who was alive and reigning at this time (538 B.C.). There does not seem in fact to be any historical evidence outside this book for the existence of "Darius the Mede" as described here and in subsequent chapters. Likewise no place can be found for his Median kingdom which, the book seems to argue, came between Nabonidus the last king of Babylon and Cyrus the first king of Persia.

Confronted with such a problem, it is important to grasp that the author of Daniel is interested not so much in an accurate historical account as in a persuasive spiritual assessment. He is writing history theologically. For this purpose he takes up traditions, legends and verifiable historical events and weaves them into the pattern of his story. It is not a matter of being "true" or "untrue" to the "facts". He is not a modern historian ferreting out the facts and checking each one against other verifiable evidence. He is a story-teller with a job to do—to offer reflection on God's ways with men, to share his own deeply felt convictions about the sovereignty of God and the powers of his kingdom and to speak a word in season to encourage and strengthen his fellow-Jews in a time of great distress, assuring them that God will be with them and will see them through.

H. H. Rowley, having concluded an exhaustive examination of this passage, makes this further comment: "God is great enough to take us, with all our imperfect thoughts and false expectations, and to make us the instruments of His service. Had there been naught of error in the book, it could not have said this to us. But its very historical mistakes add to the fulness of its religious message to our hearts, for the God who maketh the wrath of men to praise Him can also convert the mistakes of His servants, whose hearts are consecrated to His service, to good use."

JEALOUSY AND INTRIGUE

Daniel 6:1–9

It pleased Darius to set over the kingdom a hundred and twenty satraps, to be throughout the whole kingdom; and over them three presidents, of whom Daniel was one, to whom these satraps should give account, so that the king might suffer no loss. Then this Daniel became distinguished above all the other presidents and satraps, because an excellent spirit was in him; and the king planned to set him over the whole kingdom. Then the presidents and the satraps sought to find a ground for complaint against Daniel with regard to the kingdom; but they could find no ground for complaint or any fault, because he was faithful, and no error or fault was found in him. Then these men said, "We shall not find any ground for complaint against this Daniel unless we find it in connection with the law of his God."

Then these presidents and satraps came by agreement to the king and said to him, "O King Darius, live for ever! All the presidents of the kingdom, the prefects and the satraps, the counsellors and the governors are agreed that the king should establish an ordinance and enforce an interdict, that whoever makes petition to any god or man for thirty days, except to you, O king, shall be cast into the den of lions. Now, O king, establish the interdict and sign the document, so that it cannot be changed, according to the law of the Medes and the Persians, which cannot be revoked." Therefore King Darius signed the document and interdict.

(i)

If there is anything worse than being a Daniel in a den of lions, it is being a lion in a den of Daniels! Our hero had faced the second of these ordeals more than once before, confronted as he was by wise men, soothsayers and astrologers in the king's employ. He was ready now to face the other ordeal—with equal equanimity. True, Daniel was a peaceful lion. Nevertheless, he was tough, particularly when bidden to compromise those religious principles which he held so dear. He had shown this in the story told in chapter 3 of the burning fiery furnace. He was to show it again when threatened with the den of lions.

(ii)

These two stories, in chapters 3 and 6, have indeed quite a lot in common. In both, God's faithful servants undergo severe trials rather than betray their faith in God and the practice of their religion; in defiance of the king's command they remain loyal worshippers of God; by jealousy they are betrayed and condemned; an angel of the Lord comes to their rescue; their accusers meet the same fate that they themselves had planned for the Jewish youths; the king praises the God whom they worship; the youths are rewarded and promoted; a royal decree warns those who refuse to follow the requirements of the God of Israel.

In neither story (nor indeed in the rest of the stories in chapters 1–6) is the background that of the persecution of the Jews as such. In chapter 3 Nebuchadnezzar punishes them severely, not because they are Jews but because they have disobeyed his command to fall down and worship the golden image. Here in chapter 6 there is even less evidence of "persecution". On the contrary, Darius shows himself to be kindly disposed towards Daniel and is deeply grieved when Daniel finds himself in trouble, and does everything he can to help. It is hard to imagine that a writer of the time of Antiochus, faced with the dire persecutions of that king's reign, would concoct a story with such an emphasis. This is further indication that this particular story, like some at least of the others we have already looked at, belongs to traditional material going back into Persian times which was adapted to suit the purpose of our story-teller. This purpose was, once again, to encourage and strengthen the faithful Jews in his day as they, too, faced trials and tribulations. It is a story of jealousy, betrayal and threatened death in which, as in the earlier stories also, they would find comfort and reassurance—not only of God's presence with them in their hour of trial, but also of God's ultimate victory in which they themselves would surely share.

(iii)

It begins with an account of court intrigue, all too common in the experience of oriental potentates. The time is during the reign of Darius who, we are informed, had appointed 120 satraps throughout his kingdom to relieve him of unnecessary administrative burdens. Over them he had appointed three "presidents", with Daniel chief among them. So outstanding were Daniel's services that the king was minded to give him the office of Chief Minister of State. Because of this the other two presidents and the satraps felt their security threatened and so began to look for faults in Daniel's conduct of affairs, but could find none. There was no "ground for complaint" in him, i.e. no indictable charge could be levelled against him—or any "error" which might reveal dereliction of duty.

Having found no chink in his public armour, they then began to probe his private life—a familiar ploy of jealous and vindictive men before and since who snoop and spy with no regard for the privacies of home and family life. Their hope was that they might find something to fault "in connection with the law of his God". The Aramaic word used here for "law" is the equivalent of the Hebrew *torah* which in earlier writings refers to the "revelation" or the revealed "law" of God, but here signifies "religion" or "the practice of religion". Having failed to trap him in respect of his civic responsibilities which were impeccable in their execution, they tried to catch him out in respect of private religious observances which, if performed without proper state authority, were indictable offences and punishable by the laws of the land. The religious man of principle is easy prey to those who sniff and snoop and is most vulnerable at the very point where his convictions are most strong.

(iv)

The accusers, we are told, came "by agreement" to the king, for they had hatched a plot to persuade him to take action against Daniel, albeit in ignorance. They encouraged him to issue an edict requiring that, for the space of thirty days, prayers be offered to no god or man save Darius. The decree was promulgated with a solemn, unbreakable oath (cf. Esth. 1:19; 8:8). There is no historical support for any decree of this kind on the part of Darius, but the first readers of the book of Daniel would easily recognise such claims to arrogant self-deification in the claims of a king like Antiochus and certain others who had gone before him. They would just as readily identify themselves and their people with their hero Daniel and read on eagerly to know the outcome of the story—as many a reader in similar circumstances will do today; for in not a few countries similar ploys are still practised and a corresponding fate awaits the man of principle who, on religious or political grounds, refuses to "fall down and worship". There are still those who are ready to report even those of their own household (cf. Matt. 10:36) who are foolish enough to step out of line. Here as elsewhere the book of Daniel speaks with stark realism a word of encouragement in time of trial.

The penalty for disobedience, says the writer, was to be thrown into a cistern or a pit and to be devoured there by lions.

The trap was set. The following verses tell how the schemers caught their prey.

THE PLOT

Daniel 6:10–17

When Daniel knew that the document had been signed, he went to his house where he had windows in his upper chamber open toward Jerusalem; and he got down upon his knees three times a day and prayed and gave thanks before his God, as he had done previously. Then these men came by agreement and found Daniel making petition and supplication before his God. Then they came near and said before the king, concerning the interdict, "O king! Did you not sign an interdict, that any man who makes petition to any god or man within thirty days except to you, O king, shall be cast into the den of lions?" The king answered, "The thing stands fast, according to the law of the Medes and Persians, which cannot be revoked." Then they answered before the king, "That Daniel, who is one of the exiles from Judah, pays no heed to you, O king, or the interdict you have signed, but makes his petition three times a day."

Then the king, when he heard these words, was much distressed, and set his mind to deliver Daniel; and he laboured till the sun went down to rescue him. Then these men came by agreement to the king, and said to the king, "Know, O king, that it is a law of the Medes and Persians that no interdict or ordinance which the king establishes can be changed." Then the king commanded, and Daniel was brought and cast into the den of lions. The king said to Daniel, "May your God, whom you serve continually, deliver you!" And a stone was brought and laid upon the mouth of the den, and the king sealed it with his own signet and with the signet of his lords, that nothing might be changed concerning Daniel.

(i)

When Daniel heard of the plot made against him, he remained quite unruffled. His accusers tried to give the impression that he had been openly defiant in disobeying the royal edict. But this was not so. He was neither defiant nor cringing. He simply carried on as he was accustomed to do with his private devotions. In the event, he might be breaking the law of the land as decreed by the king, but there was a law of the heart that was greater still and had to be obeyed.

A thing may be lawful, but it may not for that reason be right in the eyes of God. The man of God throughout the generations has frequently shared Daniel's dilemma and faced the same kind of consequences. The "law of the land" and "the law of conscience", held in tension, present classic examples of faithfulness and heroism in almost every age as in the case of Daniel himself. There are occasions when "every person [must be] subject to the governing authorities" (Rom. 13:1); there are others when "we ought to obey God rather than men" (Acts 5:29). To distinguish between the two requires courage and faith. Daniel possessed both.

Commenting on these verses, Walter Lüthi writes: "If the beginning shows us Daniel, not in the lions' den, but hale and hearty in the King's palace, we ought not to tremble any the less for him than if he were already in the lions' den. But look! Here in the palace where Daniel has already climbed so high that he can climb no higher, a miracle happens: Daniel remains what he is. He remains one 'of the children of the captivity of Judah'. He remains a subject of the King of Kings before whom thrice daily he bows the knee." A second miracle follows, comparable with that of his deliverance from the jaws of the lions—the fear of the lions' den is taken from him and he is protected from betraying his religion and his God. Faith is the answer to fear, and Daniel's faith in God was stronger than his fear of the lions.

(ii)

Daniel was a pious man whose reliance upon God was rooted in specific religious observance, the regular discipline of prayer. He went up to his roof-chamber as was his custom and, with the lattice-windows wide open, knelt down and offered prayer three times each day facing in the direction of Jerusalem. This was no sporadic act of bravado. It was a regular and disciplined exercise by means of which he practised the presence of God.

Prescribed periods of prayer can stultify devotion, but they can also strengthen faith. Daniel felt the need of appointed hours of prayer and would not be turned aside from them.

The roof-chamber is mentioned in the Old Testament fairly frequently as a place of prayer (cf. Judg. 3:20; 1 Kings 17:19; 2 Kings 4:10; Jer. 23:14). The posture adopted in prayer takes various forms in Scripture. Standing is frequently mentioned (cf. 1 Sam. 1:26; 1 Kings 8:22; Matt. 6:5; Mark 11:25; Luke 18:11), with hands spread above the head, lifted up toward heaven (cf. 1 Kings 8:22; Ezra 9:5; Pss. 28:2; 63:4; 134:2; 141:2; Isa. 1:15; Lam. 2:19; 3:41; 2 Maccabees 3:20; 1 Tim. 2:8). Other postures include prostration before God (cf. Gen. 24:26; Exod. 34:8; 1 Kings 18:42; Neh. 8:6). Here in Daniel, as elsewhere (cf. Ezra 9:5; Ps. 95:6; Luke 22:41; Acts 7:60), a kneeling position is adopted, a sign of humility, reverence and submission.

Daniel offers his prayers facing Jerusalem. It was a custom among the Hebrews of Old Testament times to pray facing towards the Jerusalem Temple (cf. 1 Kings 8:35, 44, 48; Pss. 5:7; 138:2; Ezek. 8:16; Tobit 3:11; 1 Esdras 4:58). In later times, when the Jews were scattered abroad, those in the Dispersion were enjoined to turn towards Israel, those in Israel were to turn to Jerusalem, and those in Jerusalem were to turn to the Temple. Jerusalem and the Temple were more than religious "places", they were at the same time religious "symbols", representing the presence among them of the eternal God and standing for the unity of Israel's faith and the gathering in of the Gentiles to the "city of God".

Daniel offers his prayers "three times a day". This no doubt indicates a recognised pattern among pious Jews during the Greek, and probably also during the Persian, period. According to Ps. 55:17, the psalmist offers prayer "evening and morning and at noon", but it is unlikely that this indicates the recognition of fixed periods. That was to come later and is reflected in the book of Daniel where the thrice-daily observance of prayer no doubt corresponds to the time of the morning sacrifice in the Temple (cf. Pss. 5:3; 59:16; 88:13; Wisdom of Solomon 16:28), the evening sacrifice (cf. 1 Kings

18:36; Ezra 9:5; Ps. 141:2; Dan. 9:21; Judith 9:1) and the hour of sunset.

(iii)

The conspirators had all the proof they needed. Having confirmed the fact of Daniel's petition to his God, they went to see the king to remind him of his solemn pledge and the penalty to be executed for breach of the law. Only then did they disclose the name of the culprit. The king was greatly distressed and tried his utmost to save Daniel, but in the end had to give way to their pressure. On his command Daniel was thrown into a pit containing lions. It is known that in ancient times oriental kings kept menageries and that others hunted lions for sport. The story may suggest that the king kept the lions in a pit as a diversion as well as a means of execution. A stone was then rolled over the entrance and the king's seal imprinted, perhaps on a "filling" of clay, to prevent any interference. Daniel was left to his fate.

Commentators have drawn attention to a suggestion made by Bentzen that the descent of Daniel into the pit may in some way be related to the descent of the king in ancient mythology into the Underworld, the lions representing the demons which threaten him. As in the Psalms, the pit or cistern, on this reckoning, would represent the realm of death to which Daniel is subjected. It is most unlikely, however, that any such allusion, if it exists at all, goes beyond the use of related imagery or terminology. This is a plain story, with a plain meaning.

The Christian reader will perhaps find himself thinking of one greater than Daniel who also spent much time in prayer, and of the interesting parallels between the accounts of Daniel and Jesus. He too turned his face to Jerusalem and the Temple there. He withdrew to the quietness of Gethsemane where he prayed three times over. There he was betrayed to the rulers by a friend and given over to death, though no fault could be found in him. He descended into the depths of Hades. A stone was set over the mouth of his tomb and marked with a seal. When the stone was removed early in the morning he was found to be alive, raised from the dead by the power of God. A fanciful comparison? Maybe, but our author's belief in the resurrection, expressed in a later chapter of this book (see chapter 12), gives further content to such surmisings and underlines the message that God will not leave his people in the pit of death but will deliver those who trust in him.

DELIVERED FROM THE LIONS' DEN

Daniel 6:18–24

> Then the king went to his palace, and spent the night fasting; no diversions were brought to him, and sleep fled from him. Then, at break of day, the king arose and went in haste to the den of lions. When he came near to the den where Daniel was, he cried out in a tone of anguish and said to Daniel, "O Daniel, servant of the living God, has your God, whom you serve continually, been able to deliver you from the lions?" Then Daniel said to the king, "O king, live for ever! My God sent his angel and shut the lions' mouths, and they have not hurt me, because I was found blameless before him; and also before you, O king, I have done no wrong." Then the king was exceedingly glad, and commanded that Daniel be taken up out of the den. So Daniel was taken up out of the den, and no kind of hurt was found upon him, because he had trusted in his God. And the king commanded, and those men who had accused Daniel were brought and cast into the den of lions—they, their children, and their wives; and before they reached the bottom of the den the lions overpowered them and broke all their bones in pieces.

(i)

The king returned from the lions' pit to his palace where he spent a restless night without any food. He declined any "diversions"—a word variously interpreted to refer to food or music or dancing girls or (with a slight emendation) concubines. First thing in the morning he hastened to the scene and called out anxiously to Daniel whom he addressed as "servant of the living God". With obvious delight he heard Daniel reply from the midst of the pit announcing that God, through his angel, had shut the lions' mouths. The roaring lions had, by the

goodness of God, turned out to be "paper-tigers"! No harm had
befallen him because he was upright and innocent before both
God and the king. Orders were given and Daniel was hauled up
out of the pit. Like the young men delivered from the fiery
furnace, he was completely unscathed; and as in that incident
also, his accusers, together with their families, were dealt with
in summary fashion—they were thrown to the lions. At this
point the writer adds a dramatic touch—before their bodies
touched the bottom of the pit they were seized and their bones
were broken in pieces!

(ii)

When we think of this celebrated story certain passages of
Scripture spring to mind "like a lion from a thicket" (to coin a
phrase of C. H. Spurgeon). It is possible that the writer had in
mind a passage like Ps. 57:4f.:

> I lie in the midst of lions
>   that greedily devour the sons of men;
> Their teeth are spears and arrows,
>   their tongues sharp swords...
> They dug a pit in my way,
>   but they have fallen into it themselves.

Or Ps. 91:11ff.:

> For he will give his angels charge of you
>   to guard you in all your ways...
> You will tread on the lion and the adder,
>   the young lion and the serpent you will trample under foot.

What we have here in Daniel 6 is, as it were, a dramatised
version of such verses declaring the writer's faith in God and
giving assurance of his saving power.

It is of interest to observe that the two related stories in
chapters 3 and 6 are in fact mentioned together in Hebrews
11:3f. which commemorates the heroes of Israel's past "who
through faith...stopped the mouths of lions, quenched raging
fire", and that these stories in turn are related to the exploits of

the Maccabees who "escaped the edge of the sword, won strength out of weakness, became mighty in war, put foreign armies to flight" (Heb. 11:34; cf. 1 Maccabees 5:1ff.).

Reference to lions in terms of evil or of danger from which God in his mercy gives deliverance is to be found also in the New Testament. Peter, for example, writes of "your adversary the devil [who] prowls around like a roaring lion, seeking someone to devour" (1 Pet. 5:8). Paul writes to Timothy and says "I was rescued from the lion's mouth; the Lord will rescue me from all evil" (2 Tim. 4:17f.). Writing from Ephesus where, he says, "I fought with wild beasts" (1 Cor. 15:32), he rejoices in the deliverance of God and in the hope of resurrection. An echo of this experience is perhaps to be found in the words of 2 Cor. 1:8ff.: "We were so utterly, unbearably crushed that we despaired of life itself, but that was to make us rely not on ourselves but on God who raises the dead; he delivered us from so deadly a peril, and he will deliver us; on him we have set our hope that he will deliver us again."

(iii)

The conspirators, we are told, suffered the fate they themselves had devised for Daniel, just as in the book of Esther, Haman was hanged on the gibbet he had set up for Mordecai (cf. Esth. 9:10ff.). Here we have an example of the *lex talionis,* the law of "tit for tat", so common in the ancient world. In its origin and intention this was seen as a merciful law—a life for a life, not a whole family for a life; but again and again it is put into effect against the background of the solidarity of the family and vengeance is required of not only the evil-doer himself, but also of his kith and kin (cf. Josh. 7:24f.; 2 Sam. 14:5ff.; 21:5ff.; Esth. 9:10). Already in Israel voices had been raised against the custom of punishing the innocent in retaliation for the sins of another (cf. Num. 16:22; Deut. 24:16; Jer. 31:29f.; Ezek. 18:1ff.). The writer of Daniel, in this regard at least, lagged behind some of the great spirits in Israel and had not caught the vision of "the law of love" to be found in the New Testament which replaces revenge with reconciliation and seeks to overcome evil with good (cf. Rom. 12:17ff.)

DARIUS AND THE GOD OF ISRAEL

Daniel 6:25–28

Then King Darius wrote to all the peoples, nations, and languages that dwell in all the earth: "Peace be multiplied to you. I make a decree, that in all my royal dominion men tremble and fear before the God of Daniel,

> for he is the living God,
>   enduring for ever;
> his kingdom shall never be destroyed,
>   and his dominion shall be to the end.
> He delivers and rescues,
>   he works signs and wonders
>   in heaven and on earth,
> he who has saved Daniel
>   from the power of the lions."

So this Daniel prospered during the reign of Darius and the reign of Cyrus the Persian.

The chapter ends with Darius proclaiming a decree in which he celebrates the sovereignty of Daniel's God whose kingdom will never be destroyed. As for Daniel himself, he prospers right on into the reign of Cyrus the Persian king. The decree promulgated by Darius has a close resemblance to that in chapter 3 attributed to Nebuchadnezzar. In each of them the king recognises the God of Israel and calls on all the peoples to acknowledge him also. This recognition in our chapter well reflects the situation in 538 B.C. when Cyrus, following his conquest of Babylon, issued a decree restoring the Jewish community to Palestine and establishing their religion there (cf. Ezra 1:2ff.; 4:8ff.; 6:3ff.).

In this passage Darius confesses the God of Daniel as the *living* God, the *eternal* God and the *saving* God.

(i) The expression "living God" is a characteristic expression in the Old Testament. In contrast with worthless idols, he is active on behalf of his people as he has evidenced again and again in their long history from the time he brought their fathers out of the land of Egypt. "He is conceived not as abstracted from human life, but as revealed within it... He is Yahweh, the God of Israel known for what He is by what He does" (H. Wheeler Robinson).

(ii) He is also the "enduring God", the one whose kingdom and sovereignty are constant and stable and whose dominion is everlasting. He is the God described in the New Testament as "the Father of lights with whom there is no variation or shadow due to change" (Jas. 1:17), who is unswerving in his faithfulness and unchanging in his ways.

(iii) This living and enduring God, moreover, is the "saving God". The signs and wonders which he performs "in heaven and on earth" are of one piece with his saving of Daniel from "the power of the lions". Each is a marvel in its own right and demonstrates the goodness and power of God. Because Daniel "had trusted in his God" (verse 23), God had saved him.

The contents of this decree of Darius no doubt reflect faithfully the convictions of the author of the book, living as he does in a time of challenge and change and facing danger to life itself. In the midst of uncertainty and confronted with threats and trials, his readers would find in these assurances (as we ourselves surely do) a ground of certain hope.

"I HAVE A DREAM"

Daniel 7:1-8

In the first year of Belshazzar king of Babylon, Daniel had a dream and visions of his head as he lay in his bed. Then he wrote down the dream, and told the sum of the matter. Daniel said, "I saw in my vision by night, and behold, the four winds of heaven were stirring up the great sea. And four great beasts came up out of the sea, different from one another. The first was like a lion and had eagles' wings. Then as I looked its wings were plucked off, and it was lifted up from the ground and made to stand upon two feet like a man; and the mind of a man was given to it. And behold, another beast, a second one, like a bear. It was raised up on one side; it had three ribs in its mouth between its teeth; and it was told, 'Arise, devour much flesh.' After this I looked, and lo, another, like a leopard, with four wings of a bird on its back; and the beast had four heads; and dominion was given to it. After this I saw in the night visions, and behold, a fourth beast, terrible and dreadful and exceedingly strong; and it had great iron teeth; it devoured and broke in pieces, and stamped the residue with its feet. It was different from all the beasts that were before it; and it had ten horns. I considered the horns, and behold, there came up among them another horn, a little one, before which three of the first horns were plucked up by the roots; and behold, in this horn were eyes like the eyes of a man, and a mouth speaking great things."

Daniel 7 marks a transition from the stories of chapters 1–6 to the dreams and visions which characterise chapters 8–12. On the one hand there is a clear connection between Daniel's dream of the four beasts and Nebuchadnezzar's dream of the metal image in chapter 2, in both of which the four-empire theory is propounded with the setting up of God's kingdom at the end. On the other hand, whereas in chapters 1–6 Daniel is presented as the interpreter of other people's dreams, from chapter 7 onwards he himself is the recipient of dreams.

(i)

Throughout the whole book, then, dreams and visions (which are frequently equated) are recognised to be a medium of divine revelation. There are indications here and there that the dream recorded may reflect a genuine experience on the part of the author himself; but for the most part its description is a literary device which follows a common conventional pattern. But literary convention or not it is believed to be an important vehicle of divine truth in which the mysteries of God are made known.

In modern parlance the word "dreamer" is generally used in a rather derogatory sense to describe a "wool-gatherer", someone whose head is lost in the clouds, an idealist out of touch with reality. In the Old Testament, and in particular here in Daniel, the emphasis is quite different. Here he is the "visionary", the man who can see beyond appearance to reality, beyond events to ultimate meaning, beyond the happenings of history to the realisation of God's triumphant future. Joel tells us that one of the marks of the coming age will be that the young men will see visions and the old men will dream dreams (cf. 2:28). By the help of God's spirit they will see the far horizons of God's eternal purpose.

Two dreamers of whom favourable mention is made in the Old Testament and whom our author relates closely together, are Joseph and Daniel. Each of them, through his dreams, interprets the mind of God and each of them, as a result, falls foul of men who failed to appreciate their gift.

So it has been with dreamers and visionaries in every age. One such in recent times was surely Martin Luther King who possessed the same gift and suffered the same fate. On the wall of the motel in Memphis, Tennessee, near the spot where he was assassinated, there hangs a plaque with these words:

> Here comes the dreamer.
> Let us kill him and
> see what becomes of his dreams.

For Martin Luther King, as for Joseph and Daniel, to dream meant to live dangerously. But for each of them it meant more than this. It meant seeing beyond the limits of this present scene into the beyond of God's design.

(ii)

The message of Daniel's dream as recorded in this chapter, for all the obscurity of its presentation, is clear enough. It is that successive kings and kingdoms (symbolised by four strange beasts), which have acted arrogantly against God and treated God's people in brutal and brutish fashion, have gone as far as he will allow and must face divine retribution. It is not enough that they should be chastised and their power curbed; they must be utterly destroyed. In place of these kingdoms (as later verses show) God will set up his own kingdom, delegating his rule to the faithful among his people.

The same message comes through in the stories in chapters 1–6. But now it is given with greater urgency and from a different perspective. The new age is about to dawn—not just in "the sweet by and by" in some heavenly realm, but here and now on earth. Their enemies will be destroyed and they themselves will at last be set free from all tyranny and oppression.

Such vision and such faith have sustained the people of God in every generation and sustain them still. Few have more eloquently expressed this conviction than the latter-day "dreamer" to whom we have already referred. In August, 1963, before a congregation of 200,000 gathered in Washington to stamp out segregation, Martin Luther King preached his famous sermon on liberation. Here are some extracts from it that speak for themselves:

I say to you today, my friends, that in spite of the difficulties and frustrations of the moment I still have a dream...

I have a dream that one day on the red hills of Georgia the sons of former slaves and the sons of former slaveowners will be able to sit down together at the table of brotherhood.

I have a dream that one day even the state of Mississippi, a desert state sweltering in the heat of injustice and oppression, will be transformed into an oasis of freedom and justice.

I have a dream that my four little children will one day live in a nation where they will not be judged by the colour of their skin but by the content of their character.

I have a dream today...

I have a dream that one day every valley shall be exalted, every hill and mountain shall be made low, the rough places will be made plain, and the crooked places will be made straight, and the glory of the Lord shall be revealed, and all flesh shall see it together.

This is our hope.

THE FOUR BEASTS: THEIR SYMBOLIC PRESENTATION

Daniel 7:1–8 *(cont'd)*

(i)

Symbolism, it has been said, is the language of apocalyptic. What is more, it is symbolism of a particularly dramatic kind, the language and the style matching the inexpressible revelations it seeks to portray. The sombre language of prose will not suffice to express what comes flooding into the mind in dream and vision. It requires the imaginative, colourful and often bizarre language of poetry to do justice to what is seen and heard. The result is a riot of colour, shape and presentation of symbolic imagery of an extravagant and frequently fantastic kind—beasts with sprouting horns, dragons breathing fire, mysterious horsemen, sacred rivers, mystical mountains and great sea-monsters that defy description.

"Imagination", says Albert Einstein, "is more important than knowledge". And sanctified imagination is a gift of God which can become a vehicle of divine revelation. H. Wheeler Robinson tells of an eleventh-century Chinese artist who taught his pupils to develop their sense of artistic perception in an unusual way. He draped a large piece of transparent silk over a rough stone wall and told them to sit and look and look and look. As they looked the shape of the stones began to show; and as they kept on looking the stones and crevices and cracks became mountains and waterfalls and birds on the wing.

No doubt some at least of the imagery to be found in the apocalyptic writings owes much to the writers' vivid and, as they would claim, God-inspired imagination arising out of their experience of dreams and visions. But to them these were no mere subjective imaginings; they were divine disclosures and revelations of divine truth. It is to be recognised at the same time, however, that such symbolic language, as we shall see, was part of a literary convention and belonged to a fairly well-defined tradition which can be traced back not only into earlier

Old Testament writings but also into the ancient mythology of cultures that surrounded Israel.

Symbolic language, like symbolic objects, can become a means of revelation and a ground of assurance. Such expressions of thought and devotion are not always easily understood at first glance. Their value and meaning become plain only in the light of Scripture, tradition and experience taken together. For all their strangeness and obscurity they are worthy of contemplation as a vehicle of divine truth.

(ii)

The symbolism of the dream described in these verses is strange in the extreme. Indeed, the reader might be forgiven for concluding that what is here described is less of a dream and more of a nightmare! The four beasts that rise out of the sea belong to the species that appear only in the troubled watches of the night!

And yet, they are more than the creation of a disturbed night's sleep. They are in fact part of a mythological apparatus, part of a mythological complex of ideas, which appears again and again in later Jewish apocalyptic writings and has its likely origin in ancient Mesopotamian mythology. It has been argued that here in Daniel, in the reference to the great sea and the four fearsome beasts that emerge from it, there is a close connection with the Babylonian Creation Epic which was recited at the Babylonian New Year Festival and which may have found its way into Israelite worship also. Support for this may be found in certain Old Testament references besides the book of Daniel and more especially in certain of the Psalms where the conflict between God and evil is set forth in terms of a combat resembling that in the Babylonian myth between the Creator and a great female sea-monster *Tiamat* which was slain by the god Marduk at the time the universe was made. This reference, and that in Daniel to "the great sea", recall the reference in Gen. 1:2 and elsewhere to the *tehom,* which is philologically related to the Babylonian sea-monster *Tiamat,* and describes the watery abyss controlled and subdued by God when he made the heavens and the earth.

It is not surprising that the mythological combat between the god and the sea-monster undergoes significant modifications when taken into the Hebrew tradition. Nevertheless it is still easily recognisable in certain Old Testament passages where it is identified, for example, as the Dragon (cf. Job 7:12; Ps. 74:13; Isa. 51:9; Ezek. 29:3; 32:2), or Leviathan (cf. Job 41:1; Pss. 74:14; 104:26; Isa. 27:1), or Rahab (cf. Job 9:13; 26:12; Ps. 89:10; Isa. 30:7; 51:9) or the Serpent (cf. Job 26:13; Isa. 27:1; Amos 9:3). Reference is often made in this connection to such a passage as Ps. 74 which reflects ancient mythological lore. In verses 13 and 14, for example, it is said of God:

Thou didst divide the sea by thy might;
Thou didst break the heads of the dragon on the waters.
Thou didst crush the heads of Leviathan.

Later on, in verse 19, the Psalmist prays that he may not be delivered to "the wild beasts", where the Hebrew word used corresponds to the Aramaic word in the Daniel passage.

(iii)

It would be misleading, however, to see in this account in Daniel a direct dependence on Babylonian mythology or to read into it the meanings and nuances of the Babylonian story. The writer is taking over the stock-in-trade of symbolic imagery handed down in those religious circles in which he moved, using them to convey a message relevant to his own day affirming the victory of God over evil forces ranged against him and his faithful people.

There is one respect in particular in which the message of this chapter differs clearly from that of its Babylonian precursors, despite the similarity of the imagery and the symbolic language used. The evil forces represented by the wild beasts are not so much malevolent powers associated with *creation* as in the Babylonian Epic. They are rather those brute forces of evil which become only too evident in the unfolding of *history*–

kings and rulers who tyrannise the people of God, empires and kingdoms which terrify for a time but those "doom is writ". Brute beasts they may be, but let the faithful be assured, they are under God's control and utterly subservient to his all-powerful rule.

THE FOUR BEASTS: THEIR HISTORICAL IDENTITY

Daniel 7:1-8 *(cont'd)*

(i)

The four beasts which rise out of the troubled sea, we are later told (cf. 7:17,23), represent four kings or kingdoms. Such use of animal figures to symbolise men and nations is found elsewhere in the Old Testament (cf. Ps. 68:30; Ezek. 17:1ff., etc.) and appears frequently in later Jewish apocalyptic writings. It is not, of course, uncommon even in modern times. Thus, we have the Scottish lion, the Welsh dragon, the Russian bear, the American eagle and so on. The animals in Daniel 7, however, are much less easy to identify and, as we have seen, belong to no recognisable species.

Their symbolic representation has led to much speculation and has produced many different answers. It is generally accepted that they stand for the four great empires of Babylonia, "Media", Persia and Greece and so correspond to those depicted in the metal statue of chapter 2. Some of the symbolic descriptions associated with the four beasts, however, are quite obscure and should not be unduly pressed.

The first beast is *a lion with eagles' wings* symbolising the Babylonian kingdom. The winged lion was a familiar enough motif in Babylonian art and provided a readily recognisable symbol. The readers, moreover, would recall that already in Scripture Nebuchadnezzar, the Babylonian king, is depicted as a lion (cf. Jer. 49:22; 50:44) and Babylonia itself as an eagle (cf. Ezek. 17:3). The plucking of the eagles' wings might well remind them of the chastisement of Nebuchadnezzar (cf. 4:16), and the substitution of a man's heart for a lion's at his ultimate restoration (cf. 4:34). Interpretations differ on this last point.

Some see in it a restoration of Babylonia to a position of dignity and sanity; others see in it the substitution of the timidity of mortal man for lion-hearted courage.

The second beast is *a bear,* second only to the lion as silver is to gold (cf. 2:39), and feared for its ferocity (cf. 1 Sam. 17:34; Prov. 28:15; Amos 5:19; Hos. 13:8). In the mind of the writer this would be a fitting symbol for Media whose reputation for cruelty and rapine was amply evidenced by the prophets (cf. Isa. 13:17f.; 21:2ff.; Jer. 51:11,28).

The third beast is *a leopard with four wings and four heads,* symbolising Persia. The four wings may represent the speed of Persia's conquest (cf. Isa. 41:3). The four heads perhaps refer to the four Persian kings known to the Jews—Cyrus, Xerxes, Artaxerxes and Darius (cf. 11:2)—or may simply have the same symbolic significance as the four wings.

At last the writer comes to the fourth beast, the one that matters most of all—*a beast which defies description,* with great iron teeth (cf. the iron feet in 2:40) that devour and break in pieces, and feet that trample and crush. This great monster, resembling in many ways the mythological monster Leviathan (see previous comment), no doubt symbolises the Greek kingdom under Alexander and his successors. The kingdoms that had gone before had not unduly interfered in the internal life of Israel, but under this kingdom and its continuation in the Seleucid line, Israel and its religion had suffered grievously.

This is brought out clearly in the symbolism of the beast's ten horns (cf. the ten toes of the image in 2:41f.) which probably represent Alexander the Great and successive rulers of the Seleucid line. The little horn which springs up and uproots the other three horns no doubt symbolises Antiochus Epiphanes and his rooting out of the three others who laid claim to the throne before him. The human identity of this little horn is evidenced by its possession of human eyes and a mouth that speaks presumptuously. The brazenness (cf. 8:23) and arrogance (cf. 11:36; 1 Maccabees 1:24; 2 Maccabees 5:17) of Antiochus were characteristics of that king, of which the readers of the book were only too well aware.

(ii)

This form of visual presentation is strange indeed to the modern reader, but we should not be put off by its extravagant mythological language and fail to see its penetrating insight into the movements of history and the relevance of its message for our modern world. Here again some words of Walter Lüthi are apposite: "From the heaving sea of the nations we see shapes and forms rise up, of which we don't know the final significance, nor how they will develop, nor what we shall have to expect from them...figures that did not exist in our previous world-conception, and which are really hardly less strange to us than lions and leopards with wings, or wild beasts with ten horns. We have lived to see what our education would not even let us dream about. We have seen a world-war, a world-bolshevism, a world-capitalism; we have seen the summit of all folly—a world-crisis, which originated in over-production and was followed by unemployment. Out of the universal mists of our time we have seen the fantastic contours of a world-godlessness rising up...like ghosts, we have seen them come nearer and nearer and now they are here. We don't know what to think of them."

THE ANCIENT OF DAYS

Daniel 7:9–12

"As I looked,
thrones were placed
and one that was ancient of days took his seat;
his raiment was white as snow,
and the hair of his head like pure wool;
his throne was fiery flames,
its wheels were burning fire.
A stream of fire issued,
and came forth from before him;
a thousand thousands served him,
and ten thousand times ten thousand stood before him;
the court sat in judgment,
and the books were opened."

I looked then because of the sound of the great words which the horn was speaking. And as I looked, the beast was slain, and its body destroyed and given over to be burned with fire. As for the rest of the beasts, their dominion was taken away, but their lives were prolonged for a season and a time.

(i)

The divine judge. In contrast to the four fearsome and frightening beasts the seer now catches a vision of Almighty God himself, a majestic and venerable figure, seated on his throne preparing to judge the nations of the earth.

The scene is that of a great assize, with God surrounded by a great retinue of heavenly attendants. Other thrones are set up alongside his, presumably (though this is not stated) for the celestial assessors in God's judgment of the nations. Attention, however, is focused on God himself as judge. He is described as one "advanced in years", a picture not of senility but of venerability. He it is who existed before the world began (cf. Isa. 44:6; Pss. 55:19; 90:2), who exemplifies wisdom as well as might. His raiment, like his hair, is the purest white, reflecting that dazzling brightness which is a mark of divine or celestial beings (cf. Matt. 28:3).

The picture thus presented recalls that of the heavenly Council alluded to in such passages as 1 Kings 22:19ff., Job 1:6ff. and Isa. 6:6ff., where God presides over the proceedings of his heavenly court whose members are to carry out his word of command. He is "a God very terrible in the council of the holy ones [i.e. the angels]" (Ps. 89:7), who "judgeth among the gods" (Ps. 82:1). He is represented here, as elsewhere in the Old Testament, by the figure of a man sitting on a throne (cf. Ezek. 1:26; 43:6f.; Isa. 6:1), the throne having "wheels with burning fire", reminding us of the chariot-throne of Ezekiel's vision from which fire came flashing forth (cf. Ezek. 1:4,13,15ff.; 10:2, 6ff.). The association of the fire of judgment with God the judge is again a familiar one (e.g. Ps. 50:3), being a feature of Old Testament theophanies (e.g. Ps. 97:3ff.).

The picture of God as arbiter and judge of all the earth is, as we have seen, a fairly common one in the Old Testament

Scriptures (cf. Gen. 18:25; Pss. 7:8; 50:4f.; 82:8; 94:2; 96:10; Isa. 2:4; 33:22) and appears again in the New Testament (cf. Rom. 3:6; Heb. 10:30; 12:23, etc.; Jas. 4:12). It is of significance that the writer of the book of Revelation (cf. 1:13ff.; also 10:5f.) takes up the imagery of this passage and transfers it to "one like a Son of man" who is in this instance none other than the Messiah, and that in Matthew's Gospel the same Son of man will sit on "his glorious throne", judging "the twelve tribes of Israel" (Matt. 19:28; cf. 25:31). Elsewhere Jesus is described as the one to whom men will have to give account, "who is ready to judge the living and the dead" (1 Pet. 4:5; cf. Acts 10:42 and Jas. 5:9). He it is who, during his lifetime, claims to serve as judge together with the Father (cf. John 8:16) and will, with the coming of his kingdom, be judge of all the world (cf. 2 Tim. 4:1). This responsibility, according to Paul, he will share with "the saints" who, with him, "will judge the world" (1 Cor. 6:2f.); and, in a different context, Jesus himself assures his disciples that those who have followed him "will also sit on twelve thrones" (Matt. 19:28; cf. Luke 22:30).

There is a sense in which the follower of Jesus must not judge, lest he himself be judged (cf. Matt. 7:1). But there is another sense in which he must do so, for "the spiritual man judges all things" because he has "the mind of Christ" (1 Cor. 2:15f.).

(ii)

The divine judgment. The court sits in judgment and the books are opened. It has been suggested that this idea is to be traced back to the "tablets of destiny" which played a significant part in the Babylonian New Year ritual in the ceremony of fixing the destinies of men and nations. But Babylonian mythology apart, we find ample reference to such books in the Old Testament itself where, it is said, the records of men's evil deeds are written down before God (cf. Isa. 65:6f.) as are the deeds of those who fear the Lord (cf. Mal. 3:16; cf. Ps. 56:8), whilst in God's book of life (cf. Exod. 32:33; Rev. 13.8) are recorded also the names of those who fear him.

In this Daniel passage no indication is given of the actual

contents of the books. Perhaps we are to assume they are opened for examination at the place where the sins of the four great kingdoms are recorded. In any case, judgment is pronounced and the sentence carried out without delay. First to suffer its fate is the fourth indescribable beast with the horn that speaks arrogantly. The beast is slain and given over to be burned with fire. Antiochus Epiphanes and the whole Seleucid line will be utterly destroyed. Here is the message the readers of the book must understand. The mighty tyrant who mocks and blasphemes Almighty God and who crushes and kills God's people will himself be consumed.

The other three kingdoms are also judged and their dominion is taken away. Their lives, however, are spared at least for a time. H.H. Rowley puts forward an historical explanation for this, the kingdoms of Babylonia, "Media" and Persia which had been incorporated into Alexander's empire and had come under the rule of the Seleucids would, on the demise of that empire, become independent though subservient states for a while until such time as they were brought under the control of the coming kingdom of God. A second explanation, by E. W. Heaton, is complementary to this: ancient prophecy had foretold that the nations would at last come to acknowledge and serve the people of God (cf. Isa. 41:1f.; 49:22f.; 60:12; Zech. 8:22; Ps. 86:9) and for this purpose they would be spared.

Individuals, like Antiochus, stand condemned. But so do whole nations, kingdoms and empires (cf. Joel 3:2ff., etc.). Divine judgment is corporate as well as individual. Institutions, like men, may become corrupt and set themselves up in opposition to God and so must come under divine judgment. Only by the mercy of God and for the sake of the coming kingdom can they be spared.

SON OF MAN: AND THE COMING KINGDOM

Daniel 7:13–14

> "I saw in the night visions,
> and behold, with the clouds of heaven

> there came one like a son of man,
> and he came to the Ancient of Days
> and was presented before him.
> And to him was given dominion
> and glory and kingdom,
> that all peoples, nations, and languages
> should serve him;
> his dominion is an everlasting dominion,
> which shall not pass away,
> and his kingdom one
> that shall not be destroyed."

The scene now changes. The four beasts have been sentenced and the last of them destroyed. Then suddenly, with the clouds of heaven, there is ushered into the presence of the Ancient of Days "one like a son of man". It is a royal investiture like that in ancient Israel when God's chosen king was crowned or like that in Babylon when the god was seated on his throne. To this "son of man" God gives "dominion and glory and kingdom", a kingdom "that shall not be destroyed".

The expression "son of man" is a translation of the Aramaic *bar enash* (Hebrew, *ben adam*) and means "a human being". The context makes it clear, however, that this human figure so honoured by God is, like the four beasts, to be interpreted symbolically and in a collective sense. Just as the beasts represent the Gentile nations in their opposition to God, so the "son of man" represents the kingdom of God, given to the people of God, who will have world-wide dominion for ever and ever.

This coming kingdom, for which the people had longed and prayed, has certain marked features:

(i)*It is universal in its scope.* The dominion and authority which belong to all the other kingdoms under heaven will be transferred to this coming kingdom. That is, it will be greater than any of the kingdoms that have been before it. These kingdoms subdued their neighbours and made them their servants. But they in their turn will be made to serve and obey "the people of the saints of the Most High" who are the heirs of that kingdom which is to come. These "people", as we shall see (see comment on 7:15–18), probably represent the faithful people of Israel. Their authority will be supreme over all mankind.

(ii) *It is an everlasting kingdom.* According to popular belief history moved in ever-recurring cycles, kingdoms and empires rising only to fall away. This indeed is what had happened to all other kingdoms that had gone before. They had disappeared, the victims of enemy attack or of their own internal corruption and strife. But the coming kingdom is altogether different. It will never be destroyed (cf.2:46; 4:3; 6:26; 7:14,27). It will not be succeeded by another, but will endure for ever. Its universality in space is thus paralleled by its universality in time and as such it reflects the very nature of God himself.

(iii) *Its authority comes from God.* The dominion it possesses is something given, not achieved. The kingdom is God's creation and God's gift and not the outcome of man's striving. It may have the appearance of being purely human, belonging to the natural order, but in fact it is superhuman and supernatural, having its origin in God. This is suggested by two references in these verses—the symbol of the "son of man" himself and the symbol of the "clouds of heaven" with which he comes. In the Old Testament, and even more so in later apocalyptic writings, "beasts" frequently symbolise nations and "men" symbolise supernatural beings, whilst the clouds are a common accompaniment of such beings as they are of God himself. It is the author's way of saying that, in contrast to the bestial kingdoms of men, the coming kingdom is divine as well as human and belongs to that supernatural order where God is.

(iv) *It comes through weakness to glory.* This is not stated in so many words, but it is the clear implication of certain Old Testament passages which, there is reason to believe, lie behind the writer's use here of the expression "son of man". One of these is Ps. 8:4f. where "man" or the "son of man", in his weakness and creaturely dependence, is "visited" by God and given a new dignity over against the rest of creation, being crowned with glory and honour. This same picture of dependence replaced by dignity, of subjection replaced by honour, is given also in Ps. 80 (where, interestingly enough, "son of man" is used again as a collective symbol, representing Israel over against the nations which are depicted as a wild beast from the forest, cf. verse 13). Here, we are told, the "son of man" in his human frailty is "the man of God's right hand" whom God will make strong and to whom he will grant salvation (cf. verses 17ff.). Of interest too in this connection is the book of Ezekiel with which Dan. 7 has obvious affinities (cf. the references in Ezek. 1 to God's chariot-throne and to the four beasts). There the expression "son of man" occurs no fewer than 87 times where the picture is again that of man in his human frailty honoured and dignified by God. It is as if the writer of Daniel is saying: the coming kingdom and the people to whom it is to be given may be weak and vulnerable, sharing the human frailty of the "son of man"; but the day is coming when it will be invested with a dignity and an authority that will be recognised throughout all the earth.

(v) *It belongs to this earth.* In certain later apocalyptic writings the coming kingdom takes on an other-worldly character, but here in Daniel it is essentially earthly; it is of the stuff of history. Its blessings are material as well as spiritual; it marks the fulfilment of Israel's political dreams as well as of its religious aspirations. Such a concept of the kingdom falls far short of what we find in the New Testament, but this at least they have in common: there is a continuity between the life of this world and the life of the coming kingdom. The events of human life are woven into its very texture. In no way is this kingdom to be confused with a man-made utopia, nor will it come as the result of some social or political programme. Nevertheless, as I have written elsewhere, "the concerns and pursuits of secular history have meaning and worth in terms of the kingdom. The contributions of technology, science, economics and politics towards the creation of a just and equitable society are not of mere incidental significance. . . . It [the kingdom] has to do with our common humanity and is being created now out of the raw material of our common life."

(vi) *It represents a new humanity.* Over against the beastly and the bestial the kingdom represents the human and the humane. Old Testament writers had looked forward to the coming reign of God whose two-fold foundation was righteousness and peace. In later Jewish writings and in the New Testament the same theme is taken up and developed. In the coming kingdom all evil will have been destroyed and God will reign as king. The kingdom will introduce a new world order indwelt by a new humanity, God's own people, which for the Christian will be after the pattern of Christ himself. It will be marked, not just by righteousness and peace, but above all by love, that divine love made known pre-eminently in the life, death and resurrection of Jesus Christ and demonstrated, however imperfectly, in and through that "new creation", his Church.

(vii) *Its coming is imminent.* The writer was convinced that the beast, in the person of Antiochus and his kingdom, would speedily be destroyed and that on his destruction the promised kingdom would suddenly be ushered in. For him it was no far-off event on the dim horizon of history. It was in the immediate tomorrow. Destruction and deliverance were both inevitable and imminent. The kingdom of God was at hand.

This, of course, is a theme taken up in the New Testament. The promised kingdom finds its fulfilment in Jesus. The consummation of that kingdom remains a mystery which will one day be revealed, but in a very real sense it is already present in him. To proclaim the events of his life, death and resurrection is to preach the good news of the kingdom. To respond to him in repentance, faith and love is to enter the kingdom. To be "in Christ" is to be part of that "new humanity" which is God's "new creation".

SON OF MAN: AND JESUS

Daniel 7:13–14 *(cont'd)*

(i)

We have seen that in Daniel 7 the expression "son of man" is to be understood symbolically and is to be interpreted in a collective or corporate sense with reference to the coming kingdom and its embodiment in "the people of God". Israel, or the faithful within Israel, are to be delivered by the power of God from the hand of their enemies and to be given the authority and the rule in a kingdom which will never be destroyed.

It is unlikely that we are to see in this figure any direct allusion to an individual Messiah. Some scholars, it is true, have argued that, just as the fourth beast, for example, symbolises both the Seleucid kingdom and the Seleucid king Antiochus, so the "son of man" symbolises both the coming "messianic" kingdom and the Messiah himself. This suggestion, however, is very tenuous. The fact is that the expressions "son of man" and "Messiah" represent originally two quite separate and distinct traditions which, until the time of Daniel, had no direct connection far less identification.

It is not surprising, however, that in course of time "son of man" did in fact come to be given an individual reference and to be associated with, and indeed to be identified with, the Messiah who now assumes the character of a transcendent deliverer of his people. This was made possible by reason of the Hebrew concept of "corporate personality" whereby the community can readily be represented by an individual member of it and vice versa. "There is no evidence", writes E. W. Heaton, "that the writer [of Daniel] ever thought of a messianic leader ... but when later such an interest did arise, it is understandable that there should have been a close connection between (and therefore terminology common to) the People of God, referred to here, and the individual figure who came to be thought of as its principal and embodiment."

(ii)

There is reason to believe that Jesus, in his reading of the Scriptures, was deeply influenced by Dan. 7 and by what he read there of the "son of man". The coming kingdom, embodied in the People of God, was already embodied in himself. This was the message of so much of his teaching, especially his

parables. It was the message, too, of his miracles and acts of
healing which were demonstrations that in him the powers of
the kingdom were already at work among men (cf. Matt. 12:28).
And it was a message set forth supremely in his death and
resurrection which announced that in him the kingdom was
present "with power" (Mark 9:1; cf. Rom. 1:4). He himself, as
the representative embodiment of the kingdom, was in very
truth the Son of Man.

The relationship between this concept of "son of man" and
that of "Messiah" is a most complicated one. In particular
scholars are divided as to whether or not the two had come to be
identified before the time of Jesus. What is clear is that, for him
at any rate, the connection between them was of prime importance. The title "Son of Man", which he assumes for himself, is
one that has depths of meaning for his profound messianic
consciousness.

A third concept whose influence on the mind of Jesus was
perhaps even stronger still is that of the "servant" and more
especially the "Suffering Servant" of Second Isaiah (cf. Isa. 53
etc.). This too is a collective rather than an individual figure,
representing God's suffering people Israel. Indeed some scholars maintain that Daniel's vision of the "son of man" was
dependent originally on the "Suffering Servant" poems in
Second-Isaiah and that the "son of man" in the one is representative of the "Suffering Servant" in the other. Here again, it
would seem, Jesus recognised in himself the representative and
the embodiment of "the Servant" whose life was given as "a
ransom for many" (Mark 10:45). In this connection it is of
interest to observe that, alongside Isaiah 53, the early Church
used as *testimonia* or "proof-texts" in support of Jesus' mes-
siahship those very passages in Pss. 8 and 80 which, as we have
seen, speak about the frailty and weakness of the "son of man".
Such passages spoke to them clearly of the Son of Man who
through suffering would come to glory.

In a quite remarkable way, then, Jesus brings together in his
own person the three concepts of Messiah, Son of Man and
Suffering Servant, interpreting each in terms of the others as an

expression of his messianic awareness. The Messiah/Son of Man is also the Suffering Servant of the Lord who will be exalted through suffering to glory and to whom will be given a kingdom that will have no end.

(iii)

We have seen then, in the mind of Jesus and of the early Church, the collective symbol of the "son of man" spiralling inwards, as it were, to find its focus in him. He in his own person is the representative of the new humanity, the embodiment of the kingdom. But we see too the reverse process taking place. From Jesus as its focal point we see the symbol spiralling outwards to become what he represents—a new creation, a new humanity, a holy nation, a new Israel, the redeemed of the Lord, the Church of the living God to whom will be given the kingdom. "Fear not little flock", he says to his disciples, "for it is your Father's good pleasure to give you the kingdom" (Luke 12:32). His disciples will sit on thrones judging the twelve tribes of Israel and will eat and drink with him in his kingdom (cf. Luke 22:28ff.). As they die with him so also they will live with him; as they endure with him so also they will reign with him for ever (cf. 2 Tim. 2:11f.).

SAINTS AND ANGELS

Daniel 7:15-18

> "As for me, Daniel, my spirit within me was anxious and the visions of my head alarmed me. I approached one of those who stood there and asked him the truth concerning all this. So he told me, and made known to me the interpretation of the things. 'These four great beasts are four kings who shall arise out of the earth. But the saints of the Most High shall receive the kingdom, and possess the kingdom for ever, for ever and ever.'"

(i)

Daniel, we are told, was anxious and the visions of his head alarmed him. The same kind of reaction is recorded in other parts of the book as well. Thus, in 9:28, with the coming of the dream, his heart is troubled; in 7:28, he is bewildered and terrified. So overpowering is the experience that he cannot adequately express it in words (cf. 10:32, 55f.; 2 Cor. 12:4); he even loses the power of speech (cf. 10:15) or becomes unconscious (cf. 8:18; 10:9).

It is tempting to conclude that such reports of dreams and visions are more than expressions of a stereotyped literary convention, but are a genuine reflection of the writer's own state of mind and suggest an inspirational experience on his part corresponding to the dream or vision thus described. Conventional expression and inspirational experience are not mutually exclusive. The validity of a revelation is not to be judged by the vehicle through which it is made known.

(ii)

The dream having been described, Daniel (like Nebuchadnezzar before him) looks around for someone to give its interpretation and chooses for this purpose one of the angels who actually appears in his dream! This strange device is again part of the same literary convention which had been long established (cf. Ezek. 40ff.; Zech. 1ff.). This particular interpreter is described as "a standing one" which is a technical term for "an angelic attendant", one of many thousands who wait upon the Ancient of Days (cf. 7:10)

There is, from this time on, in the Jewish writings, a remarkable growth in angelology, far beyond anything to be found in the Old Testament. Myriads upon myriads of angels serve God day and night. In so doing they exercise many different functions: they intercede on behalf of men, they guard and guide the nations, they record divine secrets and they unfold the mysteries of dreams. Here, in 7:16, the mystery about to be disclosed and the interpretation to be given concern the coming kingdom.

(iii)

First of all the angel identifies the four beasts of the vision (who are said here to arise "out of the earth" and not "out of the sea" as in 7:3) as four "kings" who represent four "kingdoms" (cf. 7:23; 8:20ff.). Then comes the interpretation that really matters—the meaning of the investiture of the "one like a son of man" in 7:13 is that the kingdom of God will be given to "the saints of the Most High" who will possess it for ever and ever.

The word used here for "saints" is an unusual one, meaning literally "holy ones". Elsewhere in the book (cf. 4:13, 17, 23), as in the apocalyptic writings generally and the *Hodayot* or Hymns from Qumran, it is used with reference to angels.

(a) Some scholars take this to be its meaning here, a suggestion that fits in with the symbolism which represents nations as beasts and angels as men. If this explanation is accepted, then the reference in verse 27 to "the *people* of the saints of the Most High" is either to Israel as the people who are in the care of these "holy ones" or to the *company* of celestial beings who will oust the evil powers which are believed to be entrenched in the earth and indeed in the cosmos itself and will receive the sovereignty from God for ever and ever.

We are reminded in this connection of the "principalities and powers" which Paul, for example, describes as "the rulers of this age", who were directly responsible for the crucifixion of "the Lord of glory" (cf. 1 Cor. 2:8). In the cross, he says, Christ "disarmed" them and "made a public example of them, triumphing over them in it" (Col. 2:15, RSV margin). The picture presented is that of a cosmic deliverance in which demonic forces at enmity with God (cf. Rom. 8:38), are utterly routed. They may not be for the apostle the *archons* of popular Greek belief who are thought to govern the planets and the stars. Nevertheless they represent for him forces that are powerful and menacing—the sum of all those forces in the universe opposed to Christ and his Church. Like Paul, we may have to try and "demythologise", but we must be careful not to empty the picture of its meaning which takes seriously the demonic nature of evil from which the world is to be redeemed.

(b) But a second explanation of "saints" or "holy ones" is possible. Most scholars argue that the word refers not to angels but to the Jewish people, or rather the faithful element among them. With this meaning it occurs only three times (in its Hebrew equivalent) outside this present chapter—in 8:24, and in Pss. 16:3 and 34:9—though the notion is found elsewhere of Israel as God's "holy people" (cf. Exod. 19:8; Deut. 7:6; Dan. 12:7). Such an interpretation fits in with the plain meaning of verse 27 which, as we have seen, speaks of "the *people* of the saints of the Most High". This expression "the Most High" is a plural of majesty which suggests, according to E. W. Heaton, that "the writer wished to emphasize that the Jews symbolised by the figure were no ordinary members of Israel, but a special group nearer to the ideal of 'a kingdom of priests, a holy nation' (Exod. 19:6) than the rank and file of Judaism." On this interpretation, then, the righteous and godly Jews will be given authority over the nations and will rule the earth in God's kingdom which will be for them a universal and everlasting possession.

The same theme is taken up in the New Testament (cf. Rev. 5:10; 20:6) where there is no doubt about the identity of "the saints": they are Christ's people, the Church. The Apostle Paul is even more explicit. "Do you not know", he says, "that the saints will judge the world?"—and then for good measure he adds, "Do you not know that we are to judge angels?" (1 Cor. 6:2f.).

The history of the Church contains many sad stories of sincere but mistaken men who have taken these words of Paul too literally and have exercised judgment on their fellows as emissaries of the kingdom. With fire, faggot and sword they have sought to destroy evil and to establish the rule of God by force. Jesus taught that the saints of God are to live not assertively or judgmentally, but humbly and confidently, knowing that already "the ruler of this world is judged" (John 16:11).

(c) But a third possibility has been suggested. It is that the expression "holy ones" refers to *both* angels and men and that what we have here is an assimilation of the faithful in Israel to the angelic hosts with whom they share God's covenant and

God's kingdom, i.e. there is a correspondence between the heavenly and the earthly, between the cosmic and the historical. This finds some corroboration elsewhere in the writings of the intertestamental period and not least in the writings from Qumran. In the War Scroll, for example, the "sons of light" who fight against the "sons of darkness" in the final battle— "the war to end all wars"—are represented by certain tribes of Israel. In other words, they are men. But it is no ordinary army and no ordinary battle, for angels as well as men are involved in it so that the struggle assumes cosmic and not simply earthly dimensions. So here in Daniel, it has been argued, there is a community or communion of "saints" in which men and angels share and to whom God will give the kingdom.

A somewhat similar picture is presented also in the New Testament in, for example, the Epistle to the Hebrews, which tells us that in "the heavenly Jerusalem", men and angels will no longer be separated as they were long ago by the terror of Sinai; for there "innumerable angels" will be united in one great company with "the assembly of the first born" (cf. 12:21f.). Angels as well as men long to hear the good news of God (cf. 1 Pet. 1:12) and share together in adoration of the Lamb (cf. Rev. 5:11ff.).

Whatever the exact interpretation of such passages may be, they declare that the coming kingdom has a transcendent as well as an earthly dimension in terms of which its ultimate meaning is to be found.

HOW ARE THE MIGHTY FALLEN!

Daniel 7:19-28

"Then I desired to know the truth concerning the fourth beast, which was different from all the rest, exceedingly terrible, with its teeth of iron and claws of bronze; and which devoured and broke in pieces, and stamped the residue with its feet; and concerning the ten horns that were on its head, and the other horn which came up and before which three of them fell, the horn which had eyes and a mouth that spoke great things, and which seemed greater than its fellows. As I looked, this horn made war with the saints, and prevailed over them, until the Ancient of Days came, and judgment was given for the saints of the Most High, and the time came when the saints received the kingdom.

"Thus he said: 'As for the fourth beast,
there shall be a fourth kingdom on earth,
   which shall be different from all the kingdoms,
and it shall devour the whole earth,
   and trample it down, and break it to pieces.
As for the ten horns,
out of this kingdom
   ten kings shall arise,
   and another shall arise after them;
he shall be different from the former ones,
   and shall put down three kings.
He shall speak words against the Most High,
   and shall wear out the saints of the Most High,
   and shall think to change the times and the law;
and they shall be given into his hand
   for a time, two times, and half a time.
But the court shall sit in judgment,
   and his dominion shall be taken away,
   to be consumed and destroyed to the end.
And the kingdom and the dominion
   and the greatness of the kingdoms under the whole heaven
   shall be given to the people of the saints of the Most High;
their kingdom shall be an everlasting kingdom,
   and all dominions shall serve and obey them.'
Here is the end of the matter. As for me, Daniel, my thoughts greatly alarmed me, and my colour changed; but I kept the matter in my mind."

(i)

Having heard the all-too-brief interpretation given by the angel, Daniel is not satisfied but presses for more information concerning the fourth beast which is again described in the same way as in verse 7, with the additional detail that it has "claws of bronze". The following two verses (20-21) repeat the earlier reference to "the ten horns" and "the other [little] horn" and add that it "made war with the saints". Some scholars regard verses 21-22, which refer to "the saints", as secondary and as an intrusion into the text by another hand. As they stand their reference to harassment and conflict prepare the reader for the statement in verse 25 about "wearing out the saints".

(ii)

The fourth beast, says the angel-interpreter, is the fourth kingdom which, as we have seen, is no doubt to be identified as the Greek kingdom under Alexander and his successors. "It is a sobering reflection", writes Norman Porteous, "that it was this empire, for all that it mediated to the ancient peoples of the East the achievements of Greek culture, that could appear, in the eyes of a member of a subject people, to be worst of all tyrants." Its awesome power and its world-wide dominion will be brought low and destroyed (cf. 7:11) and will be replaced by a universal kingdom decreed by God and given to his "saints".

It is the meek—and the weak—who will inherit the earth, not the haughty and the strong (cf. Luke 1:51ff.). There is a moral factor in history which brings its own judgment. That judgment falls not only on individuals who arrogantly assert their own importance or claim the prerogatives of God, but also on institutions, governments and nations which, for all their record of good deeds, defy God's right to reign. "If once we admit that the moral factor operates in this way in history at all, then we today must feel ourselves to be living in one of those remarkable periods when judgment stalks generally through the world and it becomes a question whether the orders and systems to which we have been long attached can survive the day of reckoning" (Herbert Butterfield).

(iii)

This fourth beast and the judgment it incurs is epitomised in the little horn and the fate that befalls it. This horn, as again we have seen, signifies none other than Antiochus Epiphanes himself. Not only does he speak arrogantly (cf. verse 8), he also speaks blasphemously against the Most High (cf. verse 25). He "wears out" (or perhaps "afflicts") the saints—a reference no doubt to the persecution meted out by Antiochus and calculated to "wear out the holy ones" among the Jews who resisted his claims.

The measures taken by Antiochus against the Jews are specified in verse 25. It is his intention "to change the times and the law". This is no doubt an allusion to the steps taken by the king, as recorded in 1 Maccabees 1:4ff., to wipe out the Jewish religion altogether (see comment on 1:1-2). The "times" refer to the great seasonal festivals of the Jews and other recognised religious observances; the "law" is the sacred Torah of Moses with its precise regulations concerning the observance of sacred rites and duties such as the rite of circumcision, the dutiful reading of the Law, the observance of certain sacrifices and festivals and the following of dietary requirements. Another interpretation has been suggested. In 2:21 it is God alone who "changes times and seasons" in the same way that he alone "removes kings and sets up kings". Antiochus' attempt to "change the times" is to fly in the face of providence and to assert that he can act as God in decreeing the how and when of imperial power. In this context the word "law" (*dath* in Aramaic) would not correspond to the Hebrew *torah,* but have the sense of "decree" or "judgment" as elsewhere in Daniel (cf. 2:9, 13, 15). In this case it refers to the vain attempt by Antiochus to avert God's decree of judgment upon himself and his kingdom.

At the time Daniel was written, the persecution of Antiochus had not yet come to an end. But the readers are given the assurance that it will soon cease. The faithful Jews will remain under his tyranny "for a time, two times and half a time", the word "time" being used, as elsewhere in the book, for "year". In 4:32 it is said concerning the duration of Nebuchadnezzar's madness, "Seven times shall pass over you", the reference being to "a sabbatical year". In our present passage Antiochus' power will last for half that time and in this context may have only a general reference, like our "half-a-dozen", and not signify any precise period. If, on the other hand, it is to be taken as a precise number, then the prediction is not far off the mark. One possible starting point for this particular calculation is the treacherous attack on Jerusalem by Apollonius, "the officer of the Mysians" (1 Maccabees 1:29), in June 167 B.C. Three and a half years later (in December 164 B.C.) the Temple was rededicated by Judas Maccabeus—an event which, from the vantage point of the writer, had not yet taken place.

Whatever element of precise prediction there may be in this passage, later apocalyptic writers take the matter seriously and, with much juggling of figures try to forecast not just future historical events, but the end itself. The three and a half years (*c.* 1,277 days) of this passage set the fashion to be followed by others and approximate to the 2,300 evenings and mornings of 8:14 (i.e. 1,150 days) the forty-two months (*c.* 1,260 days) of Rev. 11:2 and 13:5, the 1,260 days of Rev. 11:3, the 1,290 days of Dan. 12:11 and the 1,335 days of Dan. 12:12.

Behind and beyond all such speculation was the firm faith of these writers that the times were in God's hand and that his purpose would at last prevail. This affirmation was made at a time when the writer of Daniel could not have known the outcome of these events that led up to the deliverance of Jerusalem and the rededication of the Temple there. He should be remembered for his faith more than for his fantasy, an example to all who believe in the controlling providence of God. Like so many others in our own day living and witnessing under a hostile regime, he lived by faith and not by sight, confident in the final triumph of the Most High.

(iv)

The court which the seer had described in verse 10 now sits in judgment (verse 26). The dominion of the little horn, and so of the fourth beast, is taken away and it is destroyed. Another kingdom takes its place which is both universal and eternal (see comment on 7:13–14) and is given by God to "the people of the saints of the Most High" (see comment on 7:15–18).

In the book of Daniel these "saints", if they are not angels, are, as we have seen, the *élite* among the Jews, the party of the faithful who remain loyal to the law and the tradition of the fathers. In the New Testament it is a word used to describe *all* who are "in Christ Jesus" (Phil. 1:1), who have been sanctified by his divine "call" (cf. Rom. 1:7; 1 Cor. 1:2). As such they will inherit his promise given to Daniel's "son of man" at "the coming of our Lord Jesus with all his saints" (1 Thess. 3:13; cf. Col. 3:4). They are not a religious *élite,* "saints in stained-glass windows"; they are ordinary people sanctified by Christ, "saints in homespun". To such belongs the kingdom.

(v)

The concluding verse of this chapter has suggested to some scholars that at one time the book ended at this point and that the visions which follow in chapters 8–12 are from a different hand, perhaps in the form of separate pamphlets, subsequently collected together and added to chapters 1–7. Others contend that the seer's perturbation of mind and his hint that he is not yet completely satisfied point to more visions still to come. Whatever the answer may be, the reader from now on is to be introduced to a world of thought and imagery very different from those in chapters 1–6, with chapter 7 forming a bridge in between.

A CHANGE OF GEAR

Daniel 8:1–2

> In the third year of the reign of King Belshazzar a vision appeared to me, Daniel, after that which appeared to me at the first. And I saw in the vision; and when I saw, I was in Susa the capital, which is in the province of Elam; and I saw in the vision, and I was at the river Ulai.

(i)

This chapter records a vision that came to Daniel "in the third year of the reign of king Belshazzar" and is said to have been experienced "after that which appeared to me at the first". Both these allusions refer back to chapter 7, indicating that the two chapters belong together. There are certain significant differences between them, however, which are in part at least hidden from the reader of the English text and which mark a distinct "change of gear" on the part of the author. This shows itself in two ways:

(a) The first is that the writer, who has been expressing himself in Aramaic ever since 2:4b, now reverts to the use of Hebrew. Several explanations of this have been offered, e.g. his use of "the sacred language" at this point lends greater authority to the pronouncement he is about to make, or perhaps the change of language marks a change in authorship. Whatever the reason, the quality of the writing markedly deteriorates in form, style and imaginative expression. The prose becomes more pedestrian and artificial and the sense is sometimes broken by what may be interpolations from another hand; all this is accentuated by obscurities in the text making the meaning none too clear.

We are reminded that language is an important vehicle of truth and that words are "verbal symbols" conveying meaning, sometimes clearly, sometimes obscurely. There are, of course, other vehicles and other symbols conveying meaning and truth. For Helen Keller, blind, deaf and dumb, it was the language of touch. For Beethoven, clumsy in speech and writing, it was the language of music. For most, however, it is the language of words— in spoken or in written form—that provides the best vehicle of thought and expression. By its very nature, of course, it has its limitations of perception and expression. "There are certain things the meaning of which cannot be unfolded at all by any words of human language, but which are made known more through simple apprehension than by any properties of words" (Origen, *De Principiis*). Hebrew, Aramaic and Greek are "the sacred languages" of Scripture. They are "sacred", not because they are necessarily more expressive or spiritually perceptive than other forms of language, but because through them God has spoken in a particular way to a particular people and made himself known as nowhere else, in "the Word made flesh" (cf. John 1:14).

(b) The second feature to be noted is that, beginning with chapter 8, the imaginative story-form of chapters 1–6 is replaced by a description of visionary experience somewhat similar in form and content to that of chapter 7. The language of dream and vision, like that of speech, can also be a vehicle of truth, conveying meaning about oneself and about God. The apocalyptists, like the prophets before them, saw in them revelations of the divine mind and will. "When a pious, deeply religious member of such a race turns his whole attention to God, he sees more than we see, he hears what we do not hear, and his apprehension of God is, as he himself claims, immediate and intuitive" (A. Guillaume). To such men the dream or vision was more than vivid imagination or a picture thrown on to the screen of the mind from the sub-conscious. It was nothing less than a divine disclosure, a revelation straight from God himself whose interpretation he alone could make plain.

The subject matter of the dreams and visions about to be disclosed in chapters 8–12, from the point of view of the author, is concerned with the immediate past history of surrounding empires and rulers, culminating in the events of the author's own day. Attention is focused on Antiochus Epiphanes and especially on his desecration of the Jerusalem Temple and the promise of its restoration. The fateful events recorded here all point forward unerringly to a single irrefutable fact: the end is near, God's people will soon be delivered and the kingdom of God will speedily be ushered in.

(ii)

In the vision about to be recorded Daniel finds himself in Susa, the winter capital of the Persian Empire and the residence of Persian kings, a city renowned in ancient times as a mighty fortress (cf. Neh. 1:1; Esth. 1:2,5; 2:3,5) and a centre of Persian power. He is beside "the river Ulai" (some would read the "Ulai Gate") which is no doubt the Eulaeus of classical antiquity near which the fortified city of Susa was situated, in the province of Elam, the finest and fairest part of the Persian empire.

Some take the reference in verse 2 to mean that Daniel was in fact in Susa when the vision came to him. Hence the existence there of a legendary tomb of Daniel which has been a centre of pilgrimage from as early as the sixth century and is still a tourist attraction. A more likely interpretation, however, is that, whilst still in Babylon, Daniel had a vision in which he saw himself in Susa beside the river Ulai, an experience reminiscent of Ezekiel who was transported by the Spirit to Tel-abib by the river Chebar (cf. Ezek. 3:12f.; 8:3; 40:1ff.).

In this very location, then, surrounded by all the signs of invincible empire, Daniel sees the inevitable downfall of the mighty and with it the sure triumph of God's kingdom. The grandeur and the power of Susa cannot compare with the glory and the greatness of God. A word in season for the people of God in every age!

THE RAM AND THE HE-GOAT

Daniel 8:3–8

> I raised my eyes and saw, and behold, a ram standing on the bank of the river. It had two horns; and both horns were high, but one was higher than the other, and the higher one came up last. I saw the ram charging westward and northward and southward; no beast could stand before him, and there was no one who could rescue from his power; he did as he pleased and magnified himself. As I was considering, behold, a he-goat came from the west across the face of the whole earth, without touching the ground; and the goat had a conspicuous horn between his eyes. He came to the ram with the two horns, which I had seen standing on the bank of the river, and he ran at him in his mighty wrath. I saw him come close to the ram, and he was enraged against him and struck the ram and broke his two horns; and the ram had no power to stand before him, but he cast him down to the ground and trampled upon him; and there was no one who could rescue the ram from his power. Then the he-goat magnified himself exceedingly; but when he was strong, the great horn was broken, and instead of it there came up four conspicuous horns toward the four winds of heaven.

(i)

The animal symbolism in these verses is much less bizarre than that in chapter 7 and its meaning much more plain. The Medo-

Persian empire is represented by a ram and the Greek empire by a he-goat which came into conflict with it and utterly defeated it. These two animals appear fairly frequently in the Old Testament as symbols of power (cf. Ezek. 34:17; 39:18; Zech. 10:3). Reference to them in this passage, it has been suggested, may be influenced by the fact that, in the astrological lore of the East, the zodiacal sign of Persia was the ram (the Persian king is said to have worn a golden ram's head on his helmet) and that of Syria (with which Greece shared a large part of the Seleucid empire) was the he-goat.

The ram, we are told, had two great horns, the one that came up last being the greater. The reference here is to the Persians who arose later than the Medes but exceeded them in power. From Susa the ram came charging "westward and northward and southward", as the Persians had done in their military campaigns. No-one could resist its aggressive power, and to aggression it added arrogance (cf. verse 4).

There now appears on the scene, coming from the west, a he-goat with a single conspicuous horn between its eyes. As the later interpretation makes plain (cf. 8:21), this is the Greek kingdom with Alexander the Great at its head. As in the case of Cyrus before him (cf. Isa. 41:3) the speed of Alexander's conquests is such that his feet seem hardly to touch the ground. The he-goat's onslaught on the ram is decisive, as indeed was Alexander's crushing defeat of Darius III, the last Persian king. The ram's horns are broken—the Medo-Persian power is shattered once and for all.

But once again pride comes before a fall. The great horn on the he-goat's forehead is broken off—Alexander at the height of his power meets sudden death (in 323 B.C.)—and in its place there come up "four others"—representing the four areas into which Alexander's kingdom came to be divided: Macedonia, Asia Minor, Syria and Egypt.

(ii)

E. W. Heaton likens this account to a newspaper cartoon which has no need of interpretation beyond itself. By intent or by

implication it suggests three things whose truth is as valid now
as on the day it was first written:

(a) In the light of the fast-approaching end and in terms of
the coming kingdom, the rise and fall of empires and the
resounding victories of their rulers are mere incidentals. Their
account in the annals of God merits little space. Even though
they may claim the protection of their "lucky stars" and feel
secure under the magical spell of their zodiacal signs, nothing
will in the end protect them or save them. Their fate is certain;
their destruction is assured.

(b) Twice over in these few verses reference is made to
arrogance as the prelude to disaster, a constantly recurring
theme throughout this whole book. First the Persians, then
Alexander and later (as we shall see) Antiochus—all are
inflated with a sense of their own importance and all, as a result,
come under the condemnation of God. Arrogance is a display
of wilful pride; as such it is a denial of the sovereignty and the
rule of God and brings judgment upon itself.

(c) The contribution of great cultures and civilisations is to
be assessed not in terms of apparent achievements but in terms
of God's eternal purpose (see comment on 7:19-28). Few
civilisations, if any, have brought greater benefits to mankind
in such a short space of time than that of Alexander the Great.
The spread of the Greek language, the penetration of Greek
thought, the establishment of great cities and the consequent
acceptance by the "civilised world" of the Greek culture—
all this and much more brought immeasurable benefit to mankind and as immeasurably enriched the entire world ever
since.

It is a salutary thought that it is this very culture and this very
civilisation which, for all its benefactions, comes under the
judgment of God. The blessings bestowed by great empires are
not always viewed as unalloyed blessings by subject nations in
receipt of them. The real worth of such empires is to be
measured not in terms of size or wealth or culture or military
power, but in terms of justice, fair-play, dignity and human
freedom. When judged by the requirements of the coming

kingdom all earthly rulers and their kingdoms stand condemned.

THE EXPLOITS OF THE LITTLE HORN

Daniel 8:9–12

> Out of one of them came forth a little horn, which grew exceedingly great toward the south, toward the east, and toward the glorious land. It grew great, even to the host of heaven; and some of the host of the stars it cast down to the ground, and trampled upon them. It magnified itself, even up to the Prince of the host; and the continual burnt offering was taken away from him, and the place of his sanctuary was overthrown. And the host was given over to it together with the continual burnt offering through transgression; and truth was cast down to the ground, and the horn acted and prospered.

(i)

The little horn. The author now comes to the nub of the vision—the exploits of the "little horn" which clearly refers to the notorious Antiochus Epiphanes. No particular interest is shown in the "four conspicuous horns" or kingdoms mentioned in the previous verse, except to observe that out of one of these (presumably the Syrian, representing the Seleucid line of kings) there sprouted this little horn. Small though it was, it "grew exceedingly great", thrusting to the south, to the east and to "the glorious land", referring no doubt to Antiochus' invasion of Egypt, Parthia and Palestine itself.

The succeeding verses are somewhat obscure and the text may well be at fault; but on the whole the sense is fairly clear.

(ii)

The host of heaven. Having successfully attacked earthly powers, Antiochus now turns his attention to the powers of heaven. The horn, we are told, "grew great even to the host of heaven", identified here as "the host of the stars".

(a) This reference to the celestial bodies reminds us of the popular astral worship to be found over several centuries in the countries of the ancient world and of the belief that the stars in their courses controlled the destinies of men. In ancient Babylonia, for example, the movements of the heavenly luminaries, and especially the seven planets, were thought to influence and determine the affairs of the nations—a belief that still holds a fascination for many whose daily reading is not the Scriptures but the astrological tables in the columns of the popular press.

(b) In the popular imagination these heavenly bodies were none other than gods and as such featured prominently in heathen worship. These very stars Antiochus attacked and cast down to the ground, a reference no doubt to the onslaught he is believed to have made on the heathen religions and cults in different parts of his kingdom. This is substantiated later on in 11:36ff. and also in 1 Maccabees 1:41f. where it said that the heathens were forced to forsake their own laws and to acquiesce in his decree.

(c) The sheer arrogance of the man is emphasised in verses 10 and 11. His overwhelming bumptiousness leads him to attack heaven itself. Not content with calling himself "[God] made manifest" (Epiphanes) he brooks no rival and tramples all other gods underfoot. In this he resembles a certain king of Babylon who declared, "I will ascend to heaven; above the stars of God I will set my throne on high. I will make myself like the Most High" (Isa. 14:13f.). Not content with attacking the gods of the heathen, Antiochus dares attack the only true and living God, "the Prince of the host".

(iii)

The Prince of the host. Elsewhere in Daniel the word here translated "prince" is used with reference to an angelic being (cf. 10:13,20; 12:1). If that is the meaning in this passage it refers to the chief of the angel host who is identified in 10:21, for example, as the archangel Michael. Most commentators, however, take the expression to refer to God himself. This identification would seem to find support in the context which describes the attacks made by Antiochus on the worship of God and the practice of religion in the Jerusalem Temple. Three clear illustrations of this are given in verses 11 and 12.

(a) Antiochus, we are told, abolished the regular morning and evening sacrifices which were required by the law of Moses (cf. Exod. 29:38ff.). Their meticulous observance was of primary importance; nothing must interfere with this unbroken chain. Like the "eternal flame" at the Arc de Triomphe, its very continuity was a sacred symbol expressing the very soul of the people, except that to the Jews it was much more besides. It was a visible expression of their religion and a sign of their unbreakable loyalty to their God. But now at one fell stroke the light was extinguished, the daily sacrifices were made to cease. Having challenged the gods of the heathen, Antiochus dared now to challenge the living God himself.

(b) More than this, he ravaged the Temple. This he did in two respects—he despoiled the sanctuary by overthrowing "the place" (or "the stand") of the sanctuary, i.e. the altar, and he desecrated it by setting up a heathen altar in its place.

His despoiling of the sanctuary finds ample corroboration in 1 Maccabees 4:38f. which describes what Judas and his brothers saw when later on they came to purify and dedicate that holy place: "They saw the sanctuary desolated and the altar profaned, the gates burned up, and weeds growing in the courts as in a forest or as in one of the mountains, and the priests' chambers torn down."

The exact nature of the desecration of the sanctuary and the altar is obscured by the difficult and doubtful Hebrew of verse 12. But the sense seems to be that Antiochus set up in the place of the altar a "transgression" which defiled it. This finds support in 8:13 and in 9:27, 11:31 and 12:11 where reference is made to an "abomination". It has been argued—and it makes good sense—that this was a heathen altar and cult-symbol erected on top of the altar of burnt offerings on which sacrifices were to be offered to the god Zeus (see comments on 8:13–14; 9:25–27, *cont'd*). Whatever its exact nature was, the place was so utterly defiled that, when in due course it came to be rededicated, Judas decided to tear down the sacred altar and store away the stones till a ruling concerning their use could be given and to construct a new altar in its place (cf. 1 Maccabees 4:46).

It has been suggested that the Temple which was thus profaned "is not just an edifice in Jerusalem for the author; it is also the people of the Saints" who have been ravaged and despoiled (André Lacocque). Whatever its significance may be in Daniel, it is certainly true that in the New Testament a deeper meaning is given to God's Temple than simply that of a sanctuary made of stone. It is none other than the people of God themselves (cf. 1 Cor. 3:16f.), a sanctuary made up of "living stones" (cf. 1 Pet. 2:5). That sanctuary will be attacked, despoiled and desecrated, but the warning is given: "If anyone destroys God's Temple, God will destroy him. For God's Temple is holy, and that Temple you are" (1 Cor. 3:17). His people will suffer with him; but he will vindicate them in the end.

(c) And thirdly, Antiochus destroyed "the truth". This refers not to some abstract concept which the king is calling into question but to that religious faith and practice made known by divine revelation and contained in the sacred Torah. (For fuller detail see comment on 1:1–2, *cont'd*). The practice of circumcision, the reading of the Law, the observance of sacrifices and festivals—all these were forbidden on pain of death. Devout Jews were forced to eat swine's flesh, to offer up ritually unclean animals and "to defile themselves with every kind of uncleanness and profanation" (1 Maccabees 1:45ff.). The very Law itself was taken from them. The books of the Law which their enemies found in their possession were torn in pieces and burned. Indeed, "wherever a book of the covenant was found in anyone's possession, or if anyone respected the Law, the decree of the king imposed the sentence of death upon him" (1 Maccabees 1:56f.). Many, we are told, "preferred to die . . . and they did die. Great was the wrath that came upon Israel" (1 Maccabees 1:63f.).

The story told here is a tragic one, repeated many times over in the history of both Synagogue and Church. Jews and Christians together, as "people of the Book", again and again have shown a like devotion and a like courage in their defence of "the truth" as it is found in the Scriptures which are for them the very word of God.

Antiochus, we are told, "acted and prospered". Subsequent verses will show that already God had set a limit to his arrogant rebellion and would bring to an end the suffering of his people.

HOW LONG?—A CRY OF ANGUISH

Daniel 8:13-14

> Then I heard a holy one speaking; and another holy one said to the one that spoke, "For how long is the vision concerning the continual burnt offering, the transgression that makes desolate, and the giving over of the sanctuary and host to be trampled under foot?" And he said to him, "For two thousand and three hundred evenings and mornings; then the sanctuary shall be restored to its rightful state."

The author of Daniel and the faithful Jews of his day longed for an end to the troubles through which they were passing. How long would it be before God would vindicate his people and set right the wrong done to his sanctuary and altar? It is a cry that has been echoed by the Jewish people and many others ever since; a cry for liberation from the oppressor, for the restoration of human justice and for the right to worship and serve God free from molestation.

This vision gives the assurance the people seek. Soon, very soon, Antiochus will receive his deserts; liberation will come and the holy Temple and its rites will be restored.

(i)

The assurance is given in a conversation, which Daniel overhears, between two "holy ones" or angels who appear in his vision. The scene recalls that described in Zech. 1:12ff. where the same question is asked, "How long?", and a similar reassuring answer is given. In the Daniel passage one angel asks another the key-question: How long will this situation last—the cessation of the burnt offering, "the transgression that makes desolate" and the destruction of "the sanctuary and the host"?

This last word has been interpreted variously in this context as the host of heaven or the Jewish army or the Temple service. Together with the sanctuary it has been "trampled under foot".

Of greater interest, however, is the expression "the transgression that makes desolate" which corresponds to "the abomination that makes desolate" (Hebrew, *shiqquts shomem*) in 11:31 and 12:11 and recalls "the abomination of desolation" in Matt. 24:15 and Mark 13:14. In this phrase we are probably to detect a play on the name of the god *Baal Shamen* (Lord of Heaven), the Syrian counterpart of the Greek *Zeus Olympios* (the Olympian or Heavenly Zeus) of whom Antiochus believed himself to be a manifestation, to whom he dedicated the Jerusalem Temple (cf. 2 Maccabees 6:2) and whose altar and cult-symbol he set up "on top of the altar of the Lord" (cf. I Maccabees 1:54,59). The pious Jews changed the name *Baal* to *shiqquts* (abomination) and the word *shamen* to *shomem* (desolation), thus changing *Baal Shamen* by a contemptuous pun into "An Appalling Abomination".

It was an abomination indeed which defiled the very stones on which it was laid (see comment on 8:9–12). Something of the same sense of revulsion must have been felt in more recent days by Jews in London who found the grave-stones in their local cemetery daubed with swastikas. To them, and to their forebears in the time of Antiochus, what they saw was an obscenity, a spitting in the face of God.

More than that, it would be regarded as a premeditated act of sacrilege, comparable to what happened in a Hindu Temple in Vellore, India, some years ago. The Muslims and the Hindus were "daggers drawn" against each other. Many acts of cruelty and revenge were perpetrated. But the most heinous of all took place when the Muslims desecrated the Hindu holy place by killing within its precincts a sacred cow. From that day to this the Temple has stood deserted and empty and Vellore, it is said, became—

> a bridge without a river,
> a fort without soldiers,
> a Temple without a God.

(ii)

In setting up this altar to Baal Shamen, however, it must be said that Antiochus had probably no intention of introducing the worship of some new god in place of the Jewish God. To him and no doubt also to the Jewish Hellenizers in Jerusalem, Baal Shamen, Zeus Olympios and the Jewish God of Heaven (cf. Ezra 7:12; Dan. 2:18) represented one and the same god under different local names. To the loyal Jews, however, the dangers of such an action were only too obvious and had to be resisted with might and main. Their fathers had faced a similar danger when, long ago after their entry into the promised land, they were confronted with the temptation to worship God in the form of Baal. Now under Antiochus they were faced with the same danger and the same temptation, the infiltration of heathen worship and the pollution of foreign gods. To Antiochus and the Hellenizers there was little to choose between Baal Shamen and the Jewish God of Heaven. After all, the name was the same! But to the author of Daniel this action of the king was a grievous transgression, an abomination which must be resisted at all costs.

An incident of this kind is illustrative of a problem to be found still today in the missionary task of the Church. One man worships Brahma, another Allah and another the Christian God. All of them, it can be argued, worship the same God in the sense that there *is* only one God. And yet we know that they are *not* the same in the sense that the different names represent quite diverse understandings of the divine being. The difficulty is compounded when a new convert to Christianity from another faith brings over with him heathen notions which belong to his former faith and superimposes them on the Christian image of God. When does absorption of alien faiths into the Christian faith become dangerous syncretism? When does *rapprochement* with alien ideologies become compromise? When does toleration become betrayal?

Such questions are not always easy to answer. What is clear, however, is that to the author of Daniel the answer to his particular problem was unequivocal: the altar to Baal Shamen, superimposed on the altar of the God of Heaven, was an abomination!

HOW LONG?—AN ASSERTION OF HOPE

Daniel 8:13–14 *(cont'd)*

(iii)

The outstanding question for the writer of Daniel was, How long will God allow this thing to continue? The same question had been asked many times before by the psalmists (cf. Pss. 6:3; 80:4; 90:13) and by the prophets (cf. Isa. 6:11; Hab. 2:6) and was to become a popular plea in later apocalyptic writings (cf. 2 Esdras 6:59; Rev. 6:10). How long will it be before the tribulation of God's people will come to an end? There is more in this question than simply a cry of anguish; it is at the same time an assertion of hope that God will come speedily to their rescue and deliver them.

In this the apocalyptist had much in common with the prophet, for although their messages may be presented in a different way, the hope expressed is the same. And even in their method of presentation they may not be as far apart as is often suggested. The distinction is sometimes made, for example, between prophecy as forth-telling (i.e. spoken to the circumstances of the time) and apocalyptic as "fore-telling" (i.e. addressed to a future time). There is some truth in this, but it needs qualification, for prophecy is about fore-telling as well as forth-telling, and apocalyptic is about forth-telling as well as fore-telling. These verses are a case in point, for although the setting of this book in the Persian period gave to its readers the impression of ancient prediction now about to be fulfilled, the writer of the book was declaring his message of hope for the very situation in which he and they now found themselves. In the guise of fore-telling he is in fact forth-telling that the tribulations under Antiochus will soon be over and God's people will again worship in his sanctuary without let or hindrance.

(iv)

But in one respect at least the writer of Daniel differs from the Old Testament prophets. To the question, "How long?", he supplies a precise answer—right down to the very day! This concern for numbers and measurements is quite marked in the apocalyptic writings as a whole and lends itself at times to an artificial and stylised interpretation of history in which future events are seen to be determined beforehand, to be revealed in advance only to the chosen few.

The author of these verses is writing at a time when the tribulation he describes is not yet over. Not content with a general word of assurance, he predicts the time of its end. How he arrived at the precise date he gives we do not know. It may have been from his own observation of events or a result of premonition or a pure guess! By whatever means it came it was received by him as a revelation and announced as an act of faith. The tribulation, he says, will continue "for two thousand and three hundred evenings and mornings", i.e. for 1,150 days during which the evening sacrifices and the morning sacrifices will continue to be forbidden. In fact this prediction was not far off the mark, for according to 1 Maccabees 1:54,59 the foreign altar was set up in December 167 B.C. and according to 2 Maccabees 4:52,59 was removed exactly three years later in December 164 B.C. This span of 1,150 days is appreciably less than the "three-and-a-half times" or years mentioned in 7:25 (see comment on 7:19–28). It has been suggested by way of explanation that chapter 8 may have been written somewhat later than chapter 7, or that the starting point of the prediction in 7:25 was earlier than that in 8:14. The preciseness of the figures matters less than the assurance itself that God will in the very near future bring their tribulation to an end.

(v)

In a number of apocalyptic books which come after Daniel we find an almost obsessive interest in chronology and numerology used in an attempt to forecast "the end". Ancient prophecy is interpreted and re-interpreted by means of figures, cycles and number patterns which were believed to point unerringly to that great day. When the day came and passed and nothing happened, the interpretation or re-interpretation was itself re-interpreted with fresh calculations and the building up of fresh hopes. The rabbis in later years were most disparaging of these "calculators of the end", as they called them. One of them, Rabbi Jose, went so far as to say, "He who announces the messianic time based on calculations forfeits his own share in the future". Such speculation, however, continued and had a fascination for many people from the Maccabean period onwards.

We recall that in the Gospels Jesus too had some strong things to say about those who seek "a sign" of the coming end (cf. Mark 8:12) and indulge in speculation, trying to predict the day and hour of its coming (cf. Mark 13:32). "The kingdom of God is not coming with signs to be observed; nor will they say, 'Lo, here it is!' or 'There!' for behold, the kingdom of God is in the midst of you" (Luke 17:21f.).

Despite these warnings, however, there are those who still spend much time and ingenuity in calculating times and seasons, indulging in predictions and prognostications of the end, the knowledge of which the Father has reserved for himself alone (cf. Matt. 24:36). This use of Scripture as a wire to pick the lock of the future not only disregards the warnings of Jesus, it fails to take seriously the working of God in history and instead sees men and nations as pawns in a great game of chess whose fate is determined from the beginning.

This is not the way of Jesus, nor should it be the way of his disciples. The "signs" of the kingdom are not to be detected by spectacular proofs, occult prediction or allegorical arithmetic but by recognising, through prayer and the study of the Scriptures within the fellowship of his Church, the working out of his prevailing purpose and the promise through Christ of the consummation.

GABRIEL: GOD'S MAN

Daniel 8:15-19

When I, Daniel, had seen the vision, I sought to understand it; and behold, there stood before me one having the appearance of a man. And I heard a man's voice between the banks of the Ulai, and it called, "Gabriel, make this man understand the vision." So he came near where I stood; and when he came, I was frightened and fell upon my face. But he said to me, "Understand, O son of man, that the vision is for the time of the end." As he was speaking to me, I fell into a deep sleep with my face to the ground; but he touched me and set me on my feet. He said, "Behold, I will make known to you what shall be at the latter end of the indignation; for it pertains to the appointed time of the end."

Daniel, we are told, was puzzled by what he had seen in his vision and sought to understand its meaning. Suddenly there appeared alongside him an angelic figure "having the appearance of a man". The Hebrew word used here for "man" is *geber* which represents the first part of the name *Gabriel* meaning "man of God". This unidentified "man" is presumably Gabriel himself whom a mysterious voice now summons by name to supply the interpretation.

(i)

We have already observed (see comment on 7:15-18) that during the Hellenistic period belief in angels and spirit-beings generally underwent a considerable development within Judaism, so that as early as the writing of Daniel there had emerged a prolific angelic tradition in which, it is said, "ten thousand times ten thousand" stood before God (7:10; cf. Rev. 5:11). The angels, moreover, are arranged in a descending order of authority with their officers and "other ranks" just like soldiers in a great army. Those belonging to the "officer-class" are given specific responsible duties to perform. Thus they "minister before the Lord continually" and guard God's throne; they intercede on behalf of men and act as mediators between God and men; they make known the secrets of God's hidden purpose and guide men in the right path.

These high-ranking angels, moreover, now assume titles such as "watcher" or "wakeful one" (see comment on 4:10-18) which indicate their peculiar functions. Highest in rank are the seven archangels (in another tradition they are four in number) whose names are given as Uriel, Raphael, Raguel, Michael, Saraqel, Gabriel and Remiel. The number seven possibly reflects Babylonian influence and the worship there of the five planets together with the sun and the moon.

But there is a further development of some significance: now for the first time in Hebrew literature angels appear with *personal names*. This reference in verse 16 to Gabriel is indeed the first occurrence of such a name in Scripture. He is mentioned again in 9:21 and, of course, as the angel of the annunciation in Luke 1:19,26. He appears also in the book of Enoch and fairly frequently in other Jewish writings of the period.

A development of this kind is of significance for our understanding, in the Old Testament and in the New, of the notion of divine mediation. In the Old Testament we read of "the angel of the presence" who acts as mediator between God and men, being virtually identifiable with God himself. As soon, however, as the angel or archangel becomes known by his own name, thus acquiring a personality and identity distinct from that of the Godhead, he becomes a representative of God rather than, in the truest sense, a mediator. This representative function, rather than the mediatorial, is indicated in such a passage as Gal. 3:19ff. where reference is made to the tradition that the Law at Sinai was given, not directly by God, but through his angelic representatives with the result that it lacked the glory of the true life-giving Word. In contrast to this, it can truly be said of *Jesus,* who is so much superior to angels (cf. Heb. 1:4), that he is "the one *mediator* between God and man" (1 Tim. 2:5). This indeed is the prevailing theme of the Epistle to the Hebrews where Jesus is presented as mediator of the New Covenant by reason of the fact that he "reflects the glory of God and bears the very stamp of his nature", surpassing the angels, "having inherited a more excellent name than they" (1:3,4).

(ii)

The presence of Gabriel standing close to Daniel had a devastating effect on him: "I was frightened and fell on my face" (see also comment on 10:1-9). The reaction is familiar enough in the Old Testament Scriptures. In the presence of God or of his angelic messenger the beholder is struck with awe or is completely overcome (cf. Gen. 17:3; Exod. 3:6; Judg. 13:20). So too in the New Testament as when John on the Isle of Patmos fell at the feet of the "son of man" as though dead (cf. Rev. 1:17) or when Peter, James and John were confronted by their glorified Lord—"they fell on their faces and were filled with awe" (Matt. 17:6). In that moment they were made deeply aware of "the numinous", that quality of awe and reverence that worshippers sense in the presence of the living God himself. Or we think of Luke's story of Peter's confrontation with Jesus following the miraculous draft of fishes. Peter, we are told, fell down in amazement at Jesus' feet. But what impressed him on this occasion was not so much his glorious appearance as his moral quality which no angel, however great, could emulate. Sinful man that he was he prostrated himself before his Master: "Depart from me, for I am a sinful man, O Lord" (Luke 5:8). The angels are described as "holy ones"; but there is a holier than they in whose presence we fall down in reverent worship and awe-ful praise.

Having fallen down before this awesome presence, Daniel now falls into "a deep sleep" with his face to the ground. This is no gentle slumber whilst he is relaxed. The word signifies a trance-like sleep associated elsewhere with the reception of a divine revelation through a dream or vision. Several times over in the book of Daniel the mental and physical effects of such experiences are recorded: he undergoes emotional disturbances which alarm his thoughts (cf. 7:28) or make him physically sick (cf. 8:27), pangs come upon him (cf. 10:16) or he becomes dumb (cf. 10:15), or as here he loses consciousness altogether (cf. 8:18; 10:9). Such reactions are so psychologically accurate that it is tempting to see in them a reflection of the actual experience of the writer himself.

Ecstatic experience of this kind has its place in the history of Christian devotion as the testimony of men like Paul (cf. 2 Cor. 12:2) and John Wesley, for example, make plain and as the life and worship of many charismatic groups today bear witness. But, as Gabriel demonstrates, the man of God's place is not on his face but on his feet. He touched Daniel and set him on his feet so that he arose and "went about the king's business" (8:27).

THE TIME OF THE END

Daniel 8:15-19 *(cont'd)*

(i)

Gabriel introduces his interpretation of Daniel's vision by announcing in verse 17 that it concerns "the time of the end". This word "end" occurs a number of times in the prophetic writings of the Old Testament where it signifies the time when God will exercise his judgment on Israel or, more often, on the Gentile nations which oppress Israel. In the later prophetic books we find the phrase "the latter end of the days" expressing the same kind of hope. What is envisaged is not the end of history as such, but rather the end of an historical era and the beginning of a Golden Age of peace and prosperity. Its setting is essentially "this-worldly", bounded by time and history. In it God will reign as King, sometimes with and sometimes without his "anointed one", the Messiah.

This is a theme that the apocalyptic writers, from Daniel onwards, take up with enthusiasm. Among them and their fellow-Jews of the intertestamental period, there is an air of eager expectancy which is reflected also in the books of the New Testament. The promised "end" is almost upon them. Soon they will witness the great denouement of history and the coming of the kingdom.

It must be confessed that their prognostications are much more precise than their actual descriptions of the coming great event. They remind us of the schoolboy cyclist who completely lost his way and then came across a signpost. Being good at arithmetic he could tell how far he had to go, but being bad at reading he didn't know where he was going! The apocalyptists predict with precision the "distance" to the end, but their "reading" of that event often lacks clarity and consistency.

Indeed, the pictures given in these apocalyptic books of the "end" and the coming kingdom are kaleidoscopic in their variations. In some it marks simply the end of one historical era and the beginning of a new. In others it marks the end of time itself, the termination of history as men have known it, the folding up of the physical universe and the ushering in of a timeless eternity in a transcendent world far beyond this temporal scene. In others again it introduces a purely temporary kingdom established here on earth—a "millennium"—to be followed by an eternal kingdom in heaven. Sometimes too the "end" involves the rout of Israel's enemies by force of arms. At other times it takes the form of a great cosmic conflict where the powers of darkness are locked in battle with the powers of light and where the armies of Satan are destroyed by the angelic hosts of God.

In all of them, however, the "end" is imminent. From the vantage point of the supposed ancient author, of course, it is a long way off. But from that of the actual author and his readers it is there at the very door. So it is with the author of the book of Daniel who recognises the long-expected "end" in the crisis brought about by Antiochus Epiphanes and his treatment of the Jews. In him wickedness has reached its zenith and will be speedily and utterly cast down. His destruction, soon to be accomplished, will mark the end of a long, long chapter in Israel's history of suffering and subjection. The day is about to dawn when a new era in the life of Israel will begin when God's people will triumph over all their foes and will receive their just reward. This new era will witness the introduction of a universal kingdom here on earth in which Israel will enjoy for ever the rich blessings of God (see comment on 7:13–14).

(ii)

In verse 17, then, Gabriel announces that the vision concerns "the time of the end". Later on, in verse 19, he repeats this pronouncement but refers now to "the latter end of the indignation" or "the latter part of the wrath". In the Old Testament this last word is used almost invariably with reference to "the wrath of God", indicating God's judgment on evil-doers who transgress his moral laws.

Here in Daniel it signifies that period during which God has been angry with his people and has subjected them to harassment at the hands of their enemies. Just as in olden times he had used Assyria as the rod of his anger and the staff of his fury (cf. Isa. 10:5), so now he is using Antiochus for the same purpose to chastise his people. But just as he had put a limit to Assyria's punishment of Israel (cf. Isa. 10:25), so now he will bring their troubles under Antiochus to a determined and speedy end. (For a development of this idea of the "wrath" of God in terms of the "Messianic woes" or "signs of the end" see comment on 12:1–4).

Everything is under God's control. Antiochus will flourish and prosper right up to the end; but that end is sure. We are reminded here, as perhaps the writer of Daniel himself was, of the certainty of the promise given in the prophecy of Habakkuk: "For still the vision awaits its time; it hastens to the end—it will not lie. If it seem slow, wait for it; it will surely come, it will not delay" (Hab. 2:3). The "great wrath" (cf. 1 Maccabees 1:64) that had fallen on Israel will soon be at an end and Israel will enter into the promised kingdom.

The message comes through with strong conviction that God is sovereign Lord. The wickedness and cruelty of Antiochus are not beyond God's control; they are running their course only because God allows them to; let them be assured that the end— and the end of Antiochus—will soon be here.

It is the conviction of prophet and apocalyptist alike that God in his infinite power and wisdom can make even the wrath of men to praise him (cf. Ps. 76:10). Though they may not be aware of it and though they may reject him and blaspheme his name, he is able to use men and nations to serve his holy purposes. They continue only by the permissive will of God. Their end is determined by him who will not allow the righteous to perish.

ANTIOCHUS EPIPHANES: A PORTRAIT

Daniel 8:20–25

> "As for the ram which you saw with the two horns, these are the kings of Media and Persia. And the he-goat is the king of Greece; and the great horn between his eyes is the first king. As for the horn that was broken, in place of which four others arose, four kingdoms shall arise from his nation, but not with his power. And at the latter end of their rule, when the transgressors have reached their full measure, a king of bold countenance, one who understands riddles, shall arise. His power shall be great, and he shall cause fearful destruction, and shall succeed in what he does, and destroy mighty men and the people of the saints. By his cunning he shall make deceit prosper under his hand, and in his own mind he shall magnify himself. Without warning he shall destroy many; and he shall even rise up against the Prince of princes; but, by no human hand, he shall be broken."

Now we come to Gabriel's interpretation of Daniel's vision. It is perfectly clear that he is not particularly interested in the ram with the two horns representing the Medo-Persian kingdom, or the "shaggy" he-goat with the horn between its eyes representing the Greek kingdom and Alexander the Great, or the four others which arose in his place representing his successors, the Diadochi, who continued Alexander's rule, though not as successfully as he. His attention is focused rather on one character and one character only—Antiochus Epiphanes whose portrait he now paints in both dark and lurid colours.

(i)

His appearance marks the high-point of human wickedness, when transgressions (perhaps better than "transgressors") reach their peak. He is a man with an insolent face ("of bold countenance"), the kind of face that one associates with a brazen prostitute (cf. Prov. 7:13). He is one who understands riddles—but not the parlour-game variety. The expression may refer to the fact that he is skilled in political intrigue, a man given to double-talk and double-dealing or, as has been sug-

gested, to his (supposed) interpretations of the dark mysteries
of God. He is a powerful man, capable of fearful destruction,
liquidating political opponents ("mighty men") and faithful
Jews ("the people of the saints") alike. He thinks of himself as
"Mr. Big" who operates with cunning and deceit. Without any
warning he lashes out against the people, as on the occasion
when his collector of tribute, Apollonius, arrived in Jerusalem
with honeyed words, only to fall upon them and massacre a
multitude (cf. 1 Maccabees 1:29f.; 2 Maccabees 5:23–26). He is
ready to rise up even against God himself ("the Prince of
princes", a form of the superlative in Hebrew meaning "the
supreme prince"), as demonstrated in his attack on the Temple
and on the people of God. But his power will at last be broken,
without the need for any human intervention. Contemporary
sources give varying accounts of his death. It was not violent,
but it was pathetic in the extreme. According to Polybius he
became quite insane. According to 1 Maccabees 6:8ff., he died
of melancholia, "his bitter grief breaking out again and again";
and according to 2 Maccabees 9:5, of colic, being "seized with
incurable pain in his bowels and with sharp internal torments",
which was regarded as a clear indication of divine retribution
(as Josephus tells us in his *Antiquities*).

This picture of an able, unpredictable, insolent and treacherous man is confirmed by many other references in these writers
and in Josephus as well as in Daniel itself. Here is how Edwyn
Bevan sums it all up:

> He is a man of vehement impulse and high spirits...He came to
> scandalise his court by the democratic familiarity of his manners, by
> his practical jokes, by his love of some theatrical nonsense, as when
> he made Antioch for a time pretend to be Rome and sat himself in
> the market-place, dressed as a Roman aedile, to adjudge the small
> disputes of the day...Whatever stood in the way of his will must be
> beaten down, and if a vindictive impulse was provoked in him, he
> put no restraint upon it...He could nurse a deadly design...He was
> a finished diplomat...[But] there was really something not abso-
> lutely sound in his mental constitution, such an impalpable vein of
> insanity as can go with brilliant powers and extraordinary astute-

ness in dealing. We know that the popular wit changed his surname of Epiphanes into Epimanes "the madman", and his untimely death seems to have been preceded by some sort of pronounced derangement.

(ii)

The association of Antiochus with "the end" and with "the signs of the end" (see previous comment) is of significance for the belief that arose later concerning the Antichrist who in the last days would appear on the earth and do battle with God himself. The actual term is first used in Christian writings, but the idea the word conveys is much earlier and appears in different guises in the apocalyptic books of the intertestamental period. Its earliest biblical expression is here in the book of Daniel where Antichrist is identified with Antiochus Epiphanes, whose downfall, as we have seen, will mark the "end". "The figure of Antichrist", says H. T. Andrews, "is very largely the figure of Antiochus 'writ large' and thrown upon the screen of the future."

The origins of this figure, it has been suggested, are perhaps to be traced away back to the mythical monster of chaos familiar to the reader of the Old Testament, which now comes to be individualised and historicised so that by the time of the apocalyptic literature he is identified with a particular historical person, in this case Antiochus. It is hardly surprising that the Jews should see Antiochus as a personification of evil or that in the course of time the role of Antichrist should be transferred from him to some other tyrant who, like him, plays the role of oppressor. Thus in the Psalms of Solomon 2:29 the role is taken over by the Roman general Pompey who is represented as a "dragon" whose pride God will "turn into dishonour" (cf. also 2 Baruch 40:1f.).

In other passages, however, Antichrist is represented not by a human figure at all but by a satanic figure called Beliar, the personification of wickedness, who will be slain by God in the end, together with all his evil host. God's Messiah will wage war against him and rescue the faithful from his power (cf. Testament of Dan 5:10) and he will be "cast into the fire for ever"

(Testament of Judah 25:3). He will perform many signs and deceive many people, but God will burn him up (cf. Sibylline Oracles III, 63ff.).

The same theme is continued in Christian circles in the book of Revelation, for example, where the dragon with whom Michael fights in heaven (cf. 12:7) is a demonic figure corresponding to Beliar the prince of the demons. The beast which inherits the power of the dragon (cf. 13:1ff.) is its earthly counterpart and corresponds to the little horn in Daniel's vision which in turn, as we have seen, represents Antiochus. This beast, it has been suggested, may represent none other than Nero (n) Caesar, a name whose letters have a numerical value totalling 666, which is given here as "the number of the beast" (cf. 13:18).

In succeeding generations ever since, Christians have identified their persecutors and oppressors as the Antichrist whose appearance is to precede the Second Advent. In this way a long line of tyrants from Nero to Hitler has been recognised and Christians have seen in the persecution of the faithful at their hands a sure sign that the end is near.

Identification of the Antichrist has occupied the time of cranks and credulous alike. And yet the notion itself is not to be dismissed with a superior sniff, for surely the Antichrist, whether he be called by that name or not, represents a reality against which all Christians must be on their guard. That reality is the presence in our universe of what Paul describes as "principalities and powers" whose evil influence is to be found not just in evil men but also in institutions, nations and states which share man's fallenness and also his delusion that they too can be as God.

The Jews of Antiochus' day, like the Christians of Nero's day, sought to "discern the signs" and identified the Antichrist with specific individuals who were enemies of the true God. There is a sense in which modern Christians should also set themselves to read "the signs of the times", not by means of occult predictions or fanciful calculations or the unearthing of esoteric meanings from the text of Scripture, but rather by recognising those forces of evil now at work in the universe in their various manifestations and by joining forces with Almighty God to bring about their defeat. Faced by Antichrist, who appears in many shapes and guises, the Christian is assured, through the death and resurrection of Jesus Christ and the promise of his return, that there will indeed be an end to evil and that his kingdom of goodness, righteousness and truth will be established on the earth.

"SEAL UP THE VISION"

Daniel 8:26–27

> "The vision of the evenings and the mornings which has been told is true; but seal up the vision, for it pertains to many days hence." And I, Daniel, was overcome and lay sick for some days; then I rose and went about the king's business; but I was appalled by the vision and did not understand it.

(i)

Gabriel assures Daniel that the vision he has seen is no mere illusion, but something that can truly be relied upon. This, of course, is the very message the writer himself wants to impress upon his readers as he points to the demise of Antiochus and the speedy approach of "the end". The point is reinforced by his using a literary device which is fairly common in apocalyptic books of this kind he addresses his message to his readers in the form of a prediction from a bygone age which, during all the intervening years, has lain concealed and is now for the first time made known. Daniel, living in Babylon in the time of Belshazzar, is bidden to "seal up" the account of what he has seen until the time prophesied in the vision actually arrives, i.e. the time of Antiochus in which the writer himself is now living. The very fact that the account of the vision and its interpretation is now being revealed is itself a clear sign that the end is near.

(ii)

Later on in the book the instructions given to the seer are more explicit. He is to seal up what he sees and hears *in a book* (cf. 12:4). The notion of divine revelations from ancient times given to ancient worthies in dream or in vision and hidden away in secret books to be disclosed at the time of the end to "the wise" among God's people is a familiar feature of the apocalyptic literature as a whole.

Sacred books are said to have occupied the attention of the sect of the Jews called Essenes who were required to swear an oath never to divulge the contents of these secret writings. Among the Qumran Covenanters also, sacred books were preserved, sometimes in secret writing, in readiness for the day when God would bring all things to an end.

In the apocalyptic writings of the intertestamental period, besides the book of Daniel, there are two distinguishable traditions associated with two revered figures of the past within which this notion of "secret books" prevailed. The first is that associated with the name of Enoch which finds chief expression in the several writings which make up the book we know as 1 Enoch. In 82:1 for example, Enoch addresses his son Methuselah in these words: "Preserve the books from thy father's hands and [see] that thou deliver them to the [future] generations of the world." The second is associated with the name of Ezra (the "second Moses") who, under divine inspiration, dictates not only the twenty-four books of Scripture, which are to be made public, but also seventy books—signifying no doubt the apocalyptic writings—which he is to keep secret, to deliver in due course to the wise among the people (cf. 2 Esdras 14:45f.).

(iii)

The revelations contained in these "secret" apocalyptic writings follow a similar basic pattern. Using the name of an ancient seer—like Enoch or Moses or Abraham or Ezra or Daniel— they relate the broad sweep of history in the form of prediction right up to the *actual* writer's own day (in the intertestamental period) when "prediction proper" takes over and declares that the end is near.

It is all too easy for the modern reader to conclude that

pseudonymous authorship of this kind and this peculiar literary device of "secret" hidden books is a quiet unworthy attempt to deceive the original readers (see Introduction). But this is to misunderstand the mentality of such writers and to read back into ancient times a modern concept of authorship and "copyright" which would never have occurred to them. Their purpose was not to deceive but rather to emphasise that, as God's holy purpose had prevailed down through the long ages of history, so it would prevail in the days ahead and would achieve its goal. Their readers would no doubt understand what was meant. Besides all this, it was a *convenient* way of writing in the inflammatory days of Antiochus and, later on, the successors of the Maccabees and later still the Roman procurators. It was helpful for these writers to be able to pronounce the doom of their enemies in a style of writing which purported to come from the past and which only the initiated could understand!

And yet, this style of writing was more than a *mere* literary device, for the apocalyptic writers were conscious of standing in a long tradition, stretching far back into the past associated with the names of Enoch, Moses, Ezra and others, from which they drew their insights into the spiritual world and their secret knowledge of the days to come. Apocalyptic, as we know it among the Jews, first came to flower in the second century B.C., but its roots go far back in oral tradition and owe much to earlier written sources (e.g. Ezek. 38 39; Zech. 1–8 and 9–14; Joel 3 and Isaiah 24–27). As inheritors of this long tradition the apocalyptic writers were able to transmit their secret lore with the authority of "the ancients", even though the actual words they wrote came from their own pens and pointed to the events of their own day.

(iv)

Tradition, says T. S. Eliot, is innovation, not repetition. As such, in both oral and written forms, it has played an important role not only in Judaism but in Christianity as well. It is as true for us as it was for the apocalyptist that what we have we have received. We are debtors to the past, recipients of the wisdom of our fathers and transmitters of ancient truth, enriched by our own experience of it. Present experience, however vital it may be, cannot be divorced from past revelations. Together they form that sacred tradition by means of which, through the Holy Spirit, God continues to illumine the written word of Scripture which speaks to us of his prevailing purpose in the long history of mankind and points unerringly to the consummation of all things in the coming "end".

(For reference to the physical effect of the vision on Daniel as recorded in verse 27 see comment on 8:15–19. The reference to the fact that he "did not understand" what he saw prepares the reader for the chapters which follow and particularly for the detailed interpretation of chapter 11.)

THE SEVENTY YEARS

Daniel 9:1–2

> In the first year of Darius the son of Ahasu-erus, by birth a Mede, who became king over the realm of the Chaldeans—in the first year of his reign, I, Daniel, perceived in the books the number of years which, according to the word of the Lord to Jeremiah the prophet, must pass before the end of the desolations of Jerusalem, namely, seventy years.

(i)

The author takes his readers back to the first year of Darius the Mede (cf. 5:31), i.e. to the year 538 B.C., the year after the fall of Babylon when the hopes of the Jews in exile for deliverance would be running high. At that time, he says, a revelation was given to Daniel in Babylon which came, not in the form of a dream or symbolic vision, but rather as a result of his reading "the books". By this is meant presumably the books of Scripture, and in particular that part of the prophecy of Jeremiah which speaks of the "desolation" of exile lasting for a period of seventy years (cf. Jer. 25:11f.). During this time they had to settle down in Babylon and "seek the welfare of the city", with the assurance that "when seventy years are completed for

Babylon", God will fulfil his promise and bring them back home (cf. Jer. 29:7,10).

It is fairly certain that this reference to seventy years was intended by Jeremiah to be taken as a round number indicating a life-span of "three score years and ten" (cf. Ps. 90:10). At a somewhat later stage, however, as in Zech. 1:12, it seems to be understood as a precise figure and refers to the period between the fall of Jerusalem in 587 B.C. and the reconstruction of the Temple in 516 B.C. In 2 Chron. 36:20ff. a different identification is suggested; the period in question—albeit much shorter than seventy years—is that between the fall of Jerusalem in 587 B.C. and the edict of Cyrus in 538 B.C. allowing many of the Jewish exiles to return home.

To the author of the book of Daniel neither of these interpretations sufficed, for in fact the longed-for deliverance had not yet arrived. But it had been revealed clearly to him (cf. ch. 8) that that day was now about to dawn; deliverance was at hand; the end was near. And he finds justification for this conviction in an interpretation of Jeremiah's prophecy, the like of which had never been made known before. As the sequel to the story shows (cf. 9:24ff.), the prophet's seventy years represent "seventy weeks" (of years), i.e. $70 \times 7 = 490$ years, an interpretation which points decisively to the author's own day and the time of Antiochus Epiphanes! The time of "exile", the time of Israel's "desolation" is almost over. The seventy years of Jeremiah's prophecy are about to be fulfilled.

(ii)

These verses are of interest, as reflecting our writer's understanding and use of Scripture.

(a) *It is authoritative.* It is significant that he seeks corroboration of his convictions concerning "the end" in the "authoritative" word of Scripture. By his time what we know as "the prophetic canon" had come to be recognised as a corpus of sacred books, with an honoured place given to it in private and public worship. According to popular belief the voice of prophecy had fallen silent long before the second century B.C.

The prophetic word recorded in Scripture was thus all the more authoritative as a word of the Lord. To the author of Daniel the word of Jeremiah takes the place of the dreams or visions alluded to in earlier chapters of his book. Like them it too is a vehicle of divine revelation. As such the Scriptures are self-authenticating and cannot deny themselves. Hence Daniel's perplexity that the prophecy of the seventy years does not seem to have been fulfilled. Hence too his search for an interpretation of Jeremiah's words which will demonstrate their credibility and substantiate their authority.

(b) *It is contemporary.* But Jeremiah's prophecy is not only authoritative, it is also contemporary, i.e. our author sees in the word of Scripture a word for his own day. The seventy years must refer to the age in which he himself was now living. This approach to Scripture is well illustrated in the Dead Sea Scrolls from Qumran in the *pesharim* or "commentaries" on, say, the book of Habakkuk where the events described are said to refer not to the time of Habakkuk at all but to the "time of the end" in which the men of Qumran themselves were living. Similarly, two centuries or so later the writer of 2 Esdras does to Daniel what Daniel had done to Jeremiah. He takes up his reference to the fourth kingdom (cf. 12:10ff.; Dan. 7:23) and re-interprets it to refer to the Roman empire of his own day. So also in the New Testament. The words of Moses and the prophets have a meaning and a significance far beyond their own plain sense (cf. Luke 24:44ff.). They point beyond themselves to their fulfil-ment in Christ and the Good News of his salvation.

There is a sense, too, in which these same Scriptures speak to our present-day condition. They belong essentially to the situation, the society, the culture from which they emerge and to which their message is directed; and yet they have about them a timeless and timely quality whose word overarches time and space and impinges on every generation with eternal meaning. In this sense they have to be interpreted and re-interpreted in successive ages and in diverse societies in ever new and diverse ways. It is this very task of interpretation to which the preacher, for example, has to give himself week in and week out—to uncover in Scripture not just a record of past events, but a word from God which matches the need of that day and that hour. The Bible is a contemporary book.

(c) *It is predictive.* The author of Daniel sees in the prophecy of Jeremiah a prediction of what would happen many years later and which found its fulfilment in the events of his own day. We do well to distinguish at this point between the *message* of these verses and the *method* adopted to make it known. It is perhaps unfortunate that his treatment of the prophecy of Jeremiah has itself been applied by others to Daniel's own predictions so that all too often they have become a happy hunting ground for modern prognosticators and what the Rabbis called "calculators of the end". In this connection E. W. Heaton has a wise word to say:

> Prediction which concerns the immediate future, thought of as developing out of and as part of the present situation, is within the sphere of personal and moral judgment and derives from it whatever degree of validity it has. Such *prophetic* prediction, whether in its ancient or modern form, is radically different from predictive calculations, which for the most part refer to the distant and not imminent future, have no relation to the present situation, and have their origin not in moral or spiritual conviction, but mere idle curiosity. The writer's use of Jeremiah set a fateful precedent, but he himself did not fall into the trivialities his example encouraged.

The Scriptures have indeed a message for today and tomorrow, but to use them as an Old Moore's Almanac to foretell "the distant scene" is to run the risk of missing their essential message for the days in which we live. In the words of Norman Porteous, "In finding the relevance of this passage of Scripture to ourselves, we must allow ourselves to be guided by the witness of this man to the availability of God in every crisis in history, without following him in his mistake of supposing that one can calculate in advance what God will do."

"It is an obvious waste of time," writes David L. Edwards, "to comb the Bible for exact prophecies of events in today's news— or of doom (or plenty) just around the corner. But I have been driven to see that it is worth while to put the *broad pattern* of the Bible's interpretation of history alongside the news...to

hold the Bible in one hand and today's newspaper in the other."
Its true message for today is not to be found in slide-rule
calculations of coming events, the knowledge of which God the
Father has reserved for himself alone (cf. Matt. 24:36), but in
God's moral character and in the constant rebellion and
repentance of sinful man.

A PRAYER FOR THE NATION: A LITURGY

Daniel 9:3-19

Then I turned my face to the Lord God, seeking him by prayer and
supplications with fasting and sackcloth and ashes. I prayed to the
Lord my God and made confession, saying, "O Lord, the great and
terrible God, who keepest covenant and steadfast love with those
who love him and keep his commandments, we have sinned and
done wrong and acted wickedly and rebelled, turning aside from thy
commandments and ordinances; we have not listened to thy servants the prophets, who spoke in thy name to our kings, our princes,
and our fathers, and to all the people of the land. To thee, O Lord,
belongs righteousness, but to us confusion of face, as at this day, to
the men of Judah, to the inhabitants of Jerusalem, and to all Israel,
those that are near and those that are far away, in all the lands to
which thou hast driven them, because of the treachery which they
have committed against thee. To us, O Lord, belongs confusion of
face, to our kings, to our princes, and to our fathers, because we
have sinned against thee. To the Lord our God belong mercy and
forgiveness; because we have rebelled against him, and have not
obeyed the voice of the Lord our God by following his laws, which
he set before us by his servants the prophets. All Israel has trans-
gressed thy law and turned aside, refusing to obey thy voice. And the
curse and oath which are written in the law of Moses the servant of
God have been poured out upon us, because we have sinned against
him. He has confirmed his words, which he spoke against us and
against our rulers who ruled us, by bringing upon us a great
calamity; for under the whole heaven there has not been done the
like of what has been done against Jerusalem. As it is written in the
law of Moses, all this calamity has come upon us, yet we have not
entreated the favour of the Lord our God, turning from our

iniquities and giving heed to thy truth. Therefore the Lord has kept ready the calamity and has brought it upon us; for the Lord our God is righteous in all the works which he has done, and we have not obeyed his voice. And now, O Lord our God, who didst bring thy people out of the land of Egypt with a mighty hand, and hast made thee a name, as at this day, we have sinned, we have done wickedly. O Lord, according to all thy righteous acts, let thy anger and thy wrath turn away from thy city Jerusalem, thy holy hill; because for our sins, and for the iniquities of our fathers, Jerusalem and thy people have become a byword among all who are round about us. Now therefore, O our God, hearken to the prayer of thy servant and to his supplications, and for thy own sake, O Lord, cause thy face to shine upon thy sanctuary, which is desolate. O my God, incline thy ear and hear; open thy eyes and behold our desolations, and the city which is called by thy name; for we do not present our supplications before thee on the ground of our righteousness, but on the ground of thy great mercy. O Lord, hear; O Lord, forgive; O Lord, give heed and act; delay not, for thy own sake, O my God, because thy city and thy people are called by thy name."

At this point in the chapter, between Jeremiah's prophecy of seventy years' exile and their interpretation by Gabriel as seventy "weeks of years", there is inserted a passionate prayer on behalf of God's people. Perhaps its insertion here owes something to the fact that in Jer. 29:12, immediately following a reference to Jeremiah's prophecy, the people are bidden to call upon God in supplication. This is what Daniel now does, prefacing his supplication with words of confession for the sake of God's people Israel.

Before looking at the actual contents of the prayer we may make four general observations about it:

(1) Daniel purposefully *prepares himself* for this divine encounter. He turns his face towards God and consciously seeks him in prayer, i.e. he adopts an appropriate physical posture and adjusts his mind God-wards before he begins to frame the words. But even before that he had prepared by means of fasting, by wearing sackcloth and by sprinkling himself with ashes (cf. Neh. 9:1). Physical preparedness and

spiritual receptiveness are closely related in Scripture and indeed in our own experience of prayer. The act of fasting is familiar to us from our reading of the Old Testament (cf. Exod. 34:28; Deut. 9:9; Esth. 4:6) and occurs also fairly frequently in the intertestamental literature (cf. 2 Esdras 5:13,20; 2 Baruch 20:5f.) as a preparation for the disclosure of divine revelation but also as an act of contrition. So too with the wearing of sackcloth and ashes. This common sign of mourning and lamentation indicates an attitude of repentance prior to the confession of sin. (2) It is not a "free" prayer welling up spontaneously from the heart; it is *a liturgical prayer,* familiar perhaps in the synagogue worship in the second century B.C. and typifying the deep spirit of piety which pervaded many Jewish homes and groups of the faithful at that time (see comment on 2:14-23). One such group was the party of the *Hasidim* or "Pious Ones" to which the author of Daniel is thought to have belonged. Its structure and content may suggest a date of composition some generations before our author's time, by which it had become embedded in the synagogue liturgy. It is a penitential prayer that matches his mood and suits his purpose. There is no need to regard it as an interpolation here by some other hand. The author simply uses a "set" prayer that had already been tested and tried over a fairly long period of time to express his own deep feelings in addressing God. As a liturgical prayer it was no less his own prayer. But it was more than a private and personal plea to God; it was a prayer of the whole people spoken through the voice of one man and as such was a fitting vehicle for a national confession of sin (see point 4 below).

Two small but interesting points may be noted here. One is that the name "Yahweh" for God which is avoided elsewhere in the book (apart from a single reference in verse 2 which may be part of a quotation) is used here—again suggesting the prayer's independent origin. The other is that the background to the prayer would seem to be Palestine and not Babylon where it purports to have been offered by Daniel in exile. The language, however, overreaches national boundaries and shows a timeless quality, making it suitable for the purpose our author has in

mind. At one and the same time, it expresses the deep piety of
the people among whom he lived and indicates their identification with the yearnings of their fathers and the goodness of God
to their nation in all the ages past.

(3) It is a prayer that is framed *in biblical language,* using
words and concepts straight from the Old Testament. We hear
clear echoes, for example, of Solomon's consecration prayer in
the Temple as recorded in I Kings 8 and certain others such as
those in Jer. 26, 32 and 44. In particular it bears a close
resemblance to the prayers in Ezra 9 and in Neh. 1 and 9,
confirming that it had been in use in public worship for some
time before the age of our author. And yet it is much more than
simply a casual collection of scriptural quotations or scriptural
references. Together they form a unity that expresses at one and
the same time the authority of Scripture, the recognition of
common usage and the experience of personal conviction. In
these three "marks" of prayer—Scripture, tradition and experience—we are given a helpful guideline for liturgical and
spontaneous prayer alike.

(4) It is a prayer of confession and supplication *on behalf of the
nation of Israel.* It is the nation as a whole, and not just
individuals within it, that has sinned and needs to confess its
transgressions before God and receive his forgiveness. As a
prophet Daniel has not only the privilege of receiving divine
revelations on behalf of his people, he has also the responsibility of confessing their sins.

We are reminded again that evil is to be found not only in
individual people but also in institutions and perhaps most
clearly and most powerfully in the nation and state. The nation
and state can so readily assume prerogatives which belong to
God alone or, by institutionalising evil, can so perpetuate it that
it challenges the right of God to reign. It is part of the prophetic
function of the Church not only to intercede on behalf of the
nation but also to confess its sin and, when the need arises, to
denounce it in God's name. But just as Daniel does not stand
over against his nation but makes *their* confession *his* confession, so also must it be with the Church. The Church may claim

to have "the answer" to the nation's ills. But it must recognise that it is also part of the "the problem". As God's prophet it must confess the nation's sin as if it were its own so that together they may receive the forgiveness of God.

A PRAYER FOR THE NATION:
A CONFESSION OF SIN

Daniel 9:3-14 (cont'd)

The greater part of this prayer is a prayer of confession on behalf of the people of Israel who have sinned against God and have brought down calamity upon their own heads. Their sin is all the more grievous by reason of God's gracious dealings with them in the past and the love and care he has bestowed on them.

Two things are said about God which highlight the sin of the people and call for confession and repentance:

(1) *He is the God of the covenant* (verses 4-6) who shows "steadfast love" (Hebrew, *hesed*) to those who love him and keep his "commandments". Israel had been chosen and elected by God and had entered into a covenant relationship with him at Sinai, a relationship that was unique: "The Lord your God has chosen you to be a people for his own possession, out of all the peoples that are on the face of the earth" (Deut: 7:6). We are reminded here of certain basic elements in this covenant relationship:

(a) It is a covenant of "steadfast love" (verse 4). The opening words of the prayer remind us that it is not a covenant between equals in which the partners, as it were, shake hands. The Lord ("Yahweh") is "the great and terrible God" (cf. Neh. 1:5), the God in whose presence the people trembled and the mountain smoked (cf. Exod. 20:18; Heb. 12:18ff.). But his action is marked more by sovereign grace than it is by sovereign power. Of his own volition he brought the people of Israel into this unique relationship with himself. It was not because they were either great (cf. Deut. 7:7f.) or good (cf. Deut. 9:4; Dan. 9:18) that God had acted in this way. It was because of his steadfast love towards them, that he might make known to them and through them his holy purpose.

The word *hesed* is used frequently in the Old Testament to describe this covenant relationship. On the side of God it indicates the pledge of his *loyalty* to the promise he has made to them that they will be his people; he will be righteous and merciful and will save and redeem them. On the side of Israel it indicates that they will show *devotion* to him alone and demonstrate their complete loyalty to what they know of him from his past dealings with them. This will find expression in obedience to his commandments.

(*b*) It is a covenant of law. The giving of the covenant at Sinai was closely associated with the giving of his "commandments" (cf. Exod. 20). But this is no mere bargain struck between God and the people of Israel in which God lays down terms on which he will look after them. All they are asked for is the pledge of their loyalty—their confession that he had always been faithful and gracious to them, and their willing response to trust him and to walk in his ways. When they are willing so to do, God will·be in a position to give them the priceless gift of the Law which will show them clearly how to live a life well-pleasing to him. Thus seen, the Law itself is a gift of God's grace, for it shows the people how they can keep within the covenant.

(*c*) It is a covenant that must be renewed by each succeeding generation. "The Lord our God made a covenant with us in Horeb. Not with our fathers did the Lord make this covenant, but with us who are all of us here alive this day" (Deut. 5:2f.). Israel must not rely simply on something that had happened in the distant past when God had graciously entered into a covenant with her. The pledge made and the obligations accepted back must be entered into anew generation after generation. The deliverance from Egypt and the covenant at Horeb/Sinai were great objective, historical facts declaring and effecting the salvation of God. But they must be appropriated afresh again and again by the people of Israel if they were to have any real meaning and validity for them. Thus Israel of the

Exile and Israel of the time of Antiochus, as inheritors of the
covenant, were each under obligation to God.

(d) It is a covenant that can be broken. Israel had voluntarily
entered into the covenant and was not compelled to remain
within it. She had the right to accept or reject, to confirm or
repudiate. If she chose to repudiate, she would thereby declare
that she no longer wanted to be God's people. But even if this
did happen, even then the grace of God would pursue her,
seeking anew her loyalty and devotion. It was not a light thing
for God to give her up (cf. Hos. 11:8f.). He required nothing of
her except her repentance, signifying a turning again to him
from her evil ways.

Daniel here takes this responsibility upon himself on behalf
of Israel, identifying himself with his people in a powerful act of
confession and repentance. The whole nation has sinned and
done wrong; it has acted wickedly and rebelled (cf. 1 Kings
8:47).The people have turned aside (cf. Deut. 17:20) and have
broken not only the ceremonial and civil law ("commandments"), but the moral law ("ordinances") of God as well. In
particular they have not listened to God's servants, the prophets, who declared what the Sinai covenant had made plain
from the beginning, that the covenant, grounded in the revealed
law of God, was morally conditioned. That message had been
made clear to every section of society, from the kings on their
thrones right down to the common people of the land; but they
would not listen.

(2) *He is the God of righteousness* (verses 7–14).

(a) Verses 7–10. This is just another way of saying he is the
God of the covenant whose very nature it is to show mercy and
steadfast love. He is righteous in the sense that he always acts in
conformity with his own character. He never contradicts
himself. The contrast between God and his people in this regard
is most marked. To him belongs righteousness; to them belongs
"shame of face". And that applies to all of them, whether they
live in Palestine itself, or far away in the land of exile. The latter
may have been likened to "good figs" and the former to "bad
figs" (cf. Jer. 24:1ff.). But all are one in this, that they have acted

treacherously against God. This, moreover, has been done against a God who does not demand his "pound of flesh", but on the contrary is both merciful and forgiving. Far from responding to his steadfast love with that piety and devotion which is their due, they have rebelled against him and have refused to obey his commandments set before them by his servants the prophets. His people are utterly in the wrong over against the righteous God. They cannot justify themselves. Their only hope is to cast themselves on his mercy.

(b) Verses 11–14. But that mercy has an obverse side. The one complements the other. It is the judgment of God by which he disciplines and punishes his people Israel (cf. Amos 3:2). It is because of, and not in spite of, his unchanging love that he chastens Israel for her own good. The exile was such a chastening and judgment. The curse contained in the Law of Moses (cf. Lev. 26:14–45; Deut. 28:15–68) has, as a result of their sin, been poured out upon them. God has confirmed the written word of Scripture by bringing upon them this great calamity that has befallen Jerusalem. And yet, despite all this, Israel had not entreated God's favour by turning from her iniquity and practising true religion. But this very calamity is itself an indication of the loving care of God who is ever watchful over his word to perform it (cf. Jer. 1:12). His faithfulness in keeping even the promise of judgment is a demonstration of his righteousness which in turn is a confirmation of his convenanted mercies toward his people.

A PRAYER FOR THE NATION: A SUPPLICATION

Daniel 9:15–19 *(cont'd)*

Having offered his prayer of confession Daniel now comes to a prayer of supplication in which he again acknowledges the mercy and the righteousness of God and pleads for his forgiveness and deliverance to be made known to Israel. Throughout the prayer, the author of Daniel no doubt has in mind not just the calamity of the Babylonian exile but also the calamity that had befallen his compatriots in the time of Antiochus.

This prayer divides itself into three parts:

(1) *The God of mercy* (verses 15–16a). He begins by acknowledging that the God against whom Israel had sinned was the same Yahweh who had brought his people out of the land of Egypt "with a mighty hand". For the writer of this prayer, as for so many other Old Testament writers, the Exodus was the supremely creative moment in her long history. Here, as nowhere else, God had acted graciously and savingly, working a great deliverance for his people. The memory of that great event, commemorated regularly in public and private prayers and in the reading of the Scriptures, was an ever-recurring source of encouragement to them, not least during the time of their bondage under that latter-day Pharaoh, Antiochus himself. This great mercy shown at the Exodus was mirrored in other "righteous acts" through which he continued to make known his saving grace. It is against this background that Daniel now makes his supplication.

(2) *The God of wrath* (verses 16b–18a). God's judgment is an expression of his divine wrath. No attempt is made here to protest Israel's innocence or to plead extenuating circumstances. The people's sin and that of their forefathers is readily acknowledged. They can but throw themselves on the mercy of God and beseech him to turn aside his wrath. As a result of their plight they have become "a byword" among the nations round about. Taunting and mockery are difficult to bear—not least by the oriental mind. As their people had suffered jibes and scorn at the time of the Exile (cf. Ezek. 25:3,6,8; 35:10,12,13; Pss. 44:13; 79:4), so again in the time of Antiochus they were a target for the taunts of the Ammonites, Moabites and Edomites, their immediate neighbours (cf. 1 Maccabees 5:1–8).

Daniel prays that God's wrath will be turned away from Israel and names especially the city and the sanctuary. It is difficult to imagine the depths of feeling there must have been in the hearts of loyal Jews during the time of the Exile and again in the time of Antiochus for the city of Jerusalem. It stood on

God's "holy hill", the very centre of the earth (cf. Ps. 48:2). It was the city "called by thy name", literally "over which thy name has been called". Just as a conqueror would "call his name" over a conquered city to declare it now belonged to him, so Yahweh had claimed Jerusalem as his very own.

We pause to recollect that, in a sense, Jerusalem typifies every city both then and now, in the sense that God's name is called over it. The city—with its traffic and commerce, its offices and courts, its shops and business houses—belongs to him. The Church's prayer, like that of Daniel, is still that God's wrath might be turned aside from it, that it may be made more like that city whose builder and maker is God (cf. Heb. 11:10).

And as with the city so also with the sanctuary. It lies "desolate" (Hebrew, *shamem),* a word which recalls the "abomination of desolation" (cf. 8:13; 9:27; 11:11; 12:11) in the place of the sacred altar of God. Daniel prays that God will make his face to shine upon it after the manner of the Aaronic blessing (cf. Num. 6:25). The city and the sanctuary alike come under the judgment of God, the civic and the religious, the state and the Church. Both incur God's wrath and both must seek his mercy and forgiveness. The ministry of supplication becomes a ministry of intercession *for all men* and more especially for those who are of the household of faith (cf. Gal. 6:10).

(3) *The ground of hope* (verses 18b–19). The prayer now reaches a moving climax. Israel makes her plea not on the ground of her own righteousness, but on the ground of God's great mercy (cf. Deut. 7:7ff.; 9:4); not on the ground of "human rights", but on the ground of divine grace. The question of merit does not enter in at all. It is all of God's great grace.

> Not the labours of my hands
> Can fulfil thy law's demands;
> Could my zeal no respite know,
> Could my tears forever flow,
> All for sin could not atone:
> Thou must save, and thou alone.

> Nothing in my hand I bring,
> Simply to thy cross I cling;
> Naked, come to thee for dress;
> Helpless, look to thee for grace;
> Foul, I to the fountain fly;
> Wash me, Saviour, or I die.
>   (A. M. Toplady)

The final plea is not just for deliverance from captivity but for God's forgiveness. Three times over, in words that have been likened to the *Kyrie eleison* ("Lord, have mercy") of the Christian Church, it pleads that God in his mercy will hear, forgive and save. The sinful nation, like the sinner himself, is thrown back on the abundant mercy and the free grace of God.

ANSWER TO PRAYER

Daniel 9:20–23

> While I was speaking and praying, confessing my sin and the sin of my people Israel, and presenting my supplication before the Lord my God for the holy hill of my God; while I was speaking in prayer, the man Gabriel, whom I had seen in the vision at the first, came to me in swift flight at the time of the evening sacrifice. He came and he said to me, "O Daniel, I have now come out to give you wisdom and understanding. At the beginning of your supplications a word went forth, and I have come to tell it to you, for you are greatly beloved; therefore consider the word and understand the vision."

(i)

The prayer of confession and supplication being ended, the writer resumes the account given in verses 1–3. He tells how, whilst he is still praying, the angel Gabriel, who had already appeared to him in chapter 8 (cf. 8:15) in the form of a man, comes towards him "in swift flight". Elsewhere in the Old Testament other "heavenly beings" are represented in this way as winged creatures. We think, for example, of the seraphim in Isa. 6:2 or the cherubim depicted on the ark of the covenant (cf.

Exod. 25:18–20) or portrayed in Solomon's Temple (cf. 1 Kings 6:23–28) or the "four living creatures" in Ezek. 1:5f. These, however, are not "angels" in the sense that they are divine messengers with the appearance of a man. Here in Daniel, no doubt under the influence of such ancient imagery and the occurrence in Egyptian and Mesopotamian sculpture of winged demons, Gabriel is presented as an angel with wings. The same notion is developed in other literature of the period (cf. 1 Enoch 61:1; Rev. 14:6) and has influenced their portrayal in both art and literature ever since.

Gabriel tells Daniel that no sooner had he started to pray than "a word went forth", presumably from God himself. This is a divine oracle revealing to Daniel the meaning of Jeremiah's prophecy concerning the seventy years of "desolation". Gabriel is commissioned to convey the oracle to him and arrives "at the time of the evening sacrifice", i.e. at one of the set times for prayer. He has come to give him "understanding" of the prophecy which had so puzzled him and assures him that he is singled out to receive this special revelation because he is "greatly beloved" by God (cf. 10:11,19).

(ii)

There are several features about this account that would not escape the reader then and should not escape the reader now:

(a) *God is quick to answer prayer.* Gabriel assures him that just as soon as Daniel had started to pray, confessing his sins and the sins of his people, God had responded with his divine oracle, and that before he had finished, it was there ready to be revealed to him. Here, then, is a dramatised version of the same assurance given elsewhere in Scripture of the attentiveness of God to the prayer of his people and his eagerness to grant them their requests: "Before they call, I will answer; while they are yet speaking, I will hear" (Isa. 65:24); "Call to me and I will answer you, and will tell you great and hidden things which you have not known" (Jer. 33:3; cf. Job 13:22; 14:15; Ps. 91:15).

(b) *God gives spiritual insight.* Gabriel has come "to give you wisdom and understanding", literally, "to make you wise (in respect of) understanding", where "understanding" has the sense of "insight" into the hidden things of God. "One of the most important contributions of the book of Daniel", writes André Lacocque, "is its insistence on the linking of faith to understanding, by which is meant the comprehension of the 'mysteries' (or: signs, sacraments) of God's will in history. This is why the book of Daniel has so many points in common with Wisdom. In both cases it is a question of comprehending a message addressed to all men." It is the ability to interpret the hidden meaning behind the given fact, to discern the truth of God in the common event, to look at the temporal and see through it the eternal reality. In the case of Daniel it is the ability to know the inner meaning of Scripture as revealed in Jeremiah's prophecy concerning the seventy years.

(c) *Revelation comes as a word from God.* In response to Daniel's prayer of confession and repentance on behalf of his people Israel, God utters his word and Gabriel sets forth to make known the divine oracle disclosing the meaning of Jeremiah's prophecy (see verses 24–27). It contains a revelation concerning the end and gives the assurance that God will indeed deliver his people. It is no merely human interpretation which Daniel discovers for himself; it is a divine revelation which he receives from the mouth of God. Sometimes, as here, it comes through the reading of Scripture which is to the reader the very word of God himself, illumined by the Holy Spirit. In this light it takes on new proportions and uncovers the mysteries of God. So it was with the early Church which found in the ancient Scriptures things new as well as old. And so it continues to be for all who, like Daniel, seek its truth in faith and by prayer.

(d) *God makes known his ways to those who loved him.* The reason given here for God's revelation to Daniel is that he is a man "greatly beloved". By his faithfulness to the ways of his fathers, his loyalty to the commandments of God, his confession of sin and his repentance for past wrongdoings he has won the favour of God. In all this he is an example and an encouragement to the whole people of Israel to remain steadfast in their faith and to repent of their sins. They, too, despite their many lapses of faith and their proneness to sin, are still God's beloved people (cf. Isa. 43:4) to whom he will make known the mysteries of the end and the wonders of his kingdom.

BLESSINGS TO COME

Daniel 9:24

"Seventy weeks of years are decreed concerning your people and your holy city, to finish the transgression, to put an end to sin, and to atone for iniquity, to bring in everlasting righteousness, to seal both vision and prophet, and to anoint a most holy place."

(i)

Gabriel now reveals the hidden meaning of Jeremiah's seventy years at the close of which God will deliver his people (see comment on 9:1–2). What is meant is "seventy *weeks*" by which is plainly meant "seventy *weeks of years*", i.e. 490 years, the conclusion of which will usher in "the end". This idea of a week-year was familiar to the Greeks and Romans, but it has been suggested that the author of Daniel may have been influenced in his interpretation not by these sources but by such a passage as Lev. 26:18, where it is said that God will chastise his people "sevenfold" for their sins, thus indicating a period of exile seventy times seven years. Another relevant passage may have been 2 Chron. 37:21, which suggests that the seventy years' exile are to compensate for the seventy "sabbatical years" (i.e. every seventh year) which Israel had failed to observe, i.e. 490 years in all (cf. also Lev. 25:2; 26:33ff.). But whether he was influenced by such passages or not, he believed he had found corroboration in "the [sacred] books" (cf. 9:2) for his conviction that the promised end was indeed at hand.

The period has been "decreed"; it has been decided upon beforehand and determined by God; the allotted span of "exile" and "desolation", like "the end" itself, is within his control and will reach its close when he decrees. This is the essential message of this verse, not the arithmetical calculation of times and seasons.

(ii)

Before going on in the subsequent verses (25ff.) to analyse the allotted span of 490 years leading up to "the end", the author gives his readers a preview, as it were, of the blessings which that end will bring. He has in mind, no doubt, the deliverance of his people ("your people and your holy city") from the foreign oppression of Antiochus and the Seleucids, but the promised end is much more than this—it is the consummation of God's purpose for his people Israel and the beginning of a new era under his saving rule.

The blessings which are to accompany this great event are given as six-fold, in two groups of three. The one group we might entitle "cancellation" and the second "confirmation".

(a) *Cancellation.* Three times over it is stated that God will cancel ("finish", "put an end to", "atone for") the evil done ("the transgression", "sin", "iniquity"). The text of this particular verse is not at all certain and several shades of meaning can be read into the various expressions. But the general intention is plain enough. With the ending of Antiochus' rebellious rule, God will recognise an end to Israel's rebellion also. He will "finish the transgression" of Antiochus and Israel alike; he will "put an end" to sin (literally, "seal up sin") which will then have reached its "full measure" (cf. 8:23); he will "atone for (cancel, abolish) iniquity". God, as it were, will wipe the slate clean. The blessings to come will not be confined to deliverance from their enemies; they will bring too the end of sin and the cancellation of wrongs perpetrated against a holy and righteous God.

(b) *Confirmation.* God will then confirm his action by three positive steps corresponding in some ways to those three already mentioned:

He will "bring in everlasting righteousness". This new era which is soon to break in upon them will be an era of perpetual righteousness in several meanings of the word: it will be an era of *justice* in which there will be fair dealing and equal rights for all (cf. Ps. 7:8–11; Amos 5:24); it will be a time when God will effect his *salvation* (cf. Isa. 45:8,23; 41:13; 51:5f.) and bring victory to his people (cf. Zech. 9:9); it will be an age in which the *moral holiness* of God, which is so closely associated with his righteous dealings, will become a mark of this people too (cf. Lev. 20:7; 1 Pet. 1:16).

He will "seal both vision and prophet". The meaning seems to be that, just as the genuineness of a document is confirmed by the setting of a seal upon it (cf. 1 Kings 21:8; Jer. 32:10f.), so the messages of the prophets and the visions they have received will at last be confirmed and be shown to be true. Alternatively it may mean that the "vision and prophet" are "sealed up" in the sense that they have now come to an end, for with the coming of the promised time they are no longer needed.

He will "anoint a most holy place" (literally, "a holy of holies", with the meaning "most holy"). Apart from one doubtful instance in 1 Chron. 23:13, this expression is used in the Old Testament with reference to sacred places or objects and not persons. It was tempting later on for Christian (and some Jewish) writers to see in this anointing of a "most holy" an allusion to the Messiah, but there is no justification for such an interpretation in the text. The writer no doubt has in mind rather the sacred altar which Antiochus had polluted or else the Temple which he had desecrated. This "most holy place" would be "anointed", i.e. consecrated, anew to the worship and service of God. It is just possible that behind this reference there is an allusion to that "temple not made with hands", the people of God themselves (see comment on 8:9–12) who constitute a sanctuary made up of "living stones" (cf. 1 Pet. 2:5).

This pledge of deliverance, forgiveness and renewal, confirmed by ancient prophecy, was not for some far-distant age. The time of its fulfilment, for the author of Daniel and his contemporaries, was almost upon them. They had heeded the call to repent. The end was near. The kingdom was at the door.

THE FINAL COUNT-DOWN

Daniel 9:25–27

"Know therefore and understand that from the going forth of the

word to restore and build Jerusalem to the coming of an anointed
one, a prince, there shall be seven weeks. Then for sixty-two weeks it
shall be built again with squares and moat, but in a troubled time.
And after the sixty-two weeks, an anointed one shall be cut off, and
shall have nothing; and the people of the prince who is to come shall
destroy the city and the sanctuary. Its end shall come with a flood,
and to the end there shall be war; desolations are decreed. And he
shall make a strong covenant with many for one week; and for half
of the week he shall cause sacrifice and offering to cease; and upon
the wing of abominations shall come one who makes desolate, until
the decreed end is poured out on the desolator."

Gabriel now proceeds to spell out the meaning of the seventy
"week-years" leading up to "the end" when God will at last
bring about the deliverance of his people. It is the final "count-
down" which is almost complete, from 490 to zero. The critical
moment will not be long delayed. The same confident and eager
expectation is raised by subsequent apocalyptic writers. Here,
for example, is how the writer of 2 Baruch puts it: "The youth of
the world is past, and the strength of creation is already
exhausted, and the advent of the times is very short, yea, they
have passed by; and the pitcher is near to the cistern, and the
ship to the port, and the course of the journey to the city, and
life to consummation" (85:10).

It would be wrong to assume that the apocalyptic writers,
including the author of Daniel, had no concern for history as
such. Nevertheless they give the impression that they are more
concerned about the sequence of historical events than they are
about the events themselves and that history is of significance in
the light of the "end" event which is now almost upon them.

This impression is strengthened by the fact that they try to
work out history systematically in vast periods, carefully
tabulated. The schemes thus presented are many and varied,
calculated with mathematical precision. In these calculations
the number seven (or multiples of it) plays an important part—
there are seventy "generations" between the Flood and the
Final Judgment (cf. 1 Enoch 1:36); Israel's history from the

Exile onwards is ruled over by seventy angelic "shepherds" with reigns of differing lengths (cf. 1 Enoch 83:90); world history is to be calculated on the basis of multiples of a "jubilee" of forty-nine years (cf. Jubilees) or on the basis of "seven ages" of one thousand years apiece (cf. Testament of Abraham) and so on.

This systematising and schematising gives the further impression that history, thus presented, has been predetermined by God, that there is an inevitability about its course and, more especially, about its termination. The number and duration of the areas of time into which history is divided follow a pattern which cannot be broken even by the most powerful of empires or the most tyrannical of kings. The past is determined; so also is the future.

It has to be borne in mind, however, that the author of Daniel and the other apocalyptic writers came to this conclusion not by a process of philosophical reasoning, but by an act of faith. "Pre-destination" or "pre-determination" was not for them a philosophical or even theological concept. It was rather the end result of a deep conviction that God was in complete control of the affairs of men, that he knew the time of the end, now revealed to his faithful messengers, and that he knew equally well the times between and all the historical processes of humankind. It has to be remembered, too, that the writer himself invariably stands near the end of this long process so that, in the main, what he gives as prediction is in fact an account of what has already taken place. What we have, then, is no wooden theory of predestination in which everything is fixed and determined from the beginning but rather a double assertion of faith—that the whole of history is in God's control and that the end is very near.

The writer divides the period from the Exile onwards into three unequal periods of seven "weeks" (i.e. forty-nine years, presumably from 587 B.C. to 539 B.C.), sixty-two "weeks" (i.e. 434 years, ostensibly from 538 B.C. to 170 B.C.) and one "week" (i.e. seven years, from 170 B.C. to 164 B.C.) this last being divided into two half "weeks" (i.e. three-and-a-half years each, from 170 B.C. to 167 B.C. and from 167 B.C. to 164 B.C.).

(i)

The first of these periods, lasting forty-nine years, would seem
to be from the fall of Jerusalem in 587 B.C. to the conquest of
Babylon by Cyrus in 539 B.C. Some see in "an anointed one, a
prince" (verse 25), whose appearance marks the end of this
period and the beginning of a new, a reference to Cyrus himself
who is elsewhere described as the Lord's annointed (cf. Isa.
45:1); but a more likely figure is that of the High Priest Joshua
under whose leadership the Temple worship in Jerusalem was
re-established in 538 B.C. (cf. Ezra 2:2; Hag. 1:1ff.; Zech. 3:1).
The terms "anointed" and "prince" were used of the High Priest
among others in the post-exilic period. Such an identification
fits in with the fact that the writer is particularly interested in
the cult of the Temple and in the priesthood that officiated
there. The Christological interpretation of the word "anointed"
implied in the Authorised Version's use of the expression
"Messiah" has no justification. In the New Testament and later
Jewish writings it is used as a technical term, and written with a
capital "M", signifying the title of the future ideal king or the
eschatolocal figure associated with the coming kingdom. That
is not its use here or anywhere else in the Old Testament.

(ii)

The second period, lasting sixty-two "weeks", is initiated by the
arrival in Jerusalem of this "anointed one, a prince" and the
commencement of his programme of rebuilding the city and the
Temple. The text is not altogether clear or the meaning of some
of the words certain. But the sense seems to be that the city will
be rebuilt with its streets and open squares and with its moat-
like defences skirting the outer walls, i.e. it will function once
again as a city, with the people going about their normal
business. Nevertheless, this will be a "troubled time", as the
coming of "the end" will make all too clear.

The conclusion of this second period is also to be marked by
"an anointed one" who, in this instance, shall be "cut off".
Several identifications have been suggested, but the most likely
is the High Priest Onias III who was murdered in 170 B.C. (cf. 2

Maccabees 4:33ff.) at the instigation of his brother Jason who succeeded him in office. The meaning of the words translated "and shall have nothing" is not certain. They have been rendered variously to mean "there was nothing against him" or "he shall have no-one [to succeed him]" or "he shall cease to be" or "without trial" or "without a helper". The death of this "anointed one" indicates the end of an epoch in Israel's history, marking as it does the end of the high priestly line initiated after the exile by Joshua ben Jozadak.

This middle period from 539 B.C. to 170 B.C. indicates the passage of 368 years which is far short of the 434 years suggested by the sixty-two "weeks" in Gabriel's interpretation. This discrepancy is not altogether surprising when we bear in mind the dearth of historical evidence during this time. Starting with his assumption of 490 years, the writer was clear about the duration of the first period of forty-nine years between 587 B.C. and 539 B.C. which was well documented. He was confident too (such was his faith) about the duration of the third period. From the death of Onias III in 170 B.C. the end would come in seven more years. The second period in between must represent the remaining sixty-two times seven years. The fact that the calculation and the actual historical duration fail to match does not really matter. The end is decreed and the word of Scripture is fulfilled.

ONE WEEK TO GO

Daniel 9:25-27 *(cont'd)*

(iii)

The third and final period is to last one "week", i.e. one "week-year" or seven years.

(a) It is marked by the desecration of city and Temple at the hands of "the people of the prince who is to come", an allusion no doubt to Antiochus whose devastations are described in 1 Maccabees 1:31ff. and 3:45, with particular reference to the sacking of Jerusalem in 168 B.C. by his general Apollonius. "Its end" in verse 26 may refer to the city and the Temple or it may refer to "the end" as such. In either case devastation will come like a flood. Right up to the end there shall be war and desolations.

This theme of *war* is a familiar one in subsequent apocalyptic books and is to be found also in the New Testament as one of the marks or signs of "the end" and the "great tribulation" which will come before the consummation. In the book of Revelation, for example, we read of the pitched battle of Armageddon (cf. 16:16) when God will triumph over all the powers of evil. Among the Dead Sea Scrolls the same idea is illustrated in the document entitled "War of the Sons of Light against the Sons of Darkness", which describes in graphic military terms the final great battle between the forces of good and the forces of evil. But this is more than simply a military manual. It is a theological work which describes the tactics to be adopted not just against alien armies but also against "principalities and powers", for the enemy to be confronted consists of angels as well as men. This great final battle, beginning with earthly dimensions, takes on cosmic proportions. Evil, material and spiritual alike, is of one piece and has to be fought on both planes at one and the same time. The struggle against human tyranny here on earth is of one piece with the struggle against the powers of evil "in heavenly places" whose defeat hastens the coming of the end, the conquest of the hosts of evil, and the establishment of God's eternal kingdom.

(b) Throughout this last week Antiochus makes "a strong covenant with many". Most commentators take this as a reference to the Hellenising Jews (cf. 1 Maccabees 1:11ff.) who were regarded by the *Hasidim* and other faithful Jews as apostates and traitors to the covenant made with the God of Israel. There are always those who, by reason of expediency or for some other cause, are willing to exchange a divine covenant for a human.

(c) Half way through this final period, i.e. after three-and-a-half years, the author indicates the command of Antiochus forbidding "sacrifice and offering". We know from 1 Maccabees 1:54; and 4:52ff. that the daily offerings in the Temple were in fact suspended on 15 Chislev (December) 167 B.C. It is no doubt this event to which reference is made here.

But a much greater sacrilege was committed by his setting up an image of the god *Zeus Olympios,* and with it probably a cult-symbol or cult-image, on God's holy altar in the Temple (cf. 2 Maccabees 6:2). This was the *Baal Shamen* or "Lord of Heaven" worshipped among the pagans and whom the Hellenising Jews, it would seem, recognised as an expression of the God of Israel. Elsewhere in Daniel it is described as "the transgression that makes desolate" (8:13); cf. "the abomination of desolation" mentioned in Matt. 24:15 and Mark 13:14 (see comments on 2:14–23; 8:13–14). It is an abomination that horrifies because its very presence transforms the holy sanctuary into a heathen temple.

The expression "upon the wing of abominations" is not too clear. By a slight emendation the text could read "in its place shall be an abomination that appals", i.e. the altar of God is replaced by an altar and cult-symbol of a foreign god. But taking the text as it stands, it may refer to a wing of the Temple where the image is set up or, it has been suggested, to the wing of a monumental eagle representing *Baal Shamen.*

This last reference may hold a clue to the interpretation of this same phrase on the lips of Jesus when he spoke of "the abomination of desolation" as a sign of the end. It is commonly argued that this is a reference to the Antichrist, to be associated with "the man of sin" or "the lawless one" who will defile the Temple and whose coming will be a prelude to the end (cf. 2 Thess. 2:3f.). Others, however, see here a reference to the setting up in the Temple of the Roman standard bearing the image of an eagle which, on more than one occasion, caused a great furore among the citizens of Jerusalem. As objects of worship these eagle standards were an abhorrence to the Jews, as Pilate discovered for example, when, ten years or so before the utterance of these words by Jesus, he introduced eagle-ensigns into the city (Josephus, *Antiquities).* E. Stauffer narrates the account of a Christian soldier named Dasius in the time of the

Emperor Diocletian who, on refusing to bow down before the sacred ensigns was sentenced to death. Some of his friends tried to persuade him to offer incense. But "the blessed Dasius seized the vessel and scattered the incense to the winds, trampled on the shameful and sacrilegious images of the blasphemous emperors, and made the battle sign of the adorable cross of Christ on his brow, through whose power he stood firm against the tyrants."

To Jew and Christian alike, any image set up in the place of God is "an abomination that appals", be it in the form of an idol, a man, an ideology, a state or whatsoever. He and he alone is worthy of adoration, worship and praise (cf. Exod. 20:3).

(d) This state of affairs will continue for another three-and-a-half years, at the close of which disaster will overwhelm "the desolator", Antiochus (cf. 11:44f.). The writer had witnessed the terrible events of 167 B.C., the desecration of the Temple and its altar. These words were penned, it would seem, before the death of Antiochus and before the reconsecration of the Temple and the renewal of the daily offerings on 25 Chislev (December) 164 B.C., three years after its desecration. These words, then, are a genuine prediction. But their importance lies not so much in the writer's ability to foretell the future as in his affirmation of faith that the God in whom he trusted would not let his people down but would, at his own appointed time and in his own appointed way, bring about their deliverance. The fact that that deliverance did not match his expectations and that "the end" did not come with the demise of Antiochus, did not deter the author or those who in subsequent years were to read his book. Their faith was fixed, as ours must be, not on calculations or prognostications, but on the utter trustworthiness of the living and saving God.

ANOTHER VISION

Daniel 10:1-9

In the third year of Cyrus king of Persia a word was revealed to

Daniel, who was named Belteshazzar. And the word was true, and it was a great conflict. And he understood the word and had understanding of the vision.

In those days I, Daniel, was mourning for three weeks. I ate no delicacies, no meat or wine entered my mouth, nor did I anoint myself at all, for the full three weeks. On the twenty-fourth day of the first month, as I was standing on the bank of the great river, that is, the Tigris, I lifted up my eyes and looked, and behold, a man clothed in linen, whose loins were girded with gold of Uphaz. His body was like beryl, his face like the appearance of lightning, his eyes like flaming torches, his arms and legs like the gleam of burnished bronze, and the sound of his words like the noise of a multitude. And I, Daniel, alone saw the vision, for the men who were with me did not see the vision, but a great trembling fell upon them, and they fled to hide themselves. So I was left alone and saw this great vision, and no strength was left in me; my radiant appearance was fearfully changed, and I retained no strength. Then I heard the sound of his words; and when I heard the sound of his words, I fell on my face in a deep sleep with my face to the ground.

We come now to the final vision which, like those in previous chapters, concerns the last days and the momentous events leading up to them. Its description covers the last three chapters which should be read straight through, chapter 10 forming a prologue, chapter 11 giving the vision proper and its interpretation, and chapter 12 providing an epilogue.

(i)

The preparation (verses 1–3). In "the third year of Cyrus" (the date is of little significance) "a word" was revealed to Daniel—a divine oracle (cf. 9:23) to which he paid heed (better than "understood"). This "word" was "true" in the sense that the contents of the oracle were trustworthy and immovable. It was also (literally) "a great host", the reference being to the "great conflict" between the angelic hosts alluded to later in the chapter or, perhaps more likely, to the great conflict within himself brought about by his experience.

It is significant that in the Old Testament the Hebrew word for "oracle" may sometimes be translated "burden". When God speaks to his servants there is laid upon them a heavy obligation both to understand what the oracle means and to put it into effect. It is no light thing to receive God's "word" (cf. Jer. 20:9). Often it causes great anguish of heart, a wrestling of spirit that will not be stilled till the matter is resolved. "Conflict" is not too strong a word to describe the experience, as anyone who has faced up to it clearly knows.

Having received the divine "word", Daniel now wants to know its meaning and significance. For this he requires a divine revelation and begins to prepare himself for it. In the apocalyptic books generally several kinds of preparation are described. It may involve the partaking of a prescribed diet (cf. 2 Esdras 9:23ff.; 2 Baruch 29:5,8, etc.) or a special drink (cf. 2 Esdras 14:38ff.). At other times it may take the form of "fasting" which is implied here in the word "mourning". The three weeks' fast of this chapter finds an interesting parallel in 2 Esdras 6:35, the fast in each case being followed immediately by an important revelation. Physical preparedness and spiritual receptiveness, as we have already seen (comment on 9:3–19), are closely related. Jesus' teaching and the testimony of his own life make it clear that fasting is a token of obedience and an ally of prayer (cf. Mark 9:29, margin).

(ii)

The angel-vision (verses 4–9). It was the twenty-fourth day of the first month which was the month of Passover and Unleavened Bread (cf. Exod. 12:1ff). Daniel found himself on the bank of the river Tigris when suddenly he was confronted by a dazzling figure having the appearance of "a man". The vision is reminiscent of that described in Ezek. 1. The figure was that of an angel, to be identified here perhaps with Gabriel who is named later on in the chapter. His appearance was like lightning and shone like burnished metals and precious stones.

The effect of this resplendent figure on Daniel was such that his strength departed, the colour left his cheeks and he fell to the ground in a trance-like sleep. His companions, unlike Daniel, did not see the vision as he saw it, but they were deeply aware of the awesome presence and fled in fear and trembling. We are reminded of the account of Saul's conversion on his way to Damascus as recorded in Acts 9 and 22. His companions also failed to see what he saw, but were profoundly aware that something extraordinary had taken place. Like Saul, too, Daniel heard a voice; but unlike him he could not distinguish what it said, for the angel's voice was "the noise of a deep roaring".

Older Christian commentators saw in this dazzling figure the glorious Messiah whom they recognised as Jesus their Lord. They found substantiation for this in a very similar description of "one like a son of man" in Rev. 1:13ff., the resplendent figure of the risen and glorified Christ before whom John falls down as though dead (see comment on 8:15–19). Even during his earthly ministry, as we have seen, Jesus' followers were deeply conscious of that *numinous* quality about him (cf. Luke 5:8), that "otherness" which made him stand out from others as light from darkness (cf. John 1:7ff.). His "glorification" on the Mount of Transfiguration (cf. Matt. 17:2; Mark 9:2) was but a glimpse of that greater glory that belonged to him by nature and would one day be revealed, reflecting the glory of God himself (cf. Heb. 1:3). Into that same likeness his people would at last be changed "from one degree of glory to another" (2 Cor. 3:18).

A MINISTERING ANGEL

Daniel 10:10–11:1

> And behold, a hand touched me and set me trembling on my hands and knees. And he said to me, "O Daniel, man greatly beloved, give heed to the words that I speak to you, and stand upright, for now I have been sent to you." While he was speaking this word to me, I stood up trembling. Then he said to me, "Fear not, Daniel, for from the first day that you set your mind to understand and humbled yourself before your God, your words have been heard, and I have come because of your words. The prince of the kingdom of Persia withstood me twenty-one days; but Michael, one of the chief princes, came to help me, so I left him there with the prince of the

kingdom of Persia and came to make you understand what is to befall your people in the latter days. For the vision is for days yet to come."

When he had spoken to me according to these words, I turned my face toward the ground and was dumb. And behold, one in the likeness of the sons of men touched my lips: then I opened my mouth and spoke. I said to him who stood before me, "O my lord, by reason of the vision pains have come upon me, and I retain no strength. How can my lord's servant talk with my lord? For now no strength remains in me, and no breath is left in me."

Again one having the appearance of a man touched me and strengthened me. And he said, "O man greatly beloved, fear not, peace be with you; be strong and of good courage." And when he spoke to me, I was strengthened and said, "Let my lord speak, for you have strengthened me." Then he said, "Do you know why I have come to you? But now I will return to fight against the prince of Persia; and when I am through with him, lo, the prince of Greece will come. But I will tell you what is inscribed in the book of truth: there is none who contends by my side against these except Michael, your prince. And as for me, in the first year of Darius the Mede, I stood up to confirm and strengthen him."

Here, as elsewhere in the book, Daniel is confronted with the supernatural and the superhuman. It is for him an awe-inspiring experience. He trembles with fear before the majesty and the mystery of the heavenly angels. But in the end he realises that they reflect the majesty and the mystery of God who is on the side of Israel (see next comment) and whose representative he himself is.

(i)

Three times over in these verses we are told that the angel "touched" Daniel, reviving his flagging strength and restoring his faculties.

In the *first* occurrence, a mysterious hand picks him up from the ground where, as we have seen, he had fallen in a trance-like sleep and sets him trembling on his hands and knees. But this animal-like posture will not do for one who is "greatly beloved", and so he is bidden to "stand upright", to assume the stance and the dignity of a human being. His trembling is quite unnecessary. He has nothing to fear. On the contrary, he has good cause to be assured, for no sooner had he humbled himself before God in his act of fasting and self-mortification than his words were heard and the angel was sent to him. Here, then, we have the same assurance as that given in chapter 9: God is quick to answer prayer and to come to the help of those who truly seek him.

In the *second* occurrence the cause of Daniel's perturbation is not an apparition as in the first instance, but the words spoken by the angel. The angel has come to explain what will happen to his people "in the latter days". "For the vision is for days yet to come." Daniel is about to receive the vision referred to by the prophet Habakkuk (cf. 2:2f.) which will "surely come" and which will both disclose and inaugurate "the end". No wonder he is overcome with wonder and amazement. His head droops and he loses his power of speech (cf. Exod. 3:26; 24:27). But once again an angel, having "the likeness of the sons of men", touches his lips and his speech returns. Just as Isaiah's lips are cleansed by the touch of God (cf. Isa. 6:7) and Jeremiah's mouth is empowered in like manner to speak the prophetic message (cf. Jer. 1:9), so here Daniel's lips are enabled to respond to God's own word.

In the *third* occurrence he confesses that the vision has left him weak and lifeless and he writhes in pain like a woman in childbirth (this is the force of "pains have come upon me"). He acknowledges his frailty, for who is he to talk with such exalted company! And so once more the angel touches him, giving him renewed strength. Again he is bidden to have no fear. He is then addressed in language familiar in biblical times as greetings conveyed by one friend to another in the writing of letters. The opening salutation "Peace", is followed by the concluding farewell, "Be strong and of good courage". The angel is his friend. There is no reason to be afraid of either the majestic or the mysterious. Daniel is in very truth beloved by God.

(ii)

The use of these words reminds us forcibly of one who was "much superior to angels" (Heb. 1:4) who again and again bade his fearful disciples not to be afraid (cf. Matt. 10:26,28; 28:5, etc.) and gave them his blessing of peace (cf. Luke 24:36; John 20:19,21,26, etc.). They remind us too that in the ministry of Jesus the language of touch was every bit as expressive and effective as the language of words. He laid his hands gently on this one and that and offered prayer (cf. Matt. 19:13); his touch alone brought blessing as in the case of the little children who were brought to him—taking them in his arms he blessed them, "laying his hands upon them" (Mark 10:16). By this means he identified himself not only with the weak and helpless but also with the sick and oppressed. Thus, he took Jairus' daughter by the hand and restored her (cf. Matt. 9:25; Mark 5:41; Luke 8:54); stretching out his hand he healed many who were ill (cf. Mark 6:5; Luke 4:40; 13:13) and restored the powers of hearing and speech (cf. Mark 7:32; 8:23); with a touch of the fingers he gave back sight to the blind (cf. Matt. 9:29; 20:34) and lepers were cleansed (cf. Mark 1:41).

As then, so now, the touch of love and understanding brings life and healing to those who receive it. To the mourner it brings comfort; to the discouraged it brings hope; to the weak it brings strength. In the very act something powerful is both given and received, something of infinite worth.

MICHAEL TO THE RESCUE

Daniel 10:10–11:1 (*cont'd*)

(i)

These verses, containing reference to the ministering angel, introduce the reader to a very strange account of conflict in heaven among the "princes" of the heavenly host (cf. 8·11) whom God has set over the nations of the earth. The angel explains that, although he had been sent in response to Daniel's prayer and fasting, he was delayed for twenty-one days by "the prince of the kingdom of Persia" who had withstood him. This "prince" is the patron angel of Persia who presumably resented the ministering angel's mission and the revelation he brought concerning the vindication of Israel. Fortunately the (arch)angel Michael, one of the "chief princes", appeared on the scene and contended with the patron angel of Persia, making it possible for the ministering angel to continue his journey. As soon as his mission is over and his revelation made known to Daniel, he will return to take up the struggle against "the prince of Persia", and when he is through with him, in like manner he will deal with "the prince of Greece". That having been done, he will make known to Daniel "what is inscribed in the book of truth" which contains those "future" events recorded in ch. 11 leading up to the end in which the defeat of Persia and Greece are clearly "foretold". Small wonder the patron angels of these two nations opposed the bearer of such dire news. But they will have no chance against the ministering angel who will have by his side the patron angel of Israel, none other than Michael himself.

(It is possible that the first verse of ch. 11, which is very difficult as it stands, should be attached to the end of ch. 10 and perhaps reads as follows: ". . . and as for me [i.e. the ministering angel], since the first year of Darius the Mede, I have been standing by to reinforce and strengthen him" (translation suggested by H. L. Ginsberg).)

(ii)

Behind this brief reference lies a wealth of angel-lore which must have been quite familiar to the original readers of this book. The belief was widespread that God had set guardian angels over the nations, forming as it were a heavenly counterpart of the Gentile rulers into whose power he had delivered his people Israel. Wars fought out among the nations on earth had their parallel in wars fought out among the guardian angels in heaven together with their celestial retinues. When a particular guardian angel gained the ascendancy over his fellow-angels, the nation over which he had been appointed gained the ascendancy over its neighbours. Like the nations and their earthly rulers, these guardian angels hold sway only by the permissive will of God; they are answerable to him for the use they make of their authority and will be judged and punished for any abuse of it. Likewise they and the nations over which they are set will come under the same judgment of God. Thus the key to earthly history is to be found in heavenly event. The meaning of history is to be found beyond history and above history in the realm of spiritual being.

This same idea of guardian angels of the nations is to be found also in the book of Jubilees (cf. 15:31f.), 1 Enoch (cf. 89:59ff.), the Testament of Naphtali (cf. 8:4–6) and the Dead Sea Scrolls (cf. War Scroll, col. I). Behind the notion lies Deut. 32:8f. which tells how, "when the Most High gave to the nations their inheritance...he set the bounds of the people according to the number of the children of Israel (or, in the Greek text, 'the sons of God'). For the Lord's portion is his people; Jacob is the lot of his inheritance". The Greek rendering implies that all the nations of the earth are given over into the control of angelic powers, but Israel is reserved for God alone.

(iii)

This brings us to "Michael, your prince" who is the guardian angel of Israel, the people of God. This is the earliest recorded reference to Michael by name. He appears as an archangel in 1 Enoch 9:1; 20:5; 71:9 and in the War Scroll, col. XIV, as a leader against "the sons of darkness" as well as in later apocalyptic books and in rabbinic literature. Two specific references are made to him by name in the New Testament. One is in Jude 9 which alludes to a dispute between Michael and the devil over the body of Moses, a story which seems to have originated in the pseudepigraphic Assumption of Moses and is referred to in later rabbinic writings. The second is in Rev. 12:7 where he, together with his angel-host, wages war on the dragon who represents the devil. This story is graphically repeated in

Epstein's magnificent statue on the face of Coventry Cathedral where Michael stands with drawn sword ready to deal the death-blow to the great Adversary himself.

(iv)

The relevance of such a passage as this may seem at first sight none too obvious, and yet behind the imagery and angel-lore there was a powerful message for the reader of the second century B.C. which is not altogether without meaning for the reader of the twentieth century A.D.

(a) It confirms, for example, what the Old Testament as a whole makes abundantly clear, that nations and peoples, and not just individuals, are God's concern. But the book of Daniel and subsequent apocalyptic books go further and say that the nations and their earthly rulers are in the power of forces beyond themselves which are often antagonistic to the people of God and threaten to subvert even the purpose of God himself. However we may attempt to define these "forces", the truth remains that nations, like individuals and institutions, develop "personalities" of their own which can be, and frequently are, at war with the divine will.

(b) It asserts that God will defend his people, however helpless and vulnerable they may appear to be. The weak and helpless Daniel, representing the small and insignificant people of Israel, is sharply contrasted with the mighty angelic princes of Persia and Greece. But the really important thing is that God's messenger Michael is on his side to protect and save him. This, of course, is a matter of faith and not of sight; for Daniel is never introduced to Michael; he does not even see him. He has to accept in faith the assurance that he is there doing battle on his account. We are reminded of the story of Elisha's servant whose eyes were opened "and he saw, and behold, the mountain was full of horses and chariots of fire round about Elisha" (2 Kings 6:17). It is in this spirit that the oppressed can sing, "We shall overcome...at last". And it is in this spirit that Christ's own people can say "Amen, come, Lord Jesus" (Rev. 22:20).

(c) It declares that the battle being fought by God's people is already won. Gabriel is so confident of victory that he can quite readily leave Michael to cope with the matter. He himself will return later and deal with his opponent and after that with the prince of Greece. The mighty powers they represent, in the shape of great empires with great armies, do not daunt him one bit. He takes time off from the fray, as it were, to assure Daniel and all God's people that all will be well at the end of the days and that that end is coming soon. Once again we are reminded of one greater than Michael who, by his resurrection from the dead, was able to assure God's people that, through him, they were already "more than conquerors": "For I am sure, that neither death, nor life, nor angels, nor principalities, nor things present, nor things to come, nor powers, nor height, nor depth, nor anything else in all creation, will be able to separate us from the love of God in Christ Jesus our Lord" (Rom. 8:38f.). Through him and the power of his resurrection they too will overcome.

HISTORY IN ONE LESSON

Daniel 11:2–20

"And now I will show you the truth. Behold, three more kings shall arise in Persia; and a fourth shall be far richer than all of them; and when he has become strong through his riches, he shall stir up all against the kingdom of Greece. Then a mighty king shall arise, who shall rule with great dominion and do according to his will. And when he has arisen, his kingdom shall be broken and divided toward the four winds of heaven, but not to his posterity, nor according to the dominion with which he ruled; for his kingdom shall be plucked up and go to others besides these."

"Then the king of the south shall be strong, but one of his princes shall be stronger than he and his dominion shall be a great dominion. After some years they shall make an alliance, and the daughter of the king of the south shall come to the king of the north to make peace; but she shall not retain the strength of her arm, and he and his offspring shall not endure; but she shall be given up, and her attendants, her child, and he who got possession of her.

"In those times a branch from her roots shall arise in his place; he shall come against the army and enter the fortress of the king of the north, and he shall deal with them and shall prevail. He shall also carry off to Egypt their gods with their molten images and with their precious vessels of silver and of gold; and for some years he shall refrain from attacking the king of the north. Then the latter shall come into the realm of the king of the south but shall return into his own land.

"His sons shall wage war and assemble a multitude of great forces, which shall come on and overflow and pass through, and again shall carry the war as far as his fortress. Then the king of the south, moved with anger, shall come out and fight with the king of the north; and he shall raise a great multitude, but it shall be given into his hand. And when the multitude is taken, his heart shall be exalted, and he shall cast down tens of thousands, but he shall not prevail. For the king of the north shall again raise a multitude, greater than the former; and after some years he shall come on with a great army and abundant supplies.

"In those times many shall rise against the king of the south; and the men of violence among your own people shall lift themselves up in order to fulfil the vision; but they shall fail. Then the king of the north shall come and throw up siegeworks, and take a well-fortified city. And the forces of the south shall not stand, or even his picked troops, for there shall be no strength to stand. But he who comes against him shall do according to his own will, and none shall stand before him; and he shall stand in the glorious land, and all of it shall be in his power. He shall set his face to come with the strength of his whole kingdom, and he shall bring terms of peace and perform them. He shall give him the daughter of women to destroy the kingdom; but it shall not stand or be to his advantage. Afterward he shall turn his face to the coastlands, and shall take many of them; but a commander shall put an end to his insolence; indeed he shall turn his insolence back upon him. Then he shall turn his face back toward the fortress of his own land; but he shall stumble and fall, and shall not be found.

"Then shall arise in his place one who shall send an exactor of tribute through the glory of the kingdom; but within a few days he shall be broken, neither in anger nor in battle."

(i)

At last the moment comes for the angel to disclose to Daniel the "word" referred to in 10:1. It consists of a "potted" history from Cyrus to Antiochus Epiphanes in one easy lesson. The "revelation" makes dull reading, but for Daniel it declares with absolute certainty that, despite all indications to the contrary, God is in control of the affairs of men and will deliver his people from the hands of their oppressors. The "end" is at hand when God's age-long purpose for his people will be made plain.

The message is the same as that of previous chapters, except that here it is told without the help of imagery or symbol. The assurance is given in plain unvarnished historical fact. No names are mentioned, but the various figures are easily recognisable as they strut across the stage. One after another they stand in the public gaze, with the spotlight on them, relishing the plaudits of the crowd for a few short years, each to be succeeded by another... and another...and another. Power, wealth and success are brilliant, dazzling and impressive but, like "sparklers" in the hand of a child, they fizzle out and go dead leaving nothing behind. So it is with the greatness and splendour of powerful kings and mighty empires. God in his wisdom allows them to hold the stage for a brief moment and to glory in their greatness. But the final act belongs to him and to his people Israel who in the end will receive the kingdom.

(ii)

Much of the story told here is history in the guise of prediction, from the beginning of the Persian period right down to the time of Antiochus Epiphanes and the writer of our book (verses 2–39). From verse 40 onwards, as we shall see, history gives way to prediction proper when verifiable fact is difficult to define.

The might of Cyrus the Persian (verse 2) and the earth-shaking achievements of Alexander the Great (verses 3–4) are given scant recognition. Their achievements are described in a single verse apiece—as if to say that God's interpretation of greatness is altogether different from man's. Alexander's kingdom is broken up and divided among others (verse 4). Ptolemy I ("the king of the south") and Seleucus I ("one of his friends") win control (verse 5). In the course of time their two houses form an alliance through the marriage of Ptolemy II's daughter Berenice to Antiochus II, whose divorced wife Laodice wreaks vengeance on Berenice and her child (verse 6). Berenice's brother Ptolemy III ("a branch from her roots") attacks and plunders the stronghold and the temples of the Seleucids (verses 7–8) and fends off their counter-attacks (verse 9). Antiochus III (to be called "the Great"), after an early defeat by Ptolemy IV at Raphia (verses 10–12), again musters his forces (verse 13), winning the support of certain malcontents among whom are Jewish insurgents ("men of violence among your own people") (verse 14) and finally gaining control of Palestine ("the glorious land") (verses 15–16). The marriage of his daughter Cleopatra ("the daughter of women") to Ptolemy V wins no advantage (verse 17), and in the end he is utterly humiliated by the Roman "commander" Scipio at Magnesia in 190 B.C. before being compelled to return to "his own land" (verses 18–19). Reference is then made to Antiochus III's son and successor Seleucus IV and his general Heliodorus ("an exactor of tribute") (verse 20), and finally to the villain of the piece, Antiochus III's other son, Antiochus IV, Epiphanes himself, about whom more will be said in the succeeding verses.

(iii)

There is no arrogance on the part of the writer in this panorama of historical events; only a tranquil faith that "in everything God works for good" (Rom. 8:28). It is one of the greatest contributions of the Old Testament tradition that God was seen to be at work in the great movements of history as well as in the life of his own people Israel and that the people of God would at last prevail. This did not mean that Israel would be spared suffering and deprivation. On the contrary, it was precisely through suffering that she would attain her goal. Exile and exodus are closely related in the providence of God. They are the concave and convex sides of the same divine activity. In both of them the hand of God is to be seen, keeping a firm grip on the course of events, never allowing them to run out of control but making them in the end serve his divine purpose.

This same sublime faith was taken over by the Christian Church and is amply illustrated in the New Testament, supremely in the life and witness of our Lord. For him suffering and death were not a denial of God's loving care but a confirmation that in and through them his righteous will would prevail. God was still in control. This is demonstrated dramatically in Jesus' confrontation with Pilate, representing the might and power of Rome. "Do you not know", says Pilate, "that I have power to release you, and power to crucify you?" Jesus' reply sums up the faith of Daniel and the faithful of every generation: "You would have no power over me unless it had been given you from above" (John 19:10f.). Let rulers and governments be warned! Let dictators and tyrants beware! Man proposes, but God disposes.

ANTIOCHUS: THAT MAN AGAIN

Daniel 11: 21–35

"In his place shall arise a contemptible person to whom royal majesty has not been given; he shall come in without warning and obtain the kingdom by flatteries. Armies shall be utterly swept away before him and broken, and the prince of the covenant also. And from the time that an alliance is made with him he shall act deceitfully; and he shall become strong with a small people. Without warning he shall come into the richest parts of the province; and he shall do what neither his fathers nor his fathers' fathers have done, scattering among them plunder, spoil, and goods. He shall devise plans against strongholds, but only for a time. And he shall stir up his power and his courage against the king of the south with a great army; and the king of the south shall wage war with an exceedingly great and mighty army; but he shall not stand, for plots shall be devised against him. Even those who eat his rich food shall be his undoing; his army shall be swept away, and many shall fall down slain. And as for the two kings, their minds shall be bent on mischief; they shall speak lies at the same table, but to no avail; for the end is yet to be at the time appointed. And he shall return to his land with great substance, but his heart shall be set against the holy covenant. And he shall work his will, and return to his own land.

"At the time appointed he shall return and come into the south; but it shall not be this time as it was before. For ships of Kittim shall come against him, and he shall be afraid and withdraw, and shall turn back and be enraged and take action against the holy covenant. He shall turn back and give heed to those who forsake the holy covenant. Forces from him shall appear and profane the temple and fortress, and shall take away the continual burnt offering. And they shall set up the abomination that makes desolate. He shall seduce with flattery those who violate the covenant; but the people who know their God shall stand firm and take action. And those among the people who are wise shall make many understand, though they shall fall by sword and flame, by captivity and plunder, for some days. When they fall, they shall receive a little help. And many shall join themselves to them with flattery; and some of those who are wise shall fall, to refine and to cleanse them and to make them white, until the time of the end, for it is yet for the time appointed."

The writer now comes to a figure all too familiar to his readers. Already in 8:20-25, in the vision of the ram and the he-goat, he has described him in graphic terms. Now he gives an even more graphic account, declaring with utter confidence that his end is at hand. His name is not mentioned, but his readers will recognise him at once as the tyrant Antiochus Epiphanes himself.

(i)

His exploits. He is described as "a contemptible person" who obtained his power "by flatteries" (verse 21)—a not uncommon means of attaining a position of authority, be it in politics or business or whatever. Having "swept away" as by a flood all opposition including the "prince of the covenant" (a reference no doubt to the High Priest Onias III), he continues his deceitful wiles (verses 22-23). Pretending to be on a peaceful errand he pillages and robs, doling out freely the plunder he has obtained (verse 24). So confident is he that he forecasts what he will do next (verse 25). In 169 B.C. he advances into Egypt on the pretext of supporting his nephew, Ptolemy Philometor, feigning friendship but speaking lies; but all "to no avail". Nothing he can do will frustrate "the time appointed" (verses 26–27). Hearing of disturbances in Jerusalem he diagnoses the trouble as the religion of the Jews ("the holy covenant") against which he "set his heart". We know that he slaughtered many of the people there and plundered the Temple, returning to his own country a wealthy man (verse 28). A few months later he embarks on a second campaign against Egypt, but this time he is forced to turn back by the Romans ("ships of Kittim"; there is a similar reference in the Dead Sea Scrolls) (verses 29–30).

The picture is a fairly familiar one and describes equally well the despot, be he individual or collective, of this or any other age. From obscure beginnings he rises to prominence, stepping on the bodies of those who would challege his claims. With smooth-tongued flattery he curries favour. With two-faced deceit he wins his way to a position of authority. With complete disregard for lesser mortals he liquidates those who stand in his way. With unerring instinct for power, he amasses wealth by robbery and pillage. With gifts and bribes he buys "friends". With supreme confidence in his own ability he lashes out against his adversaries, using any convenient pretext to gain his ends. And, as so often happens, with complete indifference to their pleas he attacks the religion of his critics as subversive to his rule.

(ii)

His persecution. Antiochus now sets his mind to wipe out the Jewish religion altogether (verse 30). He profanes the Temple; he sets up there an altar and cult-symbol of Zeus, "the abomination that makes desolate" (see comments on 8:13–14; 9:25–27, *cont'd*), and takes away "the continual burnt offering" (verse 31). Some of the Jews give in under pressure; others who are described as "those among the people who are wise" hold their ground despite attacks on their persons and property and the threat of exile from home and country (verses 32–33). They receive assistance—an allusion no doubt to the beginnings of the so-called Maccabean Revolt under Mattathias and his son

Judas—but this is only "a little help", the implication being that their real help lies in God (verse 34). There are "flatterers" among them, but the loyalty of the "wise" is not in doubt. Some of them will fall by the sword, but by their suffering and death they will "refine" and "cleanse" the whole nation in expectation of the appointed time of the end (verse 35).

(a) This graphic account of the harassment and persecution of "the faithful" has a strong modern ring about it. Religion— more especially that of Judaism and Christianity—is an irresistible target for the power-thirsty despot or the totalitarian state, be it of the left or of the right. Statutes are enacted bringing "the cult" under control; churches and altars are destroyed; Bibles are confiscated; teaching is restricted; witness is circumscribed; congregations are "registered"; religious activities are vetted; breach of regulations is punishable by imprisonment or banishment or both. Religion is seen as a threat to the security of all such governments; it is subversive to all totalitarian claims which deny the authority or even the very existence of God. It has to be dealt with summarily. Flatteries, blandishments and concessions are offered, but they are the velvet glove over the iron fist.

(b) Allusion to the Maccabean Revolt raises the sore question of the use of force to maintain or to win freedom—for one's own people or for others. There is no easy answer, especially if it comes from those not themselves involved in the conflict. There are evils which cry out for remedy but which remain as entrenched as ever despite every peaceful attempt to change the circumstances. Resort to force in defence of human liberties and human rights raises ethical problems and questions of conscience over which Christians in our own day continue to agonise and on which "the faithful" are divided.

The author of Daniel does not condemn such a means being used to achieve the goal of freedom. On the other hand he does not seem to lay much store by it. To him it is only "a little help". His people should not be blind to the fact that theirs is essentially a spiritual battle and that their trust should be placed not in sword and spear but in the righteousness and power of

God. He is the one who will bring their conflict to an end in his "appointed time".

(c) Some of the "wise", we are told, were killed by the sword for the stand they took against the oppressor. But their death was not without avail. Their martyrdom, for such it was, was a propitiation and a purification, refining the people as metals are refined by fire and cleansing them like a piece of cloth that has been bleached white (cf. Rev. 3:18).

The language used here is strongly reminiscent of the Servant Songs in Isaiah (cf. Isa. 52:13; 53:11), as is the idea of vicarious sacrifice (cf. Isa. 53:3ff.). Through the death of the "wise", the "many" (the whole nation) are cleansed. The Qumran Covenanters saw in themselves a fulfilment of the same ministry exemplified in the Suffering Servant and in the "wise" of Daniel. They believed that by submission and suffering they would make atonement for the sins of the people and turn them to righteousness (cf. Isa. 43:1).

But there was another, greater than they, who saw in himself and in his messianic ministry a true fulfilment of Isaiah's Servant and Daniel's martyrs. Jesus on the cross voluntarily gave up his life as an "atonement" for the sin of the whole people (cf. Rom. 5:11). Through the shedding of his blood he became a "propitiation" for the sins of the whole world (cf. Rom. 3:25; 1 John 2:2; 4:10).

THE ARROGANCE OF ANTIOCHUS

Daniel 11:36–39

"And the king shall do according to his will; he shall exalt himself and magnify himself above every god, and shall speak astonishing things against the God of gods. He shall prosper till the indignation is accomplished; for what is determined shall be done. He shall give no heed to the gods of his fathers, or to the one beloved by women; he shall not give heed to any other god, for he shall magnify himself above all. He shall honour the god of fortresses instead of these; a god whom his fathers did not know he shall honour with gold and silver, with precious stones and costly gifts. He shall deal with the strongest fortresses by the help of a foreign god; those who acknowledge him he shall magnify with honour. He shall make them rulers over many and shall divide the land for a price."

To the pagan writers who recorded the life and deeds of Antiochus he was a supremely zealous king with a reputation for building temples in honour of many gods and lavishing gifts on them. But to the writer of Daniel the thing that stands out above all others is the sheer arrogance of the man and his blasphemy against the God of Israel.

He was a practical man of affairs with whom politics took precedence over religion, should the circumstances require:

(a) At all costs he must strengthen and unify his kingdom, and local and provincial deities must go. They were divisive elements and so carried too big a risk.

Antiochus, of course, has not been the last conqueror to ride roughshod over the sensitivities, the culture and the convictions of the vanquished in the interests of "the security of the state" or "the unity of the nation". However sacred their traditions may be and however revered their "gods", they must be sacrificed to the total demands of monolithic rule.

(b) But when it suited his purpose Antiochus was ready to give recognition to this god or that. A case in point was the Roman god *Jupiter Capitolinus* ("the god of the fortresses"), now combined with *Zeus Olympios,* for whom he built a temple in Antioch and on whom he lavished "costly gifts". Moreover, with the people of a foreign god he manned the fortresses in Jerusalem and in Judea (this seems to be the meaning of verse 39) and showed them favours.

This same "god of the fortresses" continues to receive high honours today and to be the recipient of many costly gifts from devoted worshippers. As god of war, the offerings he demands are of a most sophisticated kind whose price is measured not only in terms of vast armaments expenditure but even more so in terms of millions of human lives.

(c) But the honour Antiochus gave to foreign gods carried with it no recognition or respect for them. He was superior to them all and he "would magnify himself above all". Not for nothing was he called Antiochus Epiphanes, "God manifest", nor was it by accident that the head and shoulders on his coins came increasingly to resemble Zeus himself.

Such claims to divinity must have shocked the Jews, for Antiochus claimed superiority not only over these alien gods but over "the God of gods" himself, none other than the God of Israel, against whom he spoke "astonishing things" (cf. 1 Maccabees 1:24). But a limit is set to his presumption. The period of "the indignation" will soon be over. His end is already "determined" by God.

Arrogance is akin to blasphemy, for in its essence it is a denial of God and an assumption of the place reserved for God alone. In ordinary mortals it is despicable. In rulers and governments it is a challenge thrown in the face of God which brings its own retribution. It is a highly dangerous thing for any man or any institution to "play God". And yet it is being done—apparently successfully—today. Men made in the image of God are subjected to inhuman treatment; they are robbed of human dignity; they are deprived of their liberties; they are denied basic human rights. To deny man's humanity is to deny God's divinity and to set ourselves up in his place. Such arrogance is a blasphemy which incurs the wrath of God and, like that of Antiochus, brings about its own end.

PREDICTION AND FAITH

Daniel 11:40–45

"At the time of the end the king of the south shall attack him; but the king of the north shall rush upon him like a whirlwind, with chariots and horsemen, and with many ships; and he shall come into countries and shall overflow and pass through. He shall come into the glorious land. And tens of thousands shall fall, but these shall be delivered out of his hand: Edom and Moab and the main part of the

Ammonites. He shall stretch out his hand against the countries, and the land of Egypt shall not excape. He shall become ruler of the treasures of gold and of silver, and all the precious things of Egypt; and the Libyans and the Ethiopians shall follow in his train. But tidings from the east and the north shall alarm him, and he shall go forth with great fury to exterminate and utterly destroy many. And he shall pitch his palatial tents between the sea and the glorious holy mountain; yet he shall come to his end, with none to help him."

(i)

At this point in the narrative history proper ends and prediction begins. Antiochus is attacked by the king of Egypt but replies with a devastating counter-offensive. He drives south, occupies "the glorious land" of Palestine causing the death of tens of thousands. He advances between the river Jordan and the coast, bypassing Edom, Moab and Ammon which lie toward the east. He conquers Egypt and captures its treasures. Then, like Sennacherib of old (cf. 2 Kings 19:7), he hears a rumour of happenings in the east and north that alarm him and, as a result, retreats in great fury. Then, in fulfilment of ancient prophecy, that the enemy of God's people would at last be destroyed "on the mountains of Israel" (cf. Ezek. 38:14–16; 39:2–4; Joel 3:2; Zech. 14:2), he meets his death between Mount Zion and the Mediterranean Sea with none to help him.

(ii)

The events described in these verses find no corroboration in the known facts of Antiochus' last days as recorded in other historical writings. We know, for example, that after his desecration of the Temple and his persecution of the Jews he made his way eastward early in 165 B.C. to establish his frontiers against the threat of the Parthians. In the winter of that same year he died of a mysterious disease at Tabae in Persia. The indications are that our author had not heard this news or the news of the rededication of the Jerusalem Temple by Judas Maccabeus—simply because these events had not yet taken place. If this is so, it is an important factor in ascertaining a fairly precise date for the composition of the book of Daniel as it now stands.

(iii)

The value of these verses is to be found not in the accuracy or otherwise of their precise predictions, but in the assurance they give that the tyrant's end is certain and the purpose of God for his people is near to its fulfilment. Sincere and devout Christian readers are sometimes concerned about the "unfulfilled" character of predictions or the implied "inaccuracy" of such scriptural references. It is of help to know that even within Scripture itself there are instances of prophecies or predictions, apparently or obviously unfulfilled, being taken up and re-interpreted in the light of the changed circumstances of that age. It is of help too to recognise that the real value of prophetic predictions is to be found not simply in their prognostications of the future but much more so in their pronouncements of faith in the prevailing purpose of Almighty God. Their spiritual worth is to be assessed not by ferreting out corresponding "fulfilments" in recorded history or by "proving" their veracity by the calculation of precise dates or by projecting them into the far-distant future, using them as a kind of cryptogram to identify contemporary happenings and claiming them as "signs" that in our own day the "end" is near. It is to be found rather in the confident assertion of faith that God is in control, that he will surely bring to pass what he has decreed, that he will bring to naught the designs of evil men and in his own appointed time will establish his righteous rule and justify his faithful people in the eyes of the world. In this light these few verses predicting Antiochus' end are of the utmost worth. The writer's certainty of faith is far more impressive than any accurate forecasting of events could ever be.

PER ARDUA AD ASTRA

Daniel 12:1–4

"At that time shall arise Michael, the great prince who has charge of your people. And there shall be a time of trouble, such as never has been since there was a nation till that time; but at that time your people shall be delivered, every one whose name shall be found written in the book. And many of those who sleep in the dust of the earth shall awake, some to everlasting life, and some to shame and everlasting contempt. And those who are wise shall shine like the brightness of the firmament; and those who turn many to righteousness, like the stars for ever and ever. But you, Daniel, shut up the words, and seal the book, until the time of the end. Many shall run to and fro, and knowledge shall increase."

This is a remarkable passage providing a seed-bed, as it were, for the growing belief in life after death. It falls very far short of the Christian expectation and the hope born by the resurrection of Jesus Christ from the dead; nevertheless it registers a great breakthrough in religious thought and prepares the way for the fully developed presentation we find in the New Testament Scriptures.

(i)

The death of Antiochus did not immediately usher in the kingdom. The "time of trouble" must run its course. The forces of evil, epitomised by Antiochus but not confined to him, would be unleashed as never before. But Michael, the patron angel of Israel, would stand by God's people and deliver "everyone whose name shall be found written in the book", i.e. all those who have remained faithful in face of trial and persecution, the "wise" who by their teaching and example have turned the "many" to righteousness.

This picture of conflict and tribulation, coupled with a confident expression of hope in God's final triumph, recalls the Old Testament picture of "the day of the Lord" (cf. Amos 5:18; Zeph. 1:18; 3:8, etc.), which would be ushered in by supernatural portents and signs (cf. Joel 3:1ff.), and culminate in the triumph of God over all his foes. The idea is developed and enlarged in later apocalyptic writings and also in the New

Testament. One early illustration comes from the second century B.C. book of Jubilees which declares that in that day "calamity follows on calamity, and wound on wound, and tribulation on tribulation, and evil tidings on evil tidings, and illness on illness...and all kinds of calamities and pains" (23:13ff.). Other writers describe these tribulations in terms of war or earthquake, famine or destruction by fire. Mysterious powers take over the control of nature. Even the sun, the moon and the stars behave strangely and fail to appear at their proper time.

In the Hymns of Thanksgiving among the Dead Sea Scrolls the birth of the "messianic kingdom" is likened to the birth of a firstborn child by a woman in great travail: "with pains of Sheol he bursts forth from the crucible of the pregnant one" (III, 10). This picture recalls that in Mark 13 where the "messianic woes" are called "the beginnings of the birth pangs" (13:8, cf. Matt. 24:8) or in Rev. 12:1-6 where the birth of the Messiah or the messianic community from the womb of the true Israel is likened to a woman who "crieth out, travailing in birth, and in pain to be delivered" (12:2).

(ii)

God's kingdom is assured, but it is to be born out of great tribulation. This is the message of Scripture; it is the message too of experience. Evil is the enemy of good and will do its utmost to destroy it—not only at the time of the consummation but also at *every* point in time, wherever the powers of the kingdom assert themselves. To represent the kingdom and the powers of the kingdom and to live as citizens of the kingdom now means to run the risk of violent opposition or even violent death. But this can hardly come as a surprise, for the story of the Gospel is that strength comes through weakness, victory comes through defeat, resurrection comes through crucifixion. The pattern of God's kingdom, like the pattern of our redemption, is that of life through death, triumph through tribulation.

A safe stronghold our God is still,
A trusty shield and weapon;
He'll help us clear from all the ill
That hath us now o'ertaken.
  The ancient prince of hell
  Hath risen with purpose fell;
  Strong mail of craft and power
  He weareth in this hour;
On earth is not his fellow.

With force of arms we nothing can,
Full soon were we down-ridden;
But for us fights the proper Man
Whom God Himself hath bidden.
  Ask ye, Who is this same?
  Christ Jesus is His name,
  The Lord Sabaoth's Son;
  He, and no other one,
Shall conquer in the battle.
          (Martin Luther, tr. Thomas Carlyle)

The mediaeval legend is told of how Satan was cast out of heaven. "What is it you miss most?", he was asked; to which he replied, "The sound of the trumpets in the morning".

SHEOL AND THE SHADES

Daniel 12:1–4 *(cont'd)*

These verses have been described as "a great breakthrough in religious thought", making it possible to penetrate much more deeply than ever before into the mysteries of life beyond death. They fall very far short of the "glorious hope" set forth in the New Testament, but the light they give is enough to guide the steps of devout men in the years that followed, preparing them for the revelation of eternal life made known through Jesus Christ our Lord.

(i)

In earlier Old Testament times, survival was commonly recognised in the "name" of one's offspring. The name, which indicated identity, perpetuated the remembrance of the deceased and in a sense passed on his life in sons and grandsons generation after generation. Men and women, together with their forebears and their descendents, formed a single whole, a family unity, whose members were bound together in the common bundle of life.

This, of course, is a quite different concept from that of belief in individual survival in life beyond the grave. Nowhere in the older prophets do we find any such belief clearly enunciated. No doubt they were dissuaded from following such a path by, for example, the threat to the Hebrew faith of necromancy with its accompanying ghosts and mediums which were a menace to the true worship of God (cf. Isa. 8:19) and also by the dangers inherent in the practice of heathen religions depicting the changing seasons in terms of the death and rising again of the gods.

To the Hebrews, as taught by the prophets, there is no *life* for the individual beyond death, only a shadowy existence in the land of Sheol to which at death a man's ghost or "shade" descended. It is a land of no return (cf. 2 Sam. 12:23; Job 7:9) where "the dead know nothing...for there is no work or thought or knowledge or wisdom in Sheol to which you are going" (Ecc. 9:5, 10). It is a "land of dust" (cf. verse 2) where only a weak and shadowy replica of the once-living man persists, bereft of all those qualities and characteristics that once identified him as a human being during his lifetime on earth.

(ii)

How gloriously different is the Christian hope: not a lone existence cut off from God the source of life, but life itself in all its fulness (cf. John 10:10); not a life of fear and forboding, but a life of complete fulfilment; not a life of forgetfulness and oblivion, but a life of growth in the knowledge of God; not a life of gloom, but a life of supreme joy in the presence of a living Lord. "We would rather be away from the body and at home with the Lord", says Paul (cf. 2 Cor. 5:8). "For to be with Christ is far better" (Phil. 1:23).

The teaching of the New Testament (as indeed of the Old) is not that of "natural immortality", of natural survival, either in the form of heavenly bliss or reincarnation. It concerns rather the gift of eternal life which cannot be destroyed by death, but remains intact, set free from earthly limitations and finding its ultimate expression in intimate fellowship with God. It is "eternal" not just in the sense of "everlasting", but in the sense that its source is to be found in the eternal life of God himself. The assurance the Apostle has for such a hope is not just that of wishful thinking; it is nothing less than the love of God from which no powers on earth, in heaven or hell, can separate us. In Rom. 8:37ff. he lists these powers—headed by "death" itself—and concludes that none of them "will be able to separate us from the love of God in Christ Jesus our Lord."

As one who quite recently had to look death straight in the face, the present writer has found great assurance in these words of his former College Principal, H. Wheeler Robinson:

How then ought a Christian to anticipate the incidence of physical death? With the prayer that he may be given patience to bear whatever pain may accompany it; with the confidence that the transformation of character begun in him and so far from its completion will be continued under new conditions; with no senti-mental musing on the retrospect of his life and its many failures, but with a humble penitence that casts itself joyfully on God's love... with the zest of one who is undertaking a new adventure, and with no fear of its outcome, but in the spirit of John Bunyan, when facing the imminence of death and crying, "I will leap off the ladder even blindfold into eternity, sink or swim, come heaven, come hell; Lord Jesus, if Thou wilt catch me do; if not, I will venture for Thy name".

> In the hour of death, after this life's whim,
> When the heart beats low, and the eyes grow dim,
> And pain has exhausted every limb—
> The lover of the Lord shall trust in Him

When the will has forgotten the lifelong aim,
And the mind can only disgrace its fame,
And a man is uncertain of his own name—
The Power of the Lord shall fill this frame.

For even the purest delight may pall,
And power must fail and the pride must fall,
And the love of the dearest friends grow small—
But the glory of the Lord is all in all.

THE HOPE OF RESURRECTION

12:1-4 *(cont'd)*

(i)

Here and there in the Old Testament we detect a glimmering of hope that, instead of the gloomy prospect of shadowy existence in Sheol, men will truly survive the trauma of death (cf. Job 14:13-15; 19:25-27; Pss. 16; 49; 73). Nowhere, however, does this become a firm assertion of faith—except in two late passages, Isaiah 24-27 and Daniel 12:1-4. It is significant that in each of these two references life beyond the grave is seen in terms of resurrection. It is as if a formula, as it were, had at last been found in terms of which the mystery of death could finally be explained. In Isa. 26:19 we read: "Thy dead shall live; their corpses shall arise; they that dwell in the dust shall awake and sing, for the dew of lights is thy dew, and the earth shall give birth to the shades." But this is no general resurrection. It is reserved for the pre-eminently righteous who will rise from Sheol to participate in the new creation which God will establish at the end of the days.

So also with these verses in Daniel. Why should those who have suffered martyrdom for their faith be deprived of the glories of the coming new age? Surely they will not be denied the benefits of the kingdom! The "many", says our author, will be awakened from their "sleep" in Sheol and rise to share "everlasting life" in that kingdom which is itself eternal. Among them are the "wise" and "those who turn many to righteousness" who will share the "brightness" of the new age and be like the very stars in heaven whom the heathen worship as gods. Their dwelling-place will be on earth—for it is an earthly kingdom—but their glory will be that of heaven. But the author does not stop there. Why, he asks in effect, should the pre-eminently wicked be allowed to rest in peace, albeit in Sheol? They too will be raised—"to share an everlasting contempt". For all the rest, Sheol remains their eternal abode.

We are not to read into these verses any doctrine of heaven or hell. That theme was to be taken up and developed in later apocalyptic books, with their graded compartments in the after-life and their diversified rewards and punishments for the righteous and the wicked. The New Testament does not balk this issue, but points unerringly to the very core of the Christian hope—the resurrection of Jesus Christ who, it is claimed, is "the first-fruits of those who have fallen asleep" (1 Cor. 15:20).

(ii)

Consideration of these verses suggests certain reflections which find fuller content in the teaching of the New Testament Scriptures:

(a) The essential belief adumbrated in the Bible—and particularly in the New Testament—is not the immortality of the soul but the resurrection of the body. In a number of apocalyptic books later than Daniel the departed are described in terms of "souls" which have left their bodies behind in death, after the manner of popular Greek thought. But at best these discarnate souls are but truncated personalities awaiting the resurrection for the fulfilment of their true selves. Behind this notion lies the convinced Hebrew belief that man in all his "parts" is a unity of personality and cannot be adequately expressed simply in terms of soul or spirit apart from body. The nature of "the resurrection body" was a matter for deep debate in the days of the early Church (cf. 1 Cor. 15:35ff., etc.), but its reality was not in doubt. The redemption wrought by Christ was a redemption of the whole man and the resurrection would make this plain.

(b) Man's survival beyond death is not just a natural phenomenon which is his by virtue of his humanity, as a doctrine of immortality might assume. The resurrection declares that it is in fact an act of God. "Belief in the immortality of the soul", writes Oscar Cullmann, "is not belief in a revolutionary event. Immortality, in fact, is only a negative assertion: the soul does *not* die, but simply lives on. Resurrection is a *positive* assertion: the whole man, who has really died, is recalled to life by a new act of creation by God. Something has happened—a miracle of creation! For something has also happened previously, something fearful; life formed by God has been destroyed."

(c) The Daniel passage, as distinct from that in Isaiah 24–27, raises the difficult question of the punishment of the wicked. There are those who would dismiss any such possibility as unworthy of the revelation of God in Scripture and falling far short of that divine love made known through Jesus Christ his Son. Such a conclusion, however, is hard to justify in the light of New Testament evidence. Again and again in the Gospels and elsewhere, reference is made to the coming judgment and the possibility of rejection. "Nothing could exceed the gravity and solemnity of the warnings about this which are given in the teachings of Jesus and Paul. All the strands of tradition which are woven together in the New Testament bear witness to this. We would part company with the New Testament altogether if we ignored it" (Lesslie Newbigin). But the same writer adds pointedly: "The question of eternal salvation and judgment is not for speculation about the fate of other people; it is an infinitely serious practical question addressed to me."

(d) It is important to note, however, that belief in life after death according to the Scriptures, is not confined to the individual; it is essentially corporate in character, for it relates directly to life in the coming kingdom. This is set forth clearly in this Daniel passage where the emphasis is not on individual survival but on participation in the ongoing life of the people of God. So it is also in the New Testament itself. Individual believers, to be sure, will rise in resurrection as Christ himself has risen. But they are part of that mystical body which is the Body of Christ, the redeemed of all the ages, to whom has been given the gift of eternal life. "The resurrection of the body", writes J. A. T. Robinson, "like Christianity itself, is something social; it is 'put on' as we are brought into Christ and built up into his body. That is why the resurrection of the body is always associated in the New Testament with the *Totus Christus,* the Complete Man, the revelation of Jesus Christ with all his saints." This glorious community of the resurrection, for such it is, will share the eternal life of God and show forth that love which is the hallmark of the new humanity which bears the likeness of the risen Christ our Lord.

IT'S IN THE BOOK

Daniel 12:1-4 *(cont'd)*

The angel now tells Daniel to seal up these revelations in a book. The reference is presumably not just to the concluding vision but to all the material that has gone before. It is to be kept a secret "until the time of the end". The fact that it is now being disclosed to the readers is a sure sign that the end is at hand.

We have already observed (see comment on 8:26-27) that the tradition concerning secret books preserved from antiquity whose mysteries were to be revealed in the last day, was a fairly common feature to be found in apocalyptic writings from the second century B.C. onwards. Its purpose was not to deceive; rather it was a necessary and accepted device, given the form of pseudonymous authorship popular at that time. The vision, purporting to have been given in the sixth century B.C. and hidden ever since, is now made known. Many shall "run to and fro", as in the days of Amos (cf. Amos 8:11f.), seeking knowledge of God. This book, presumably, is thought to contain all the knowledge they need!

For the writer of the book of Daniel, the dreams and visions that had come to him were none other than divine revelations. They spoke to him, and through him to others, of the purpose of God for his people and indeed his whole creation. In this connection we can perhaps identify five significant factors which have cropped up throughout the book and which find focus in these few verses:

(1) God's revelation is to be transmitted in literary form. The writer is bidden to write down *in a book* what he has seen and heard. The apocalyptic tradition, including that of Daniel, is essentially literary in character. In this it is unlike the prophetic tradition, at least in its earlier expression. To the prophet God says, "You shall speak to them this word" (Jer. 13:12). To the apocalyptist he says, "Write what you see in a book" (Rev. 1:11). In each case it is an authoritative word, uttered with a divine imperative.

There are, of course, disadvantages about the *written* word over against the *spoken* word. There is a danger, for example, that the spontaneous utterance might become stereotyped and "frozen" in "cold print", isolated from the historical event that produced it. But such contrast can be overdone. The spoken and the written word are in fact complementary as vehicles of divine revelation. The fluidity of the spoken word in history is counter-balanced by the fixity of the written word in literature. The declaration of the word in preaching is an expression of the writing of the word in Scripture. Through both, and both together, the Incarnate Word is made known, who is greater than the book and more powerful than the prophet.

(2) This revelation is "secret" in the sense that it contains the "hidden mysteries" of the divine purpose made known to the people of God (see comment on 2:24-30). Jesus came to interpret to "his own" the ineffable mysteries of God and to uncover for them the secret of the kingdom (cf. Mark 4:11). He is the key to the written word of Scripture within which the divine disclosure concerning himself has remained hidden for ages past but is now made known (cf. Rom. 16:25f.). He gives the promise that the Holy Spirit, sent from the Father, will reveal the Scriptures to them and lead them into all the truth (cf. John 16:13). Through him the hidden mystery becomes an open secret.

(3) It is a revelation that can be traced into the ancient past and is also mine, as a member of the age-old people of God.

God's truth made known to me may be personal but it is never private in the sense that it belongs to me alone (see comment on 8:26–27). I belong to "the body of the Church" to which "the body of truth" is revealed. God by his Spirit may speak intimately to me, in some quiet moment of prayer; his divine truth may flash in upon me in a moment of blinding revelation as I stand alone before him. But behind me and around me and before me are the people of God to whom I belong and with whom I share his goodness and grace. I am what I am because of what I have received. I stand in line with prophets, saints and sinners of all the ages past who, together with myself, have received the revelation of God and are privileged to pass it on.

(4) It is a revelation that is contemporary in its application. It is an *open* book; it is a *revealed* secret; it is for this very moment in time in which I live. It speaks to my given situation. This is the message of the New Testament concerning the living Christ and God's revelation in and through him. Because he is risen and has sent his Spirit he is our great Contemporary. By the help of the Spirit the preached word and the printed word reveal the living Word, the Son of God. Where Christ is preached, Christ is present; and where the Scriptures are read there he stands in the midst of his people. The revealed word of God, which is from ages past, is for now.

(5) It is a revelation that relates to the end and is to be understood in terms of tomorrow. It is the ultimate purpose of God that makes sense of all our todays, and discloses the meaning of the mystery of life itself. "Then", says Paul, "I shall understand fully even as I have been fully understood" (1 Cor. 13:12). The future is the key to the present, not the other way round. And because that "end" and that "purpose" find their expression in Christ (for in him tomorrow is here), the Christian can live in confidence *now*, as if these were the last days, for all the promises and all the purposes of God find their "yes", their fulfilment, in him (cf. 2 Cor. 1:20).

BLESSED IS HE WHO WAITS

Daniel 12:5-13

> Then I Daniel looked, and behold, two others stood, one on this
> bank of the stream and one on that bank of the stream. And I said to
> the man clothed in linen, who was above the waters of the stream,
> "How long shall it be till the end of these wonders?" The man clothed
> in linen, who was above the waters of the stream, raised his right
> hand and his left hand toward heaven; and I heard him swear by him
> who lives for ever that it would be for a time, two times, and half a
> time; and that when the shattering of the power of the holy people
> comes to an end all these things would be accomplished. I heard, but
> I did not understand. Then I said, "O my lord, what shall be the issue
> of these things?" He said, "Go your way, Daniel, for the words are
> shut up and sealed until the time of the end. Many shall purify
> themselves, and make themselves white, and be refined; but the
> wicked shall do wickedly; and none of the wicked will understand;
> but those who are wise shall understand. And from the time that the
> continual burnt offering is taken away, and the abomination that
> makes desolate is set up, there shall be a thousand two hundred and
> ninety days. Blessed is he who waits and comes to the thousand three
> hundred and thirty-five days. But go your way till the end; and you
> shall rest, and shall stand in your allotted place at the end of the
> days."

And so we come to the epilogue. The curtain is about to fall on
the drama enacted in story and vision over twelve chapters.
Many characters have crossed the stage and many strange
dreams have taken shape before our eyes. The tale has been
told. The end is near.

These concluding verses refer back to the scene recorded in
10:4, from which emerged the long final vision described
in the intervening verses. It shows Daniel standing by the river
Tigris and with him "a man clothed in linen", and on either side
of the river another angelic figure. In this extended account we
are told of four things:

(1) *A promise made.* Daniel asks the question he had asked
before (cf. 8:13f.): How long will it be till the end of these
terrible events perpetrated by Antiochus? The angel replies in

words already given in 7:25: they will last for three-and-a-half years when the "shattering" of Israel by Antiochus will have come to an end. This promise is given by a most solemn oath. Two hands are raised to heaven, and not just one as was the custom (cf. Gen. 14:22; Deut. 2:40; Rev. 10:5). The angel, moreover, swears "by him who lives for ever", whose spokesman he is. God's word is his bond. It cannot be broken. What he promises will come to pass. The word of God endures and will accomplish that for which it has been sent (cf. Isa. 55:11).

(2) *A mystery unresolved.* Daniel, by the river Tigris, fails to understand what has just been said. He asks for further elucidation. Can he have an interpretation of these things? The angel is quite adamant—the revelation is finished; it is sealed and settled. From now on it is a closed book. But let him be assured that the "many" and the "wise" who will live in the last days will understand and be ready for the great event that is to come.

The man of God has to learn to live by faith and not by sight. Not every divine revelation is clear in its meaning or in its application. Many mysteries remain, the answers to which we should dearly like to know. But such knowledge is withheld from us. Only at the end of the day will God by pleased to make their meaning known.

(3) *A prophecy re-interpreted.* Verses 11 and 12 are seen by some as interpolations or glosses, whose intention is to extend the 1,150 days of waiting mentioned in 8:14, which follow the cessation of "the continual burnt offering" and the setting up of "the abomination that makes desolate" (see comments on 8:13–14; 9:25–27, *cont'd*). The argument is that the author, or some other writer, recognising that the end has not come after the 1,150 days, extends the period of waiting to 1,290 days and subsequently another hand extends it still further to 1,335 days. It has been suggested that the 1,290 days do in fact represent the three-and-a-half years (with the addition of an intercalary month) referred to in 7:25, and again in 12:7. The significance of the 1,335 days, it would seem, defies explanation. Whatever the precise explanation of these figures may be, we know that during the intertestamental period there was a great interest in

the interpretation and re-interpretation of Scripture (see comment on 9:1–2). The "plain" meaning was not always its *real* meaning. It spoke of things yet to be whose interpretation would be made known at the end of the days.

This was the convinced belief of the New Testament writers and of the early Church. In the coming of Jesus they saw clear signs of the breaking in of the kingdom. To them the Scriptures took on a new meaning in the light of that coming. They found in him the climax of God's age-long dealings with his people and the fulfilment of the promise given of old through Moses and the prophets (cf. Luke 24:44). What was hidden is now revealed. In him the kingdom comes and with it the true meaning of God's prophetic word to man.

(4) *An assurance given.* Daniel is bidden to await with patience the unfolding of God's purpose. He has to go his way until his end comes in God's good time. In due course he will go to his rest—a reference probably to the grave. But for Daniel his death will not be irretrievable loss, for he will stand in his "allotted place" at the great consummation, when God's kingdom will come and the new age will at last be ushered in.

The assurance given to Daniel—and to all who believe—is not dependent on power politics or armed revolutions. It is a quiet confidence that, come what may, God will remain in control and will bring in the kingdom. In that kingdom those who trust in him will fully share. This was the assurance too of another writer who, like Daniel, also received a divine revelation relating to the end—"the revelation of Jesus Christ which God gave to show to his servants" (Rev. 1:1). His book, unlike that of Daniel, was left unsealed (cf. Rev. 22:10), for it pointed to one in whom the kingdom had come and through whom it would come in power and glory at the end of the days. His assurance is the assurance of the whole Church in every age: *Maranatha.* "Come, Lord Jesus" (Rev. 22:20).

> For thine is the kingdom,
> the power and the glory,
> for ever and ever. Amen.

NOTES

1. *Dan. 1:1:* It is stated that Nebuchadnezzar, king of Babylon, besieged Jerusalem in the third year of the reign of Jehoiakim, king of Judah. Nebuchadnezzar (605–562 B.C.) did not in fact come to the throne until the fourth year of Jehoiakim (cf. Jer. 25:1) who reigned from 609 to 598 B.C. It was not until a year after Jehoiakim's death that he besieged Jerusalem, i.e. in 597 B.C. (cf. 2 Kings 24:10–15).

The date given in this verse is presumably based on a combination of 2 Chron. 36:5–8, which records a tradition that there was an attack on Jerusalem during the reign of Jehoiakim, and 2 Kings 24:18 which records that Jehoiakim became subject to Nebuchadnezzar for three years. It has been suggested that one possible reason for the dating given in Dan. 1:1 is that it provides a more exact confirmation of the seventy years' exile foretold by Jeremiah (cf. Jer. 25:11ff.; 2 Chron. 36:21; Dan. 9:1f.).

2. *Dan. 1:6-7:* The Hebrew names given to Daniel and his friends are to be found in name lists in the book of Nehemiah, indicating perhaps that our author purposely made use of names familiar to the Jewish community in Babylon at that time. More interesting, however, is the name of Daniel himself which appears elsewhere, in 1 Chron. 3:1 and Ezra 8:2 and also in Ezek. 14:14, 20 and 28:3. The Ezekiel references are of particular interest, for there Daniel is introduced as a proverbially wise man ("You are indeed wiser than Daniel; no secret is hidden from you", 28:3), and is bracketed with Noah and Job as one renowned for his righteousness before God (cf. 14:14, 20).

For many years scholars have detected in the Daniel of this passage a legendary figure known from ancient times, a surmise that has found likely confirmation in the Ras Shamra tablets from Ugarit in northern Syria reflecting Canaanite legend. There mention is made of one "Dan'el" who has a reputation for righteousness in caring for the orphan and the widow (see Introduction). These references would seem to suggest some connection at any rate between our hero and his namesake of antiquity. E. W. Heaton suggests that "if the writer did borrow the name of an ancient hero, it is likely that he also took over some of the ideas associated with it in tradition" and concludes that though the adoption of the name "does not add anything material to the writer's presentation", it nevertheless "sharpens our response to it and predisposes us to share more fully his elusive learning and the profound theological thought of which it is the medium."

3. *Dan. 1:21:* "Daniel continued until the first year of King Cyrus". This may mean simply that he "continued alive" till then, though this would contradict what is said in 10:1 which states he was still alive three years later. More likely it indicates that Daniel was among those who returned to Palestine on the publication of Cyrus' edict in 538 B.C. which allowed his captive subjects to return to their homes (cf. Ezra 1:1). Such a statement would give fresh hope to all faithful Jews scattered throughout the Dispersion that they would at last be gathered in and restored—a hope alive to this very day.

4. *Dan. 5:1:* Belshazzar was a historical person, the son of Nabonidus, the last Babylonian king who was fourth in succession after Nebuchadnezzar. To the best of our knowledge Nabonidus was unrelated to Nebuchadnezzar either by birth or marriage. The records show that during Nabonidus' sojourn in Tema, Belshazzar served as regent until his father's return shortly before the fall of Babylon in 539 B.C. Nowhere, however, in contemporary inscriptions is he designated "king" but is described simply as "the king's son". That he was not recognised as king is suggested by the fact that on several occasions the New Year Festival, in which the king as such played a central role, could not be held in Babylon, apparently because Belshazzar as regent did not qualify to serve in this way. It would appear that the author of Daniel, in common with the historians Herodotus and Xenophon, is using traditional material to tell a tale with a "moral" without the need—far less the means—to check the historical veracity of every detail in the story.

5. *Dan. 5:31:* Reference is made here to one "Darius the Mede" who came to the throne when sixty-two years of age. No king of this name is known at this time from any other historical source. Valiant attempts have been made to identify him with Cyaxares II (Cyrus' uncle), Cyrus himself, Gobryas (Cyrus' general who captured Babylon), Cambyses (Cyrus' son) and Astyages (the last king of the Medes). None of these identifications, however, is all that convincing.

The explanation of the name may be found along one of two lines. The first is that a literal fulfilment of prophecy would require the conquest of Babylon by the Medes (cf. Isa. 13:17; 21:2; Jer. 50:9, 41; 51:11, 28) and the founding of a "Median empire" (see comment on 2:31–45). The conviction of our author that prophecy must be fulfilled and that this is what actually happened would perhaps find support in the fact that Cyrus the Persian had previously become ruler of the

Medes who were now included within his Persian empire. The second explanation is that Cyrus, conqueror of Babylon in 539 B.C., could quite readily have become confused with Darius I, its conqueror in 520 B.C. The reference to Darius the Mede succeeding to the kingdom at the age of sixty-two may reflect yet another strand in the tradition and may be reminiscent of, say, Gobryas or some other figure in the tangled skein.

FURTHER READING

The following is a small selection of commentaries and other books which the reader may find helpful in further exploring the Book of Daniel and the times with which it deals. The "easier" books among them are marked by an asterisk.

COMMENTARIES

*Joyce G. Baldwin, *Commentary on Daniel* (The Tyndale Old Testament Commentary), 1978
 J. Barr in *Peake's Commentary on the Bible,* 1962
*R. H. Charles, *The Book of Daniel* (Century Bible), 1913
 R. H. Charles, *A Critical and Exegetical Commentary on the Book of Daniel,* 1929
*S. R. Driver, *The Book of Daniel* (Cambridge Bible), 1900
 Louis F. Hartman and Alexander A. Di Lella, *The Book of Daniel* (Anchor Bible), 1978
*E. W. Heaton, *The Book of Daniel* (Torch Commentaries), 1956
 André Lacocque, *The Book of Daniel,* 1979
 J. A. Montgomery, *The Book of Daniel* (International Critical Commentary), 1927
*J. J. Owens in *The Broadman Bible Commentary,* vol. 6, 1972
 Norman W. Porteous, *Daniel* (Old Testament Library), 1965
*D. S. Russell in *The Jews from Alexander to Herod* (Clarendon Bible), 1967
 E. J. Young, *The Prophecy of Daniel,* 1949

BACKGROUND LITERATURE

*E. R. Bevan, *Jerusalem under the High Priests,* 1904
*Walter Lüthi, *The Church to Come,* 1939
 S. Mowinckel, *He that Cometh,* 1956
 H. H. Rowley, *The Relevance of Apocalyptic,* 1944 (revised 1963)

H. H. Rowley, *The Servant of the Lord* (ch. 7), 1952

*D. S. Russell, *Between the Testaments,* 1960 (revised 1963)

D. S. Russell, *The Method and Message of Jewish Apocalyptic* (Old Testament Library), 1964

*A. C. Welch, *Visions of the End,* 1922